LAW AND ECONOMICS

CONTRIBUTORS

Josef M. Broder, Department of Agricultural Economics, University of Georgia

Ronald C. Faas, Department of Agricultural Economics, Washington State University

Nicholas Mercuro, Department of Economics, University of New Orleans

Warren J. Samuels, Department of Economics, Michigan State University

A. Allan Schmid, Department of Agricultural Economics, Michigan State University

James D. Shaffer, Department of Agricultural Economics, Michigan State Univsity

LAW AND ECONOMICS: AN INSTITUTIONAL PERSPECTIVE

Edited by

Warren J. Samuels
A. Allan Schmid

Martinus Nijhoff Publishing
Boston/The Hague/London

Distributors for North America:
Martinus Nijhoff Publishing
Kluwer Boston, Inc.
160 Old Derby Street
Hingham, Massachusetts 02043

Distributors outside North America:
Kluwer Academic Publishers Group
Distribution Centre
P.O. Box 322
3300 AH Dordrecht, The Netherlands

Library of Congress Cataloging in Publication Data

Samuels, Warren J 1933–
  Law and economics.

  Bibliography: p.
  Includes index.
  1. Law – Addresses, essays, lectures. 2. Economics
– Addresses, essays, lectures. 3. Trade regulation
– Addresses, essays, lectures. I. Schmid, Alfred
Allan, 1935– joint author. II. Title.
K487.E3S36   343'.07   80–13735
ISBN 0–89838–049–9

To Alice and Sylvia

ACKNOWLEDGMENTS

Chapter 1: "Welfare Economics, Power, and Property" reprinted with permission of the Institute for Research on Land and Water Resources, The Pennsylvania State University, from *Perspectives of Property,* G. Wunderlich and W.L. Gibson, eds. (University Park: Institute for Research on Land and Water Resources, Pennsylvania State University, 1972), pp. 61-127.

Chapter 3: "Interrelations between Legal and Economic Processes" reprinted with permission from the *Journal of Law and Economics* 14 (October 1971): 435-50. Copyright 1971 by the University of Chicago Law School.

Chapter 4: "Ecosystem Policy and the Problem of Power" reprinted by permission from *Environmental Affairs* 2, no. 3 (1972):580-96.

Chapter 5: "Normative Premises in Regulatory Theory" reprinted from *Journal of Post Keynesian Economics* 1 (Fall 1978):100-14. © M.E. Sharpe, Inc., 901 N. Broadway, New York, N.Y. 10510.

Chapter 6: "A Research Approach to Institutionalist Alternatives in the Administration of Agrarian Development Programmes" reproduced from *Agricultural Administration* 2 (1975):285-305, by permission of Applied Science Publishers Ltd.

Chapter 7: "Citizen Participation in Michigan District Courts" reprinted with permission from *Citizen Participation in Natural Resource Decision Making,* Allan Randall, ed. (North Central Research Strategy Committee for Natural Resources, Department of Agricultural Economics, University of Kentucky, November 1978).

Chapter 9: "Commentary: An Economic Perspective on the Compensation Problem," *Wayne Law Review* 21 (November 1974):113-34. Printed with permission of the *Wayne Law Review.*

Chapter 10: Reprinted from "The Role and Resolution of the Compensation Principle in Society: Part One—The Role," with permission of JAI Press, Inc., from *Research in Law and Economics* 1:157-94. Copyright © 1979 by JAI Press, Inc.

CONTENTS

LAW AND ECONOMICS

INTRODUCTION

This book brings together a number of articles, for the most part already published, that develop a contemporary institutionalist approach to the study of the economic role of government. The institutionalist tradition in these matters began with the work of Henry Carter Adams on economics and jurisprudence[1] and Richard T. Ely on the relation of the institutions of property and contract to the distribution of wealth.[2] It continued with John R. Commons's monumental analytical and historical study of the legal foundations of capitalism,[3] Edwin E. Witte's work on the role of government in the economy,[4] and Kenneth Parson's study of economic development.[5] The approach to law and economics that is developed in this book centers on (1) an identification of the objective fundamentals of the interrelations between legal and economic processes and (2) the development of skills with which to analyze and predict the performance consequences of alternative institutional designs.

We must stress that our principal goal is quite simply to understand what is going on—to identify the instrumental variables and fundamental issues and processes—in the operation of legal institutions of economic significance. We envision government as an object of legal control. We also see law as an instrument of securing economic gain and advantage—that is, as a wealth-producing and -acquiring alternative. Government—the law—is (1) an institution available for the use of whoever can control it; (2) an arena of power and power play; (3) an important part of the larger social decision-making and valuational process; and (4) both an independent and dependent variable, the former insofar as other persons, groups, and institutions are law *takers*, the latter insofar as others can secure control of and use government as law *makers*. Government, in short, is a set of handles by which various power players endeavor to manipulate social structure and the distributions of opportunity, wealth, income, and welfare.

In emphasizing objective understanding, we intend to differentiate between two uses of the term *positive economics* and between both of them and *normative economics*. The form of positivism that we endeavor to pursue is principally concerned with the objective, neutral identification of what *is* the case. The other form of positivism is concerned with what *is necessary or instrumentally useful* given what ought to be done, while normativism is concerned with what *ought* to be the case. As human beings, we have our own, private sentimental and normative longings; indeed, we disagree with one another from time to time. But that level of discourse we endeavor to exclude as much as possible from our work as scholars. We are interested in identifying and analyzing fundamental legal-economic processes—in part, to understand them as a distinct and important subject in their own right and, in part, to be able to analyze and predict institutional performance, particularly those institutions in the public sector and those that reside in the legal-economic nexus. Such a viewpoint and such a limited set of objectives often are disappointing to those who want to rationalize certain general or specific arrangements as "optimal" (or criticize others as "exploitative"). We are not intellectual eunuchs in such matters, but we prefer that the great bulk of our work be positivist in the first sense, and such is what we have brought together here. This approach is taken not because we think valuation, or choice, is not important. On the contrary, we stress the ultimate normative (rather than technical) character of the fundamental operations and interactions between legal and economic processes. If anything, as scholars, we want our work to make the choosing process both more informed and more open, *whatever choices are made.*

In contrast, we find that most conventional analysis is normative, presumptive, and misleading in important respects. Accordingly, some of our work has been critical in the sense that we have endeavored to reveal the limits and faults of conventional work as a sort of ground-clearing operation, which we hope will raise the level of both analysis and debate. We find, for example, that analysis of "regulation" as a concept distinct from "rights" can mislead and selectively channel analysis. We find that the concept of efficiency as separate from distribution is false. Distribution has allocative implications; efficient solutions are distribution (rights-structure) specific (that is, efficiency has distributive assumptions and implications); and the legal system is necessarily a fundamental determinant of the distribution of economic welfare, including resource allocation. We also find that the market is not separable from government and that policy issues should be seen not in terms of more or less government, but in terms of who is using government for what purposes. In general, we find that the role of government is important, not aberrational— that it is indeed a fundamental decision-making process whose operation is channeled by, among other things, beliefs relating to the dysfunctional or aberrational nature of government. (These beliefs are typically highly specific, if only implicitly, in regard to whose interests should count.) The decision-making process is also channeled by beliefs amounting to wishful thinking about what is circumstantially or fundamentally possible for government to accomplish.

Thus, part of our work has assumed a demythicizing role. We have attempted to transcend the modern Western economy's view of itself, in part to identify the rationalizing or ideological role of more conventional work in law and economics, which is a blend of both explanation and rationalization. Thus, we have occasionally attempted to identify the role and substance of implicit, selective antecedent normative premises in conventional work. More generally, we have emphasized and practiced the identification of conflict, especially over the control and use of government, on terms more fundamental and more neutral or objective than those of the existing order or of certain partisans. We believe that to raise questions about the role of certain values in analysis is not necessarily to argue against them or for them. Rather, we endeavor to expose presumptive premises and arguments and to raise the level of debate vis-à-vis the more common practice of channeling the direction of debate.

Not surprisingly, then, we have stressed at least four crucial concepts: power, selective perception, interdependence, and evolution. As John Kenneth Galbraith, Robert Heilbroner, and Robert Lekachman have remonstrated on numerous occasions, although conventional work in economics grossly neglects considerations of power, power is a fundamental category of analysis, partly because it is a fundamental in the real world of law and economics. Selective perception is important because of the widespread use of concepts that require the exercise of choice if such concepts are to yield exact or definite conclusions for policy. Choice often involves implicit antecedent normative premises or identifications, which are sometimes the result of ideology, as, for example, in a choice involving the question of when an interest is a right and when it is not. Next, we stress the ubiquity of interdependence and the need to investigate whose correlative interest is sacrificed by identifying rights or externalities in one way rather than in another. We also trace the variety of exposures that economic actors have to one another and the origins, formations of limits, and consequences of those exposures. For example, the opportunities for one party to affect another are in large part a function of the character of goods and services. Those characteristics affect such things as exclusion, information, and contractual costs, whose impacts on performance are then shaped by alternative institutions and rights. Finally, we stress evolution, in part because of the kaleidoscopic nature of legal-economic interrelations and the cumulative-causation nature of general interdependence, which produces unanticipated, as well as intended, changes. Of course, these dimensions are part of a long tradition: Institutional economics has stressed holism and the problem of the organization and control of the economy and its evolution.

We may suggest and illustrate the unique character of our analysis in the following way: Consider a production possibility curve to which is tangent an actual social welfare function (or actual community indifference curve). We suggest that there are four simultaneously interacting social decision-making processes pertaining to this situation, about which conventional analysis typically makes a number of presumptive assumptions that directly channel analysis and prefigure policy conclusions. These processes are: (1) the identification of the values on the axes between which choice is to be made; (2) the determination of the technological and power bases of the creation of the production possibility curve, which governs the necessary trade-offs; (3) the learning and formation of the preferences of individuals with regard to the values on the axes; and (4) the determination of the weights governed by the power structure that are to be applied to the different preferences of individuals in the formation of the actual social welfare function (or, more accurately, the entire array of social welfare functions, inclusive of the one tangent to the production possibility curve). In one way or another, our work expresses the belief that an understanding of legal-economic fundamentals and the analysis and prediction of institutional performance—in all their interdependent complexity—must deal directly with the power, selective perception (including ideology), interdependence, and evolutionary aspects of those four processes, minimizing as far as possible presumptions as to either whose interests are to count or how interests should be made to count, and emphasizing instead how society (polity and economy) actually works out solutions to those problems or how the performance consequences of a particular institutional arrangement are achieved.

The institutionalist paradigm can be readily juxtaposed to the paradigms of neoclassical and Marxian economics (although it borrows from and builds on both). The neoclassicist begins with a given set of entitlements and seeks to identify the optimal allocation of resources and consequent distribution of income, which is specified in terms of productivity. The Marxist begins with a given set of entitlements and attempts to identify the resource allocation and income distribution of capitalist markets in terms of exploitation. Whereas the neoclassicist may offer an explanation of the initial endowments based on some notion of maximizing the value of output, the Marxist explains the initial entitlements in terms of the historical evolution of exploitative forms of accumulation. In contrast, the institutionalist attempts to explain the origins and evolution of rights (sets of entitlements) without introducing such judgmental categories as productivity or exploitation. The institutionalist's explanation of resource allocation and income distribution is made in terms of a complex causal chain involving both allocation and distribution as functions of market forces that depend in turn on power, rights, and the use of government; distribution is described in nonjudgmental terms as the result of a vast and complex contest to appropriate income.

With respect to identifying the sources of power, both the neoclassical and Marxist perspectives are limited. Both place prime emphasis on nominal factor ownership in settling claims to conflicting opportunities. The Marxian analysis supports public ownership, while the neoclassical theory supports individual ownership. Our analysis suggests that the substantive results of this simplistic dichotomy are hard to predict because in practice the results are influenced by many complementary rights not specified in these theories. The neoclassical theory focuses on the power that derives from the parties' unequal alternatives for buying and selling. Policy to secure larger number of buyers and sellers so that no one party can influence price becomes the chief instrument controlling the interdependence of individuals who are not self-sufficient. As noted above, our analysis identifies widely ranging sources of interdependence that are beyond the control of factor ownership or competition. This is not to say that public or private ownership or market shares are unimportant; rather, our belief is that additional legal details cumulate and interact to produce a particular performance.

Approaching law and economics from a different direction of analysis, Pigovian welfare economics (for example, public expenditure theory) identifies externalities, using the well-known private-social marginal-cost–marginal-benefit analysis, and proceeds to establish a general presumption in favor of governmental corrective action. Paretian welfare economics attempts to preempt or abort most forms of governmental corrective action, emphasizing the definition and assignment of property rights to permit market exchanges and thereby internalizing the so-called Pareto relevant externalities. The Marxian approach concentrates on the roles of government with regard to systemic legitimation, private capital accumulation, and the distribution of its "share" of revenues (part of surplus value) that accrue from exploitation. In contrast, the institutionalist is interested in explaining how society reaches policy decisions. For example, the institutionalist would want to know which definition of externality (given the reciprocal character of externalities) is being implemented and whose interests are being promoted to the exclusion of others' interests. In short, the institutionalist attempts to explain how government is used to reach public expenditure decisions, but does so without establishing a presumption in favor of or against any particular solution or any general category of solution, and without identifying public spending, public goods, or other policies as necessarily inadequate, excessive, or exploitative.

Many of these themes and much related substantive analysis and interpretation are developed in the articles that follow. We hope that, taken together, they will reinforce an understanding of the nonpresumptive nature and viability of the institutionalist approach to law and economics.

We are both indebted to numerous teachers, colleagues, and students, as well as to each other. We particularly want to acknowledge our debts to Jim Shaffer, Robert Solo, and Harry Trebing, all of Michigan State University.

NOTES

1. Henry Carter Adams, *Relation of the State to Industrial Action and Economics and Jurisprudence,* Joseph Dorfman, ed. (New York: Columbia University Press, 1954).

2. Richard T. Ely, *Property and Contract in Their Relations to the Distribution of Wealth,* 2 vols. (New York: Macmillan, 1914).

3. John R. Commons, *Legal Foundations of Capitalism* (New York: Macmillan, 1924).

4. Warren J. Samuels, "Edwin E. Witte's Concept of the Role of Government in the Economy," *Land Economics* 43 (May 1967):131–47.

5. Kenneth H. Parsons, "The Institutional Basis of an Agricultural Market Economy," *Journal of Economic Issues* 8 (December 1974):737–57.

I
PARADIGMATIC AND THEORETICAL STUDIES

The articles in this section develop the fundamental conceptions that we use in understanding and explaining the operation of legal and economic processes. Their purpose is, in part, to analyze and predict the performance consequences of legal institutions of economic significance. Two themes pervade these, as well as the following, writings: the ultimate exercise of choice and the reaching of choices through the accumulation of individual acts of choice by economic actors under conditions of ubiquitous interdependence. The first chapter presents a general model of choice and power applicable to all multiparty decision-making situations. It stresses the multiple foundations of the opportunity sets from which choice is made and the impact of others' choices on any actor in a system of mutual coercion or mutual impact. The analysis is extended to a general theory of the nature of externalities and externality solutions, which stresses the ultimate necessity for determining, in one way or another, whose interest is to be sacrificed to another's.

The next chapter outlines a theory for identifying instrumental institutional variables affecting who gets what. Prediction of the consequences of alternative rights requires identification of the sources of human interdependence. Nominal factor ownership controls interdependence arising from incompatible use, but it cannot speak to conflicts arising from the high-exclusion, information, or transaction-cost characteristics of some goods. Theory should help researchers to generalize and extend experience to predict how institutional change might perform in a new situation.

Chapter 3 applies the analysis developed in the first chapter to the interpretation of a particular legal case. It attempts to identify the fundamental processes, as well as the meaning of specific decisions in terms of those processes, that mark the general legal-economic nexus. In effect, the chapter presents some important elements of a fundamental model of the legal foundations of the economy and the general interdependence relations between legal and economic processes.

Chapter 4 explores the aspects of choice found in all areas of economic policymaking, here in terms of the environmental question. It stresses the circumstantial relativity of choice, the relation of power to choice, the role of power in forming costs (through choice as to whose interests count as a cost to others, through rights), and the complex interplay between criteria of structure and of results in reaching decisions.

The last chapter in this section is a critique of the role of implicit antecedent normative premises in a wide range of applied economic analysis, especially premises concerning the given structure of rights that directly govern the policy conclusions of the analysis. The chapter suggests the need to make such premises explicit and to conduct analyses that make alternative assumptions about rights. It echoes the earlier discussion of the role of costs and output definitions in giving effect to implicit assumptions as to whose interests are to count.

1
WELFARE ECONOMICS, POWER, AND PROPERTY
Warren J. Samuels

I. Introduction

In an earlier paper,[1] I undertook to show that the interrelations between legal and economic (market) processes were considerably more
intricate and subtle than recent literature has allowed. Overall, I
suggested that voluntary market exchange is both a partial emanation or dependent variable and an independent or determining or
conditioning variable so far as certain interrelations between legal
and economic processes are concerned. The implicit thrust of the
article was that certain concepts of welfare economics could be revised to reflect a broader and more viable analysis of choice. The
objective of the present paper is to begin that revision, to reconsider
certain fundamental concepts of welfare economics in terms of a
broader and more complex and yet more viable model of choice and
power.

In this paper I show the constrained character of those concepts
and how they may be extended even within the context of a methodo-

As with the paper cited in Footnote 1, the analysis in this paper relies heavily on
the writings of John R. Commons, Robert L. Hale, Frank H. Knight, and Edwin
E. Witte, as well as the literature of welfare economics. I have found clues, antici-
pations, suggestions, and reinforcements in a variety of recent writings, especially
those of E. J. Mishan, Francis M. Bator, and Gordon Tullock's *Private Wants,
Public Means*, New York: Basic Books, 1970. But I am especially indebted to the
ideas of Hale, whose general paradigm of power and mutual coercion is adopted
in Section II and applied in subsequent sections. (See Samuels, The Economy as
a System of Power and its Legal Bases: The Legal Economics of Robert Lee
Hale, mimeographed.) I am particularly appreciative of the contributions of Allan
Schmid to the clarification and constructive direction of my thinking. I am also
indebted to Glenn Johnson, John F. A. Taylor, T. Nicolaus Tideman, and Gene
Wunderlich for suggestions, not all of which have been followed. Needless to
say, I remain solely responsible for the remaining errors and for endeavoring to
combine the theory of power with that of utility.
1. Samuels, "Interrelations Between Legal and Economic Processes," *Jour. of
Law and Econ.*, vol. 14, 1971, pp. 435-450.

logically individualist[2] analysis of voluntary market exchange. In
Section II, I outline the general paradigm of choice and power which
serves as the framework for the remainder of the paper. In Section
III, I show the nature and place of Pareto-optimality in the context
of that general theory of choice and power. In Section IV, I reinter-
pret and generalize the concept of externalities in terms of the general model of choice and power, showing that conventional usage
has been unnecessarily narrow and selective and has begged critical
questions of power. In both Sections III and IV, I suggest that the
traditional usages are really incomplete partial-equilibrium concepts
which neglect basic aspects of social choice but which may be clarified and reinterpreted in a broader general equilibrum theory of
choice and power. Finally, in Section V, I discuss the Coase Rule in
the same context. Throughout I am interested in implications for the
study of the processes whereby private decision-making is organized
and structured, in large part through the institution of property.

I should make explicit that the argument of this paper does not
involve a broader definition of economics than is conventional. The
perspective is that of methodological individualism. But where traditional welfare economics considers the market as the only methodologically collectivist phenomenon, the present analysis will identify
and examine other social-choice processes relevant to welfare.

The analysis is intended as a step toward revising the character
of welfare economics. Traditional theoretical welfare economics has
been normative: it has attempted "to evaluate the social desirability
of alternative allocations of resources;"[3] "to formulate propositions
by which we may rank, on the scale of better or worse, alternative
economic situations open to society."[4] It has done this largely only to
the extent that it has identified Pareto-better solutions as the unobjectionable acceptable minimum and has generally refused to go beyond
Pareto-optimality in ranking alternatives on the stated grounds of
avoiding interpersonal utility comparisons (though this has been

---

2. By methodological individualism I mean the view which holds that meaningful social-science knowledge is best or more appropriately derived through
   the study of individuals as individuals; and by methodological collectivism
   I mean the view which holds that meaningful social-science knowledge is
   best or more appropriately derived through the study of group organization,
   forces, processes, and/or problems.

3. James M. Henderson and Richard E. Quandt, *Microeconomic Theory*, New
   York: McGraw-Hill, 1958. p. 222.

4. E. J. Mishan, A Survey of Welfare Economics, 1939-59, *in* Surveys of Economic Theory [hereafter cited as Mishan: Survey], New York: St. Martin's,
   vol. 1, 1967, p. 156.

honored often only in the breach). It is the intent of this paper, however, to pose a much more limited aim of welfare economics, namely,
a positive study of the factors and forces governing the attainment
and distribution of welfare, the study of how economic actors in a
market economy go about the quest for welfare maximization both
in their private decision making and in their participation in processes of social choice. It has been my objective to eschew normative
considerations as far as possible and make no decisive valuational or
utility assumptions. The traditional assumption that individual preferences are to count remains but it is subsumed under a concern with
the question of *whose* preferences are to count and the factors and
forces governing the social-choice solution to that question.

II.   A General Paradigm of Choice and Power

The theory of choice in neo-classical micro and welfare economics is
the logic of choice between alternatives. The individual is posited to
have an opportunity set of alternative lines of action each with a
relative cost. Each economic actor operates under the condition of
scarcity: his choice is limited by his means and by the costs of his
opportunities, e.g., by his income and/or assets and by the prices
which he must pay. Given his opportunity set, his set of attainable
choices and their respective costs, the individual chooses so as to
maximize either his profits or his utility, adjusting through the equimarginal principle to attain the marginal conditions of a maximizing
equilibrium. Diagrammatically this may be illustrated by the tangency
of the highest indifference function to the budget-constraint line. In
general, the individual chooses between alternatives within his opportunity set.

Individual choice is a microcosmic facet of collective or social
choice. Society (defined simply as the collectivity of individual economic actors and their interrelations) operates under the conditions
of *scarcity* and *interdependence,* so that the conduct of one group of
individuals has an impact on other groups and the solution of one
economic variable is intertwined with the solution of all other economic variables. This means that the choices made by an economic
actor are both a dependent and independent variable vis-a-vis the
choices of other economic actors: his choices have impact on the
range and cost of alternatives open to others, and the choices of
others have impact on the range and cost of alternatives open to him.
The scarcity that confronts society is disaggregated and distributed

among the economic actors comprising it. The distribution of opportunity sets among individuals represents the disaggregation and distribution of societal scarcity down to the level of the individual. There are many possible distributions of opportunity sets, many possible decision-making structures. There may be, and typically is, an asymmetrical or unequal distribution of opportunity, resulting in a structure of advantage and disadvantage. Social decisions are a function of the structure of opportunity sets as well as of the choices made by individuals from within their respective opportunity sets.

The individual's welfare is attained by his maximizing within the constraints of his opportunity set. But what determines the opportunity set of the individual? What factors and forces govern the available alternatives and their respective costs? What is the larger process of choice out of which is generated the actual (and changing) structure of opportunity sets which comprise the economic decision making process of any point of time and over time?

Let us understand as *choice* here not an autonomous unconstrained choice but the circumstantially limited exercise of choice between available alternatives, the scope of one's choice or freedom being a function of the range of available alternatives and of their relative cost.

Let us designate as *coercion* the impact of the behavior and choices of others upon the structure or array of one's opportunity set, that is, upon the scope of one's choice; and vice versa. I intend *coercion* as a neutral term; as Bator puts it, ". . . the fact of scarcity relative to wants implies coercion no matter by what institutional devices we choose to parcel out apples and nuts amongst people,"[5] and Samuelson, that "the price system is, and ought to be, a method of coercion,"[6] even when, under an ideal laissez faire system, it is a system of coercion by dollar votes. Needless to say, this model of choice and coercion applies to any system of economic organization, for in every system the individual has choice only with respect to the oportunity set open to him as a consequence of his interaction with others. The economy is thus a *system of mutual coercion* in which the choices of each individual have eventual impact upon the opportunity sets and choice of others—even when washed through a competitive market. All choice has both individualist and collectivist, or private and public, aspects, yet whatever the perspective it remains true "that whatever scope society accords individual choice and valuations is a conse-

---

5. Francis M. Bator, *The Question of Government Spending*, New York: Collier Books, 1962, p. 116; cf. pp. 117, 119 (footnotes 3 and 4), 120.
6. Paul A. Samuelson, *Collected Scientific Papers*, ed. Stiglitz, Cambridge: M.I.T. Press, 1966, vol. 2, p. 1415.

quence of the latitude for discretionary action which is built into the system."[7]

Injury is interpreted as a reduction in the range of alternatives and/or an increase in their costs, as a result of the impact of others' choices. It may take the form of loss of job, increased prices, unavailability of goods, destruction of the income-value of property through competition, changes in legal arrangements, etc. Conversely with *benefits*.

Let us designate as *power* the means or capacity with which to exercise choice, with which therefore to coerce; whose reciprocal is exposure to others' coercive capacity or power. By means or capacity I mean the *de jure* or *de facto* bases by, with, or on which one acts as a chooser: one's property, position in an organization, non-property rights, skill at negotiation, etc. The interaction of one's power and the power of others, as effected through institutional mechanisms, e.g., the market or the legal system, is the basis for mutual coercion and the structure of opportunity sets. While power is the wherewithal of choice, it is relative to the power of others.[8]

The opportunity set of the individual, within which he attempts a constrained maximizing equilibrium, is a function of the total structure of mutual coercion, grounded upon relative power. The individual, in attempting a maximizing equilibrium, is exercising whatever choice is open to him in his opportunity set. The activity of constrained maximization is thus part—the relatively individualist part—of a larger process, the process of mutual coercion within which the individual's opportunity set is generated, partly as a function of the impact of others' choices and partly as a function of the individual's own past and continuing choices, always under the condition of uncertainty and within the play of subjective imagination.[9] The process of the attainment and distribution of welfare is, accordingly, much larger and more complicated and subtle than individual constrained maximization. The process of equimarginal adjustment of the individual

---

7. Kenneth Parsons, Institutional Economics: Discussion, *Am. Econ. Rev., Papers and Proceedings,* vol. 47 1957, p. 26. For a similar view, in terms of the problem of valuation, see Frank H. Knight, Some Fallacies in the Interpretation of Social Cost, *Quarterly Jour. of Econ.,* vol. 28, 1924, reprinted in American Economic Association, *Readings in Welfare Economics,* Homewood: Irwin, 1969, p. 219.

8. Choice or freedom is thus a function of one's legally protected property vis-a-vis the legally protected property of others, *inter alia*; see E. J. Mishan, *The Costs of Economic Growth,* New York: Praeger, 1967, p. 73, and J.E. Meade, *Efficiency, Equality and the Ownership of Property,* Cambridge: Harvard, 1965, p. 11.

9. See, e.g., G. L. S Shackle, *The Nature of Economic Thought,* Cambridge University Press, 1966, p. ix.

actor is but a part of the total process of interdependent decision making. The individual is a choice maker but only within the range of his opportunity set; insofar as his opportunity set is given for him, he is a choice taker.[10]

To picture the foregoing, consider the accompanying diagram. Alpha has an opportunity set, representing his sphere of choice; it is a function of his power and of the process of mutual coercion, here represented by his interaction with Beta (who may stand for all other parties). Given Alpha's power and opportunity set, there is a related set of decision trees for Alpha, encompassing the totality of his choice alternatives and their personal and interactional consequences; so too with Beta. The open-ended yet constrained process of mutual coercion operates as Alpha and Beta, each choosing from within their respective opportunity sets, make choices having coercive impact on the future opportunity sets of each other. The structure of opportunity sets changes over time through the mutual exercise of choice and mutual coercion. We have a system of general equilibrium in which it is true *both* that the opportunity set of an individual is a function of the total structure of power, *and* that the total structure of power is a function of the decisions made by individuals from within the opportunity sets enjoyed by them at any point in time and over time.

---

10. The point may be expressed in terms of *security*, where there is the complex situation in which Alpha is secure *from* the coercion of others and secure *to* exercise coercion upon others, and the same for Beta (the juxtaposition is adopted from the French jurist Demogue's distinction between static and dynamic security, discussed in Jerome Frank, *Law and the Modern Mind*, Garden City: Anchor, 1963, pp. 238-244; or in terms of freedom *from* vis-a-vis freedom *to*, for Alpha and for Beta (see Frank H. Knight, *Freedom and Reform*, New York: Harper, 1947, ch. 1; Jacob Viner, Hayek on Freedom and Coercion, *South. Econ. Jour.*, vol. 27, 1961, pp. 230-236; Fritz Machlup, Liberalism and the Choice of Freedoms, *in* Erich Streissler, ed., Roads to Freedom, New York: Kelley, 1969, pp. 117-146; and Samuelson, *Collected Scientific Papers, op. cit.*, vol. 2, p. 1414.)

Even the individual's preferences are, of course, learned and part of a general equilibrium system. In terms of the present analysis, the individual's developed (really developing) preferences are a partial function of his opportunity set structure, and the availability and costs of alternatives. Even if we assume given preferences at a point in time, choices from (and reflecting) this opportunity set influence his life and future preferences; thus lower prices facilitate the development of certain preferences, e.g., street football versus golf. There is a dynamic interaction between preferences and alternatives. The individual evaluates alternatives (and their relative costs) as they arise, developing preferences in the process. He chooses between alternatives from within his opportunity set, but the contents of his opportunity set influence the development of his preferences. On the produced character of preferences, see Knight, in *Readings in Welfare Economics, op. cit.*, p. 227.

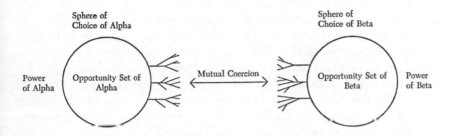

Private property, similarly, is power, part of the total decisional structure; individual property rights are relative to the rights of others; the greater the property holding, other things being equal, the greater the power, the greater the opportunity set and range of choice; but since property owners are exposed to the workings of mutual coercion, property is both a dependent variable and an independent variable. Thus, Boulding saw in the contract curve of Pareto-optima a conflict curve; for, as Radomysler insisted, "conflict is the essence of the problem,"[11] at the heart of both a viable welfare economics and a viable theory of property.

---

11. A. Radomysler, Welfare Economics and Economic Policy, *Economica*, vol. 13, 1946, reprinted in *Readings in Welfare Economics, op. cit.,* p. 92.

III.   Pareto-Optimality

A.   *The Basic Concept*

The concept of Pareto-optimality approaches the maximization of welfare through a particular decision rule. The rule states that a bundle of choices or a situation is optimal in which no change can improve the position of one individual without making at least one other individual worse off, in which, that is, "Any change which harms no one and which makes some people better off (in their own estimation)[12] must be considered to be an improvement."[13] The rule has been stated in at least three major contexts: (1) for individual maximization, essentially the equimarginal principle, that the individual is in a maximizing position when he cannot rearrange his affairs in any way that the gain involved is greater than his associated loss; (2) for transactions between two parties, that each willing trader, in agreeing to the terms of the transaction, is surrendering something less in value to him than he receives in exchange, so that both are better off because of the transaction; and (3) for the economy as a whole or for a subsector thereof, as the marginal conditions of welfare maximization.[14]

The logic of Pareto-optimality has given rise to the decisional criteria, first, of *Pareto-efficient,* a statement of the equilibrium condition of maximizing, that there can be no further gain without loss to oneself or to another, i.e., change without loss or without net loss; and second, of *Pareto-safe,* a statement of a loss-avoiding decision rule, that there should be no change unless the change is costless or acceptable in the sense that there is no loss, or no uncompensated loss, or no unacceptable loss, incurred by anyone involved. *Pareto-efficiency,* given that maximization is normative, is essentially a positive proposition, a statement of the equilibrium marginal conditions of maximization. *Pareto-safe,* even aside from more complex normative aspects to be considered later, is unquestionably normative in that it makes

---

12. This is an important qualification: first, it avoids interpersonal utility comparisons and second, it signifies the fundamental voluntarist or consensual character of the Pareto concept, yet it will be seen in the next subsection that it is very narrowly applied vis-a-vis the model of mutual coercion.

13. William J. Baumol, *Economic Theory and Operations Analysis,* Englewood Cliffs: Prentice-Hall, second edition, 1965, p. 376.

14. See C. E. Ferguson, *Microeconomic Theory,* Homewood: Irwin, revised edition, 1969, ch. 16; Henderson and Quandt, *op. cit.,* ch. 7; and Mark Blaug, *Economic Theory in Retrospect,* Homewood: Irwin, revised edition, 1968, pp. 598ff.

"a simple value judgment"[15] in accepting only changes that carry no costs or no uncompensated costs.[16] The basic mathematical and choice-theory logic of Pareto-optimality is the maximization of a linear function;[17] either the equilibrium marginal conditions of maximization obtain or nonequilibrium conditions elicit shifts (or transactions) producing a Pareto-efficient solution, whether for an individual or jointly between individuals.

The status of Pareto-optimality, at least beyond the theory of the firm, has always been controversial. Recent challenges have, for example, involved dispute over the scope of Pareto-optimality,[18] about which more below; and criticism of its alleged inadequacy as an ideological weapon in the "arsenal of economic thought."[19] But most discussion has centered on its adequacy in relation to welfare maximization and thus on the adequacy of the assumptions of Pareto-optimality. In general, with respect to the adequacy of Pareto-optimality for welfare, it is widely held that the conditions of Pareto-optimality are necessary but not sufficient for welfare maximization, which requires a Bergsonian social welfare function with which to choose between alternative Pareto-optima.[20] Criticism of the "necessary" quality (that the conditions are *neither* necessary *nor* sufficient)[21] leads to consideration of the assumptions and limits of Pareto-optimality the chief of which has to do with the problem of externalities, the subject of

---

15. Henderson and Quandt, *op. cit.*, p. 222; cf. 208.

16. This paper abstracts from consideration of compensation (i.e., the Kaldor, Hicks, and Scitovsky criteria) since it would needlessly complicate the analysis; the criteria in question follow the logic of Pareto-optimality by allowing change generating loss where the gain is at least enough to compensate for the loss, etc.

17. Tjalling C. Koopmans, *Three Essays on the State of Economic Science*, New York: McGraw-Hill, 1957, p. 49.

18. Compare the views of Richard A. Musgrave, Pareto-Optimal Redistribution: Comment, *Am. Ec. Rev.*, vol. 60, 1970, pp. 991-993; and Harold M. Hochman and James D. Rodgers, Pareto-Optimal Redistribution: Reply, *ibid., loc. cit.*, p. 999.

19. Ludwig M. Lachmann, Methodological Individualism and the Market Economy, *in* Streissler, ed., *op. cit.*, p. 90.

20. See, e.g., Henderson and Quandt, *op. cit.*, pp. 208, 217, 218 (footnote), 223; Samuelson, *op. cit.*, vol. 2, pp. 1096, 1100, 1410 (footnote); Maurice Dobb, *Welfare Economics and the Economics of Socialism*, Cambridge University Press, 1969, pp. 7, 49, 252; and F. M. Mator, The Simple Analytics of Welfare Maximization, *Am. Econ. Rev.*, vol. 47, 1957, reprinted in William Breit and Harold M. Hochman, eds., *Readings in Microeconomics*, New York: Holt, Rinehart and Winston, 1968, p. 390.

21. F. M. Bator, The Anatomy of Market Failure, *Quarterly Jour. of Econ.*, vol. 72, 1958, reprinted in Breit and Hochman, *op. cit.*, pp. 475-476, and The Simple Analytics of Welfare Maximization, *ibid*, p. 411.

Section IV below. With respect to the adequacy of the assumptions of Pareto-optimality, i.e. the social space to which it applies, there is much disagreement. There is probably wide agreement that competitive equilibrium produces Pareto-optimality or that competitive equilibrium is Pareto-optimal;[22] but this agreement coexists with other statements to the effect that perfect competition is *neither* necessary *nor* sufficient for Pareto-optimality.[23] Thus, while one of the typically stated assumptions of Pareto-optimality is the absence of monopoly, it has been argued that monopoly is consistent with or can lead to Pareto-optimality.[24] Similarly, despite the general free-market and voluntarist tenor of the concept, it has been held that Pareto-optimality can exist with central controls.[25] In this latter regard, if Pareto-optimum is to mean "only" that there can be no further gains from trade, it is hard to see how Pareto-optimality could not apply to the equilibrium conditions of a centrally controlled economy without reducing to a mere restatement of the principle of consumer sovereignty.

We come now to the assumptions and limits of Pareto-optimality. There are many assumptions which have been acknowledged or claimed in the literature, and while some are controversial, altogether they yield important insight. (I recognize that whether an assumption is or is not made is discretionary with the analyst. But if Pareto-optimality is to be used with equivalent meaning by different writers and in a non-ideological way, there should be some clarification if not standardization.) Several assumptions are discussed at length below, most of which I want only to identify, so that here an enumeration will suffice. As generally used, Pareto-optimality assumes the following (aiming at maximum exposure, and not theoretical rigor, so that some overlap is involved):

1. the existing distribution of income: either the assumption of status quo income distribution per se *or* of indifference to (what Mishan

---

22. Henderson and Quandt, *op. cit.*, pp. 202ff, 222; Ferguson, *op. cit.*, p. 446; Koopmans, *op. cit.*, pp. 42, 46ff, 49; Kenneth J. Arrow and Gerard Debreu, Existence of an Equilibrium for a Competitive Economy, *Econometrica*, vol. 22, 1954, p. 265; James Quirk and Rubin Saposnik, *Introduction to General Equilibrium Theory and Welfare Economics*, New York: McGraw-Hill, 1968, pp. 125, 128, 135; and Vivian Charles Walsh, *Introduction to Contemporary Microeconomics*, New York: McGraw-Hill, 1970, p. 182.

23. Mishan: Survey, p. 167; Dobb, *op. cit.*, pp. 60 (footnote), 64; Koopmans, *op. cit.* p. 53.

24. Quirk and Saposnik, *op. cit.*, pp. 125-126.

25. Quirk and Saposnik, *op. cit.*, p. 124; Dobb, *op. cit.*, pp. 49, 252, 253.

calls "disregard" of)[26] income distribution *or* that if an income distribution is not considered proper that collective action is undertaken to produce a proper distribution;[27] and similarly with wealth distribution, moral and legal rules, power structure, etc., below

2. the existing distribution of wealth, i.e., the initial endowments of assets, such as property rights

3. the existing system of legal and moral rules, including the rules governing the rights of access to and use of private property and income and wealth in general, and the operation of social control (this is, *inter alia,* related to No. 4)[28]

4. the existing distribution of power, or power structure, in society (important, among other things, in regard to the construction and application of the social welfare function, in part through the construction and application or enforcement of legal and moral rules)

5. existing technology, resources and tastes, i.e., consumer preferences and production possibilities (closely tied to several other assumptions, e.g., the knowledge condition of intertemporal optimality, second order conditions, the learning of preference functions, and so on)

6. the existence of a market for exchange (not necessarily for goods; Pareto-optimum is part of the pure theory of exchange and choice)[29]

7. a bounded consumption set (see below)

---

26. E. J. Mishan, Pareto-Optimality and the Law, *Oxford Econ. Papers,* vol. 19, 1967, p. 279.

27. Robert Strotz and Colin Wright, Externalities, Welfare Economics, and Environmental Problems, paper presented at meeting of American Association for the Advancement of Science, Chicago, December 26, 1970, p. 24. See also Henderson and Quandt, *op. cit.,* p. 208; Bator, *in* Breit and Hochman, *op. cit.,* p. 394; Dobb, *op. cit.,* pp. 10, 69, 90, 253; and Paul A. Samuelson, *Foundations of Economic Analysis,* Cambridge: Harvard University Press, 1953, p. 214 (footnote), and *Collected Scientific Papers, op. cit.,* vol. 2, p. 1410.

28. Koopmans, *op. cit.,* p. 54; James M. Buchanan, The Relevance of Pareto-Optimality, *Jour. of Conflict Resolution,* vol. 6, 1962, pp. 341-354; and Oskar Morgenstern, Pareto-Optimum and Economic Organization, *in* Norbert Kloten et al, eds., *Systeme und Methoden in den Wirtschafts und Sozialwissenschaften,* Tubingen: Mohr [Siebeck], 1964, pp. 573-586. See also references given in note 27, *supra.*

29. Koopmans, *op. cit.,* pp. 42, 148; Dobb, *op. cit.,* pp. 9-10.

8. the existing distribution of capacity to derive utility from consumption, and the social value structure in general insofar as it conditions individual preferences, as a function of social structure and other factors (this is obviously related to and in some ways dependent upon other assumptions, such as wealth distribution,[30] operation of social control, etc.)

9. that efficiency is comprehended in terms of maximization

10. the existence of perfect competition, i.e., the exclusion of monopoly (this is listed even though I doubt its significance or necessity; the argument below does *not* rest on noncompetitive conditions, i.e, power exists in the market even under competitive conditions; monopoly can, of course, be seen as a case of market failure through increasing returns to scale or as a barrier to reaching the marginal conditions)[31]

11. the exclusion of externalities and public goods, including interdependent utility functions and production functions (this is considered at length in Section IV below)

12. knowledge sufficient to produce intertemporal optimality[32]

13. second-order optimality or stability conditions, such as convexity and perfect divisibility[33]

14. the price-cost structure which emerges as a consequence of demand-supply interaction, given the other assumptions

15. that individual preferences are to count, given the other assumptions (e.g., social control, status quo wealth and income distribution, power structure, etc.) as well as general scarcity

16. that a local rather than the largest maximum is acceptable as optimum: even if the second-order conditions are satisfied there is no assurance of any optimal solution beyond a local maximum[34]

17. that second-best considerations, to the extent not excluded by earlier assumptions, are either nonexistent or acceptable

30. Tullock, *op. cit.*, pp. 90-91.
31. Bator, *The Question of Government Spending, op. cit.*, pp. 91ff.
32. Blaug, *op. cit.*, p. 598; Henderson and Quandt, *op. cit.*, ch. 8.
33. Mishan: Survey, p. 168.
34. *Ibid.*

A word about the assumption of a bounded consumption set is in order. Welfare theorists at least since Debreu[35] have recognized that a situation might exist in which competitive equilibrium was reached with at least some individuals living at below a subsistence level, in which case it would be Pareto-optimal for society to have them work for nothing, inasmuch as they will soon perish anyway. They have thus assumed that each individual has the resources with which to "both survive and participate in the market."[36] This has the interesting implication that the consent and no-loss requirements of Pareto-optimality operate within an assumption precluding death such that the laissez faire implications often attending the Pareto rule are inappropriate and gratuitous. Whereas welfare-state support is generally seen as a departure from Pareto-optimal conditions (except where it represents Pareto-optimal redistribution, which relaxes the assumption against interdependent utility functions),[37] constituting an involuntary loss for the support of others. Pareto-optimality seems to require by this consumption-set assumption the very existence of a welfare state. As Koopmans pointed out some time ago, aside from limiting it to a description of the case of "a society of self-sufficient farmers who do a little trading on the side," and aside also from the "hard-boiled alternative" of assuming "instantaneous elimination by starvation of those whose resources prove insufficient for survival, and . . . conditions ensuring existence of an 'equilibrium' involving survival of some consumers," "An alternative more realistic for highly industrialized private enterprise societies would be to recognize the existence of income transfers through taxation and social insurance, and to look for conditions, including tax and benefit schedules, ensuring general survival in an equilibrium."[38]

Pareto-optimality has to be recognized as a powerful concept: it points to an unobjectionable acceptable minimum decision rule and in any conflict situation it can lead to areas of minimum agreement. Nevertheless, aside from the case of individual maximization and notwithstanding the aura it has come to enjoy as the denotation of economic optimality, what it represents are *the marginal conditions of*

35. Gerard Debreu, Valuation Equilibrium and Pareto-Optimum, *Proceedings of the National Academy of Science,* vol. 40, 1954, reprinted in American Economic Association, *Readings in Welfare Economics, op. cit.,* pp. 40, 45.

36. Koopmans, *op. cit.,* p. 59.

37. Harold M. Hochman and James D. Rodgers, Pareto-Optimal Redistribution, *Am. Econ. Rev.,* vol. 59, 1969, pp. 542-556; and the references given in note 18, *supra.*

38. Koopmans, *op. cit.,* p. 62.

joint constrained maximization,[39] and this only in a formal sense and only with the no-loss provision. It is formal in the sense that the conditions of Pareto-optimality are the conditions of maximizing equilibrium independent of the limiting assumptions, such as the institutional framework. Yet while logically Pareto-optimality is independent of the limits, the *substance* of equilibrium solutions are directly dependent upon the substantive matters covered by the assumptions, and it is these substantive matters which economists have long both privately and professionally insisted upon as important for welfare, e.g., the integrity of private property, competition, economic stability, etc. Thus, the emphasis must be upon *constrained.* The social space to which Pareto-optimality applies includes most if not all exchange or conflict situations. But it only applies within the set of assumptions enumerated above and especially the no-loss provision, so that wherever it does apply it relates only to the formal condition of joint constrained maximization without loss and not to questions of substance, which is to say that it truly offers very little guidance in ranking alternatives. Joint maximization takes place only within the actual conditions to which the assumptions relate. A maximizing equilibrium that is Pareto-optimal can exist between giants, between pygmies, or between giants and pygmies—but of this more below.

We are now in a position to see the real significance of the widely recognized doctrine that there is no unique Pareto-optimum, that the contract curve represents a set of Pareto-optima with respect to which some additional value judgment, e.g., a Bergsonian social welfare function, is necessary as a basis on which to choose between the optima.[40] Not only is there a multiple number of Pareto-optima represented on the contract curve, which reflects alternative intial endowments, but there are an infinite number of Pareto-optima reflecting the many

---

39. Ragnar Frisch, *Maxima and Minima,* Chicago: Rand McNally, 1966, ch. 7; Koopmans, *op cit.,* pp. 46, 49 and *passim;* Mishan: Survey, p. 168; Ferguson, *op. cit.,* chs. 15-16, e.g., pp. 444-447; Dobb, *op. cit.,* pp. 11, 13; E. J. Mishan, The Recent Debate on Welfare Criteria, *Oxford Econ. Papers,* vol. 17, 1965, p. 225; and Bator, *The Question of Government Spending, op. cit.,* p. 86 (footnote); ". . . the equilibrium conditions which characterize a system of perfectly competitive markets will, given our assumptions, exactly correspond to the conditions implied by the solution of the mathematical maximizing problem which defines efficiency."

40. Henderson and Quandt, *op. cit.,* p. 208; Ferguson, *op. cit.,* pp. 434-435, 455; I. M. D. Little, *A Critique of Welfare Economics,* London: Oxford University Press, second ed., 1957, pp. 84, 118 and *passim;* Samuelson, *Foundations of Economic Analysis, op cit.,* p. 214 and *passim;* Mishan: Survey, pp. 163, 169, 177; Dobb, *op. cit.,* pp. 7, 11, 12, 83 (footnote), 252, 253; E. J. Mishan, *Welfare Economics,* New York: Random House, 1964, p. 177.

other assumptions and the mutiplicity of substantive contents of each of them. Pareto-optimum varies, for example, with income and wealth distribution,[41] with the power structure, and, most significantly for policy issues, with the law.[42]

We can also see that, aside from the no-loss stipulation (which will be examined in the next subsection), there is no conclusiveness to Pareto-optimality; rather it is formal, contingent, and relative. Despite the pretentiousness with which it is sometimes used (typically as a surrogate for consumer sovereignty), and notwithstanding the acknowledged utility of the concept under certain circumstances and for certain purposes, its inconclusive and even vacuous character is indicated by the fact that Pareto-optimality can exist both before *and* after any non-Pareto-optimal change occurs. Thus Samuelson has urged that Pareto-optimality is "not a theorem about ideal *laissez-faire* for it holds just as validly after good or bad (lump-sum) interferences have determined the initial distribution of wealth and earning powers. There are literally an infinite number of equilibrium states just as 'efficient' as that of laissez-faire individualism."[43] Pareto-optimality can exist before *and* after the exercise of state controls,[44] and both before *and* after the imposition of monopoly.[45] As Bator expresses the critical point, "if it is the right to choose that matters, any set of prices invented by an O.P.A. man gone berserk would do as well as any other."[46] In general, Pareto-optimality can exist both before *and* after any change in the structure of advantage and disadvantage.[47]

41. Frisch, *op. cit.,* p. 50; Walsh, *op. cit.,* p. 111; A. Allan Schmid, Nonmarket Values and Efficiency of Public Investments in Water Resources, *Am. Econ. Rev., Papers and Proceedings,* vol. 57, 1967, pp. 162ff; and Paul L. Kleinsorge, Property Rights and Behavior: Discussion, *ibid, loc. cit.,* p. 376.

42. Mishan, Pareto-Optimality and the Law, *op cit.,* and The Postwar Literature on Externalities: An Interpretive Essay, *Jour. Econ. Lit.,* vol. 9, 1971, pp. 18ff; and Paul Burrows, On External Costs and the Visible Arm of the Law, *Oxford Econ. Papers,* vol. 22, 1970; and Samuels, The Interrelation of Legal and Economic Processes, *op. cit.*

43. Samuelson, *Collected Scientific Papers, op. cit.,* vol. 2, p. 1410 (footnote); see also Musgrave, *op. cit.,* p. 991.

44. Bator, *The Question of Government Spending, op. cit.,* p. 124.

45. Samuelson, *Foundations of Economic Analysis, op. cit.,* p. 204.

46. Bator, *The Question of Government Spending, op. cit.,* p. 102.

47. "As there is no one set of inequalities that must necessarily flow from property and contract, it cannot be asserted dogmatically that a statutory rearrangement of the existing inequalities will necessarily involve more restriction on liberty and more impairment of property rights than the reverse. It may merely have the effect of weakening the liberty and property of the more favored to strengthen the liberty and property of the less favored." Robert L. Hale,

It is not surprising, then, that considerable scepticism has been expressed as to the viability of Pareto-optimality for welfare economics and the viability of a welfare economics in which Pareto-optimality is the major if not exclusive criterion of welfare improvement and which makes almost no effort beyond micro theory to articulate the processes through which welfare is attained and distributed. Samuelson, for example, has recommended "a corrosive nihilism" with regard to the exaggerated pretensions of Pareto-optimal reasoning; as he puts it, "Pareto-optimality is a definition, not an inevitable destination."[48] Others have pointed out that the concept deals with relative trivia, by avoiding the important cases. Thus Blaug writes that:

> Paretian welfare economics . . . achieves a stringent and positivist definition of the social optimum inasmuch as Pareto-optimality is defined with respect to an initial distribution of income. The practical relevance of this achievement for policy, however, is nil.[49]

As Henderson and Quandt acknowledge, "But almost every alternative to be judged by welfare economists will have favorable effects on some people and unfavorable effects on others."[50] This is echoed by Baumol, who writes of the Pareto-criterion that:

> Unfortunately, there are many policy proposals which cannot be judged with the aid of this criterion. The Pareto-criterion does not apply to any proposal which will benefit some and harm others. In other words, the Pareto-criterion works by sidestepping the crucial issue of interpersonal comparison, that is, by dealing only with cases where no one is harmed so that the problem does not arise.[51]

A similar position is taken by Dobb. After writing of "the extent to

---

Labor Legislation as an Enlargement of Individual Liberty, *American Labor Legislation Review*, vol. 15, 1925, p. 160. This is parallel to the point made in the text and suggests that policy issues similar to the ones on which Pareto-optimality takes either an explicit or implicit position (or with respect to which Pareto-optimality is sometimes (mis)used) have been debated before albeit in other terms and in different contexts.

48. Paul A. Samuelson, Pure Theory of Public Expenditure and Taxation, *in* Julius Margolis and Henri Guitton, eds., *Public Economics*, New York: St. Martin's, 1969, p. 107.

49. Blaug, *op cit.*, p. 607.

50. Henderson and Quandt, *op. cit.*, p. 201.

51. Baumol, *op cit.*, p. 376.

which the somewhat tortuous history of Welfare Economics has wit-
nessed formal sophistication serving as a cloak for deficient logic and
plain confusion," he writes that:

> The Pareto-criterion stops short, as it were, of providing an
> answer precisely within a region of decision where possibly
> the most crucial (and in practice the most difficult,) decisions
> may lie.[52]

He argues that the Pareto rule seems to lead to "a quite trivial result,
and something pretty close to a tautology," and that the maximum of
Pareto-optimality "is purely *relative* maximum."[53] Indeed, long ago
Little wrote that an optimum situation in the Pareto sense "which
corresponds to a bad distribution of income, may well be worse than
a 'sub-optimum' position corresponding to a good distribution of income."[54] (Such a judgment, of course, requires a value judgment
going beyond the "simple" value premise of Pareto-optimality; but we
shall see in the next subsection that that "simple" value premise coexists with much more subtle and important value premises.) Similar
points have been made by many others.[55] The upshot seems to be
that *as an approach to the ranking of alternatives* Pareto-optimality,
largely by self-abnegation, has a truly narrow range of significance;
that however powerful and appealing it is within that range, the limits
on Pareto-optimality required to make it acceptable and meaningful
utterly reduce its area of significance, so that its development often
appears, in Boulding's telling language, to have been an example of
a really "monumental misallocation of intellectual resources."[56] In the
following subsection I shall examine the significance of Pareto-optimality for the study of the *factors and forces governing the attainment
and distribution of welfare in society* in the context of a broader theory
of choice and power. We shall see further the limited range and role
of the Pareto-concept as an explanatory device.

---

52. Dobb, *op. cit.*, pp. vii, 11.
53. *Ibid.*, pp. 11-12.
54. Little, *op. cit.*, p. 84.
55. Mishan: Survey, pp. 175, 208; Kenneth J. Arrow, *Social Choice and Individ-
    ual Values*, New York: Wiley, second ed., 1963; J. de V. Graaff, *Theoretical
    Welfare Economics*, Cambridge University Press, 1967, e.g., p. 168.
56. Kenneth E. Boulding, The Economics of Knowledge and the Knowledge of
    Economics, *Am. Econ. Rev., Papers and Proceedings*, vol. 56, 1966, p. 12.

B. *Pareto-Optimum and Mutual Coercion*

The *descriptive* adequacy of the Pareto-criterion depends upon, first, the actual or potential scope of joint constrained maximization with the no-loss and consent requirements (i.e., no unacceptable or unaccepted losses) and, second, the coherence of the concept. The *normative* significance of the Pareto-criterion depends upon, first, the possible range of the criterion (i.e., if no-loss and complete-consent possibilities are insignificant, then the criterion, however desirable, becomes trivial); second, whether in fact it involves only "a simple value judgment;" third, the degree of adherence to it vis-a-vis other possible criteria of action (which shall not concern us here); and fourth, the coherence of the concept. The Pareto-criterion is only deceptively simple; actually it is fraught with complexities, making it far less coherent as either a description or a decision rule than is generally understood. By coherence I mean whether, whatever its alleged range, it applies to all the phenomena to which it is said to apply; that is, whether it applies to only one group of a larger set of analytically equivalent phenomena with the smaller group only arbitrarily distinguished from the larger. In other words, the coherence of the Pareto-criterion depends upon whether it really means that *no* loss is incurred in a Pareto-optimal adjustment; and whether consent is required in *all* respects in situations designated as Pareto-optimal. In this section I will attempt to show the limited descriptive utility of the Pareto-criterion with respect to the attainment and distribution of welfare *and* the limited normative significance of the criterion as a ranking concept, in each respect because, first, of its incompleteness with regard to the problem of loss and consent; second, it has a more complex normative character than is often realized; and third, it is inapplicable to the critical issues of policy, except insofar as its more subtle normative characteristics tend to involve it. Using the general model of choice and power developed in Section II, we shall see that the Pareto-criterion is incomplete *on its own terms* and that there is the need for welfare inquiry in terms of that broader model of choice and power.

1. *Pareto-Optimum as Choice Within the Status Quo Structure of Mutual Coercion*

There can be hardly any doubt that the grand thrust of the Pareto-criterion is *self-choice.*[57] Nor can there be any doubt that the corol-

---

57. Little, *op. cit.,* pp. 122, 124, 258; Mishan: Survey, pp. 156, 182, 189.

lary of self-choice under the Pareto-criterion is *consent,* consent to the point of *unanimity,* so that only that change is deemed optimal within the terms of Pareto-optimality which is by *voluntary agreement.* In order to avoid making interpersonal comparisons and choices, optimality is defined in terms of a consensual unanimity. The literature of welfare economics—at least that dealing with the "new" welfare economics—is replete with these ideas. We find, thus, that the Pareto-criterion is one in which "The definition [is one] of an improvement in the collective welfare which commands general assent . . .;"[58] the "Pareto-principle" is "that a unanimity of individual preferences implies a social preference;"[59] it is "the *unanimity rule,* that forms the basis for the *Pareto-ranking;*"[60] the Pareto rule is synonymous with "voluntary agreement."[61] The logic of Pareto-optimality is the logic of consensus, of unanimity, of voluntarism.

But the consensual agreement exists only in the form of a maximizing equilibrium between individuals as each chooses from within his respective opportunity set of available alternatives. Pareto-optimality emphasizes the individual, or individual-consent, facet of choice, the methodologically individualist facet; but the choice process is social, methodologically collectivist, and not individualist only. The logic of Pareto-optimality tends to obscure the processes whereby the structure of opportunity sets is generated; it tends to obscure the coercive impact of the behavior and choices of others, the absence of consent in basic choice processes, and that accepted opportunity costs are losses too. The choice of Pareto-optimality is choice from within the individual's opportunity set. A paradigmatic and revealing, and only seemingly extreme, example of the "voluntarist" argument is the case involving the assumption of political mobility (the option to choose exclusion from a political jurisdiction, i.e., emigration) with the inference that if one elects not to emigrate (and thereby accepts the domestic situation) then that individual is satisfied, ergo in a Pareto-optimum situation.[62] But this is only choice from an opportunity set, an acceptance of one injury (the disutilities of remaining at home) to avoid another presumably more undesirable one—as when any price is paid. The individual has a choice between the alternatives of remaining or emigrating but he has no choice as to the

58. Mishan, *Welfare Economics, op. cit.,* p. 160.
59. Arrow, *op. cit.,* p. 96.
60. Quirk and Saposnik, *op. cit.,* p. 116.
61. William F. Campbell, Adam Smith's Theory of Justice, Prudence, and Beneficence, *Am. Econ. Rev., Papers and Proceedings,* vol. 57, 1967, p. 575.
62. Hochman and Rodgers, Reply, *op. cit.,* p. 999.

range of his options and their respective relative costs. To call his choice Pareto-optimal is only to say that he made it, and to thoroughly neglect the structure of and the forces governing his opportunity set amid the total structure of decision making. It also neglects the *absence of (his) consent* which is characteristic of his having to choose between the restricted alternatives open to him because of the operation of mutual coercion, e.g., a mass psychology (stimulated by public opinion leaders) in which—certain policies having become identified with the national "ism"—the individual is told (and perhaps constrained so to act as) to either love it or leave it, or where the only alternative to (a hazardously and rarely achieved) political asylum abroad may be a politically operating "insane" asylum.

Similarly, consumer sovereignty is more than the right to choose. It signifies consumer choice with consequences for production and the allocation of resources. But even consumer sovereignty is only a choice from within opportunity sets and it involves both the individual benefiting from and the individual being injured by those consequences for production, e.g., through actual or no production, or through low rather than high prices. It is not enough to argue, or to show, that "Neither supplier nor demander, neither producer nor consumer, imposes his will on other parties to the exchange."[63] For it is not generally a question of whether the individual is under the control of another but rather a matter of the impact of others' behavior and choices upon his opportunity set. Nor is it a matter of the market being competitive or noncompetitive, for even a competitive market will give effect to the structure of power operating through it, e.g., resource allocation will tend to reflect the dollar "votes" whose pattern will depend upon the distribution of income and wealth.

The structure of the individual's alternatives, in most if not all economic situations, is given him without his own consent; e.g., even if he pays or is paid the competitive market price (or the centrally planned price), he is a price taker. To speak of willingness or volition to buy is incomplete: a Pareto-optimum situation may mean either *no desire* to change or an *inability* to change. What Pareto-optimality does is to "accept the *status quo* distribution as a measure of the relative strength of feeling of the two individuals."[64] But status quo income and wealth distribution is not a clear proxy for desire; it tells us things only in terms of the individual's selections from his oppor-

---

63. Harold Demsetz, Economics in the Industrial State: Discussion, *Am. Econ. Rev., Papers and Proceedings*, vol. 60, 1970, p. 482.

64. Baumol, *op. cit.*, p. 379.

tunity set and nothing about his preferred opportunity set or, more important, how his actual opportunity set is formed through mutual coercion. *Pareto-optimal transactions are only chosen adjustments within the opportunity set structure accorded by the status quo structure of power or mutual coercion, and the forebearance of others.* Welfare in the real world is maximized, even subject to constraints, not only by the exercise of choice from within one's opportunity set but by participation in the process of mutual coercion governing the structure and content of opportunity sets. Moreover, Pareto-optimality's meaning being limited only to choice from within opportunity sets, it neglects the structure of opportunity sets and the relative status of the advantaged and the disadvantaged; and in addition neglects the *nonconsensual* status of the *adverse* (i.e., loss-incurring) recipients of mutual coercion, in part and perhaps especially those who are in one way or another third parties to transactions. This latter brings us to the concept of externalities, which is the subject of Section IV below; but it should be clear that Pareto-optimality is limited to only one—and one relatively small—area of choice; and that the process of mutual coercion operates to make of the "voluntarist" or consensual thrust of Pareto-optimality something less descriptive and more visionary than has been generally recognized. In addition, it should be clear that what is here called coercion is not absolute or total, rather that it has meaning only within the total structure and process of *mutual* coercion, which follow from scarcity and interdependence. In this sense, coercion is ubiquitous, even though there is at work a subjective sieve (also ubiquitous) which perceives certain acts and not others as subjectively (and unjustifiably) "coercive" when they all share the general character ascribed to them earlier. The ubiquity of coercion, and the inevitability of opportunity costs, are no excuse for not making moral judgments; nor are they an excuse not to study the structure and process of mutual coercion.

Consider the case for the capitalist market system, which is generally articulated in terms of competition and private property. Competition rests on a wide diffusion of power and, like private property, upon "self-choice." Pareto-optimality is concerned with self-choice, yet there is all the world of difference between an equilibrium (Pareto-optimum) between giants, between pygmies, and between giants and pygmies. However in each of these cases there is a structure of mutual coercion; so long as there is scarcity coupled with interdependence, an individual's opportunity set, even in the case of "perfect" equality, would be a function of mutual coercion. One form of posing the point at issue is to ask if the rights of private property include the right to monopolize[65]—for Pareto-optimal solutions will emerge under either competition or monopoly: given the usual neoclassical model of monopoly, any move to a socially superior solution through increasing competition is not, or is not necessarily, Pareto-optimal for the monopolist. No wonder that Baumol maintains that "The obverse of a unanimity rule is the veto power which it gives to any one person if an arrangement is not initially optimal. It offers special advantages to anyone who can continue an arrangement whereby he profits at the expense of the rest of the community. A unanimity rule is the ideal instrument for the preservation of externalities and inequities which are already extant."[66] Pareto-optimum as a decision rule thus becomes an instrument of power play, of mutual coercion, allowing the perpetuation of privilege. But more on this later; the present point is that both competition and private property involve coercion, nonconsensual impact, and loss.

What all this means is that Pareto-optimal solutions and adjustments take place only within the opportunity set structure rendered by the status quo power structure through mutual coercion. *Pareto-optimum solutions and adjustments exist only within and as a partial function of the structure and process of mutual coercion.* When prices are paid in the market to secure or escape from something, they are

---

65. Karl de Schweinitz, Jr., Free Enterprise in a Growth World, *South. Econ. Jour.*, vol. 29, 1962, p. 103 (footnote). Writes Samuelson: "Mere voluntarism, therefore, is not the root merit of the doctrine of the Invisible Hand: what is important about it is the system of checks and balances that comes under perfect competition, and its measure of validity is at the technocratic level of efficiency, not at the ethical level of freedom and individualism." *Collected Scientific Papers, op. cit.,* vol. 2, p. 1410. It *is* the system of checks and balances that is competition which is important: the market is a grand discretion-limiting institution, but it requires competition in market structure *and* a widespread diffusion of social power if it is to produce the values historically associated with the market economy. (Mishan also argues that "the range of voluntary agreements that are, or might be, entered into within the existing legal framework cannot be vindicated, at least not on ethical grounds, by reference to invisible-hand arguments." Pareto-Optimality and the Law, *op. cit.,* p. 280.)

66. William J. Baumol, *Welfare Economics and the Theory of the State,* Cambridge: Harvard University Press, second ed., 1965, pp. 43-44. The literature of welfare economics treats, and appropriately so, many such cases as bribery, in which individuals are so positioned as to be able to secure money or other payments as the price of either restraining some affirmative action of theirs or of no longer withholding something of value to others, i.e., exacting a price for their consent. As Baumol makes clear, the Pareto-criterion, through its consent requirement, places a premium on withholding in order to be bought off.

paid in order to incur one cost so as to avoid a felt larger one; but all this—all this equimarginal adjustment—takes place within and as a function of the opportunity set structure generated by power play through mutual coercion. The individual choice involved is correlative to the social choice of which it is a part. Such things as income distribution and the choices made by others restrict and may even prohibit certain transactions by channeling the generation of opportunity sets.[67] Correlative to the selection from within opportunity sets is the mutual coercion which creates and destroys, and reduces and increases the costs of, particular alternatives and sets of available alternatives; the mutual coercion which entails loss without consent. Consensual choice is but a part, though an integral part, of this larger coercive process, a process which is no less coercive because individuals exercise choice, for paradoxically it is through the exercise of choice that mutual coercion takes place.

With Pareto-optimal adjustments taking place only within and as a function of the system of mutual coercion, the questions of "*whose* interests" and "*which* consumers" are resolved through the exercise of power, through mutual coercion. As Allan Schmid has put it,

> One cannot talk of Pareto-better trades unless property rights are first established to say who counts. Depending on the property rights, there are all kinds of Pareto-better trades possible which would produce a whole range of price sets (i.e., relative prices of paper, chemicals, fishing, and views) and other performance results in terms of growth in per capita income, inflation, employment, kinds and variety of available products, and mental health.[68]

The fundamental problem is not just self-choice or that individual preferences are to count, but *whose* choice and *whose* preferences. We have seen that there is theoretically no "unique" Pareto-optimal solution; but any *achieved* Pareto-optimal solution *is* "unique" in re-

---

67. Including through differential burdens of reaching optimal adjustments and arrangements between the parties. See Mishan, Pareto-Optimality and the Law, *op. cit.*, and The Postwar Literature on Externalities: An Interpretive Essay, *op. cit.*, p. 19; and Marc J. Roberts, Environmental Quality: Discussion, *American Economic Review: Papers and Proceedings*, vol. 61, 1971, pp. 174ff.

68. Schmid, *op. cit.*, p. 164. "The use of markets was 'justified' above in terms of their efficiency in catering to consumers' tastes. But which consumer's tastes? How much weight is to be given to Crusoe's as against Friday's?" Bator, *The Question of Government Spending, op. cit.*, p. 87. See also Dobb, *op. cit.*, p. 91.

gard to the extant structure of power. Each Pareto-optimal solution is a temporary equilibrium within the existing process of mutual coercion, generating the opportunity sets on the basis of which the next round of choices will tend to produce another maximizing-equilibrium or Pareto-optimal solution or adjustment. The Pareto-optimum actually reached is a function of the status quo power structure, or as expressed in a more conventional context but to the same effect:

> Rather than a single social welfare function there are many, each expressing the evaluations of different groups of people. Which one is chosen for the purpose of solving the problem of allocation depends upon the institutional framework within which society decides upon such matters.[69]

—it depends, in other words, upon the total structure of power, whether in the form of private property or not.

As the statement just quoted suggests, all of this is recognized interstitially and even hesitatingly in the literature of welfare economics. What the present analysis insists upon is a more complete and explicit analysis of choice and power in the generation and distribution of welfare,[70] a more elaborate and explicit analysis of the

---

69. Henderson and Quandt, *op. cit.*, p. 223. "In most actual situations we come to a point at which choices between goals must be made: do you want this kind of freedom and this kind of hunger, or that kind of freedom and that kind of hunger? I use these terms in a quasi-algebraic sense, but actually what is called 'freedom' is really a vector of almost infinite components rather than a one-dimensional thing that can be given a simple ordering." Samuelson, *Collected Scientific Papers, op. cit.*, vol. 2, p. 1414. See also Roland N. McKean, *Public Spending*, New York: McGraw-Hill, 1968, p. 19.

70. Writes Samuelson: "The game is up for abnegation of all social decision making. To 'do nothing' is not really to do nothing but to continue to do what has been done. Since coercion is willy-nilly involved, and there is no algebraic magnitude of it that can be minimized in the interests of maximizing algebraic freedom of *n* men, what can abstract reasoning deduce concerning the 'equitable' exercise of coercion, or, what may be the same thing, concerning the setting up of optimal arrangements for cooperation? Very little, as experience has shown and as Reason itself confirms." *Collected Scientific Papers, op. cit.*, p. 1416. Samuelson may or may not be right in his pessimism; at the very least, further study can help clarify policy choices, e.g., by identifying all alternatives as coercive and not some as coercion and others as freedom, thus loading the decisional scales *a priori*. The leading attempt at an analysis of setting up a theory of constitution making is in terms of Pareto-optimal analysis and shares the limitations presented here, though on the deeper level of rule making: James M. Buchanan and Gordon Tullock, *The Calculus of Consent*, Ann Arbor: University of Michigan Press, 1962. For the study of the operation of mutual coercion within government, see McKean, *op. cit.*, ch. 2 and references given therein.

processes which are nonconsensual and which administer the distribution of sacrifice, of loss, of scarcity. As for the literature of economics, I have argued elsewhere that there does in fact exist a considerable body of literature articulating the nature and scope of economic policy in terms of broader questions of choice and power,[71] and that the scope of economics historically has included the theory of power as a second, albeit unsystematized, tradition alongside economic theory (considered as micro and macro).[72] In the literature of welfare economics, the problem of power is clearly present in the writings of Mishan, Dobb, Samuelson, Schmid, Buchanan and Tullock, and others. Perhaps the most pithy statement has been that of Bator (quoting Isaiah Berlin):

> Interaction among different people's individual freedoms is only too often one of rivalry and conflict. As with other good things in life that are scarce, choice and compromise are unavoidable. "Freedom for the pike is death for the minnows."[73]

An even more powerful statement, one directly to the point of this discussion, has been given by Musgrave:

> Pareto-optimal redistribution thus constitutes a *secondary redistribution* which depends on the initial distribution of earnings. This distribution is determined by such factors as inheritance, earning capacities, education, and market structure. It may itself be changed through the political process. Such changes, referred to here as *primary redistribution*, are not a matter of voluntary giving, but of taking.
>
> How is this primary redistribution decided upon? To the extent that it operates within the legal framework, it is performed through the voting mechanism. At a normative level, this explanation is not very helpful, however, since it merely raises the next issue, i.e., how the distribution of votes and the voting rules are to be decided on. Eventually, the problem becomes one of social-contract determination. At a positive level, primary redistribution depends on the social structure and balance of power between income groups. As these change,

---

71. Samuels, The Nature and Scope of Economic Policy, *in The Classical Theory of Economic Policy*, Cleveland: World, 1966, Appendix.

72. Samuels, The Scope of Economics Historically Considered, mimeographed.

73. Bator, *The Question of Government Spending, op. cit.*, p. 120. On Lindahl's assumption of equality of bargaining power, see Samuelson *in* Margolis and Guitton, *op. cit.* p. 115.

corresponding changes occur in the voting decisions and/or voting rules.[74]

The structure of social power is what counts, and not individual choice in a power vacuum. If intellectual resources were devoted to the study of what Musgrave specifies as the problem on the positive level, welfare economics would have a very productive life indeed.

We have seen that Pareto-optimal adjustments and solutions are specific to the system of mutual coercion in which they arise, and that the very thrust of Pareto-optimality is compromised and constrained by the nonconsensual imposition of loss that takes place in and through mutual coercion, loss in terms of range of alternatives and relative cost of alternatives. This yields further insight into the important fact that Pareto-optimum solutions take place within the status quo moral and legal rules. First, it is necessary to recognize that Pareto-optimal solutions *are* specific to the state of the law.[75]

---

74. Musgrave, *op. cit.*, p. 991. It is in reply to this and other comments by Musgrave that Hochman and Rodgers brought up the case of political mobility, resisting the notion of power. This is a good example of the slipperiness of the Pareto-criterion in practice: it can be used to cast luster on any set of arrangements which the user wants to support simply by arguing that if anything better were possible then the adjustment would be made. Hochman and Rodgers thus also speak of the social contract, yet the concept of social contract is a myth, albeit one with enormous evocative power: thus Bentham, unlike Blackstone and St. George Tucker, "quite properly recognized that . . . [its] function was to provide a moral basis for authority or for the rebellion against authority." Robert M. Cover, Book Review, *Columbia Law Review*, vol. 70, 1970, p. 1484. Social contract and Pareto-optimum are both consensual myths (which *are* important in their social control effects—it is in this respect that Pareto-optimum has substituted for the doctrine of consumer sovereignty; on the social control aspect of economic thought see Joan Robinson, *Economic Philosophy*, Chicago: Aldine, 1962); but the social contract can also be seen as an ongoing process, not a once-for-all-time matter, so that even revolution can be interpreted as a mutual-coercion renegotiation of primary redistribution akin, on a larger or more time-compressed scale, to the redistribution effectuated through mutual coercion in the marketplace. Unlike social contract, Pareto-optimality has yet to legitimize a revolutionary movement, unless contemporary libertarianism is so interpreted. On the problem of power see also: Ferguson, *op. cit.*, p. 434; Dobb, *op. cit.*, p. 16 (footnote); and Tullock, *op. cit.*, who acknowledge the problem of power structure through recognizing the asymmetry of power and bargaining.

75. See Mishan, Pareto-Optimality and the Law, *op. cit.*, where he writes of "the general conclusion that the pattern of costs and outputs varies with the state of the law . . . ," p. 276, and The Postwar Literature on Externalities: An Interpretive Essay, *op cit.*; Schmid, *op. cit.*, pp. 162-164; and Tullock, *op. cit.*, pp. 91-2, 95 and *passim*. For Pareto's view, that maximum collective ophelimity is specific to the rules governing distribution, see James A. Gherity, ed., *Economic Thought*, New York: Random House, 1965, p. 411.

Pareto-optimality exudes the spirit of laissez faire but Pareto-optimality can be reached after as well as before a legal change: change the law and change Pareto-optimality. Pareto-optimality will yield a formal solution, given the state of the law; but change the law and the substance of the formal solution will change. Laissez faire markets constitute a power structure within the law; change the law and change the power structure within which Pareto-optimal solutions and adjustments are generated or worked out.[76]

Market positions relevant to Pareto-optimizing behavior are partially a function of the working rules which govern the acquisition, structure, and use of power, e.g., property rights (including any right to monopolize). The relative capacity of an economic actor to enter and participate in the market, to acquire gains and to thrust costs upon others, to reach optimal adjustments,[77] etc., all are a function of the structure of legal rights and of the legal and moral rules governing those rights.

It is also easy to see how the legal and moral rules become an object of power play and what I have called the principle of the use of government: government is a vehicle available to whomever can control or use it, so that individuals and groups seek to control government in order to formulate legal rules of benefit to them. This represents a further compromising of the Pareto-criterion: part of the nonconsensual losses which Pareto-optimality analysis ignores are the losses consequent to changes in the legal and moral rules brought about by those in a position to use government to change the rules to their advantage. Thus, Pareto-optimal solutions are a function of the jockeying for position for political control, hence political structure, which governs the change of legal rules, the structure of opportunity sets, and thereby who can inflict nonconsensual change and losses upon whom. Pareto-optimal solutions are specific to the political structure under which they are worked out.[78]

Finally, we are in a position to grasp the general equilibrium paradigm in which the Pareto-criterion is a limited partial equilibrium concept. For it is true *both* that the working rules govern the distri-

---

76. "Laissez-faire markets, as also well-policed competitive markets, constitute a particular political structure, with a particular set of rules and practices, which yields a particular distribution of the things people want." Bator, *The Question of Government Spending, op. cit.*, p. 117.

77. Mishan, Pareto-Optimality and the Law, *op. cit.*, p. 255; and Harold Demsetz, Why Regulate Utilities?, *Jour. of Law and Econ.* vol. II, 1968, p. 61.

78. *Inter alia*, see Donald Ray Escarraz, Wicksell and Lindahl: Theories of Public Expenditure and Tax Justice Reconsidered, *National Tax Jour.*, vol. 20, 1967, p. 148; Henderson and Quandt, *op. cit.*, p. 223.

bution of power *and* that the distribution of power governs the development of the working rules. It is within this general equilibrium paradigm that it is true *both* that the opportunity set of an individual is a function of the total structure of power *and* that the total structure of power is a function of the decisions made by individuals from within the opportunity sets enjoyed by them at any point in time and over time. In general, the variables are individual choice, power structure, opportunity set structure, and working rules, as well as resource allocation and income distribution. They are all interdependent, i.e., they are all both dependent and independent variables. Pareto-optimality is a product of both consent and coercion. The Pareto-criterion is a partial-equilibrium, individual-choice concept not at all representative of the general-equilibrium, social choice character of the process in which welfare is attained and distributed; consensus and consent are the heart of the Pareto-criterion but they only incompletely characterize the system of mutual coercion within the market and its set of rules and the political system and its rules which determine the market rules yet which itself is a function of power play, a dual process of interacting feedback. It is in this larger, general-equilibrium context, that we may appreciate the thrust and possibilities of what Buchanan calls "creative institutionalism,"[79] which, notwithstanding their generally conflicting approaches to welfare economics, is akin to what Mishan sees as "alterations in the legal framework that would promote Pareto improvements unattainable under the existing system," in part thereby "surely to expand the range of society's choices in a significant way," a situation superior, in terms of Pareto-optimum logic itself, to that in which there is unconcern "with the existing legal framework that acts to inhibit socially significant choices from being brought into effect."[80]

Still further ramifications of the underlying analysis are evident. First, it is possible to see that the cost-price structure existing at any time is not only a function of individuals' choices and production technologies, but also of, and indeed specific to, the status quo structure of power, mutual coercion, and working rules. The conditions of demand and supply, hence the conditions under which cost and revenue functions are generated and calculated, arise within and as a partial function of the structure and process of mutual coercion. Prices and costs, through demand and supply, reflect social power.

---

79. See discussion in Samuels, *The Classical Theory of Economic Policy, op. cit.,* p. 272 (including note 150).
80. Mishan, Pareto-Optimality and the Law, *op. cit.,* p. 281.

One implication of this, elaborated in the following subsection, is that optimizing in terms of existing cost-price ratios generated as a partial function of status quo income distribution, power structure, and working rules, serves to reenforce the existing distributional institutions. Indeed, the existing distributional institutions cast luster on the optimizing outcomes *and* the optimizing outcomes cast luster on the distributional institutions. This has been pointed out, for example, by Dobb, who argues that inasmuch as the substantive conditions of equilibrium reflect production patterns generated in part "by reference to a specific pattern of demand *(via* the influence of the latter on prices)," it "is relative to a certain distribution of income, with the 'weighting' or relative 'pull' given by this distribution to individual demands in composing the aggregate demand of the market."[81] Since not only is it the case that income distribution is a partial function of resource allocation but resource allocation is a partial function of income distribution, Dobb approvingly quotes Mishan that "a bias in favour of the *status quo* enters whenever one aims to bring the economy closer to an optimum using the existing set of prices, since this set of prices itself emerges from the existing distribution."[82]

The importance of this mutual-coercion specificity of costs and prices for the structure of opportunity sets can follow the formation of factor prices back through supply and demand to the allocation of property (and other equivalent) rights. This was long ago expressed by Alfred Marshall. In a discussion of the market position of unskilled workers (in the chapter of the *Principles* preceding his discussion of the cumulative market disadvantages of labor generally), Marshall wrote that, "There is no more urgent social need than that labour of this kind should be made scarce and therefore dear."[83] The relevant meaning of this is found in the statement of Meade that:

> If citizen A owns nothing except a factor (e.g., his own unskilled labour) whose price is low and needs for his family's welfare goods whose price is high, he will be very poor, as compared with citizen B who happens to own a factor (e.g., a scarce natural resource) whose price is high and who happens to need for his family's enjoyment goods which are very cheap.[84]

---

81. Dobb, *op. cit.,* p. 57.
82. *Ibid,* p. 59, quoting Mishan, *The Costs of Economic Growth, op. cit.,* p. 49.
83. Alfred Marshall, *Principles of Economics,* New York: Macmillan, 8th ed., 1920, p. 558.
84. Meade, *op. cit.,* p. 11.

and the statements of Schmid:

> Efficiency depends on the relevant input-output categories and
> it is collective judgment expressed in property rights which
> determines relevancy.[85]

and:

> . . . the plight of the poor man—he just does not count because
> he owns very little that is a cost to other people.[86]

Prices and costs, then, reflect not only existential scarcity, tastes, and
production technologies, but also the institutional distribution of that
scarcity through the power structure and mutual coercion, e.g.,
through the legal distribution of things that are or become cost items
to other people. And if costs and prices are partially a function of
power structure and wealth distribution, then productivity, too, is
similarly governed, which means that factor pricing according to
productivity *is* partially factor pricing according to institutional arrangements, and that to justify income as a proxy for productivity by
reference to institutions and to justify institutions by reference to
how they reward productivity is to reason in a circle, as when rights
are justified by results and results are justified by rights.[87] Quite
aside from the problem of the role of theory as ideology (the social
control function of legitimation), the problem of social efficiency is
how to maintain "equitable" background income distribution, power
structure, and other arrangements and *still* have efficiency in the sense
of prices equal to marginal costs,[88] a statement which, I urge, is a
purely positive proposition. Equity is very much mixed up with efficiency; or, to say the same thing in other words, institutional arrangements figure very much in economic efficiency.

Another ramification which also severely compromises the Pareto-
criterion, has to do with what is recognized as a loss. This will be the
heart of the discussion on externalities in Section IV, but at this stage
let me make two main points. The first is that Pareto-optimal reasoning

---

85. Schmid, *op. cit.*, p. 163.
86. *Ibid*, p. 162.
87. Hale's theories of resource allocation, income distribution, and productivity
    as a function of mutual coercion and their institutional (legal) bases are dis-
    cussed in Samuels, The Economy as a System of Power and Its Legal Bases:
    The Legal Economics of Robert Lee Hale, mimeographed.
88. Cf. Samuelson, *in* Margolis and Guitton, *op. cit.*, p. 122.

recognizes a narrow range of costs, injuries, or losses. Specifically, it neglects the wide range of losses imposed upon opportunity sets through the operation of mutual coercion. Given the individual's preferences, the individual is subject to profound income effects resulting from changes in prices and costs which emanate from the exercise of others' choice-making. The individual makes a choice in the context of the costs imposed in the form of restrictions upon his opportunity set through the coercive actions of others in the market. The choices of economic actors (as they make Pareto-optimal marginal adjustments) have ramifications upon the structure of mutual coercion and upon the power structure underlying it. Pareto-optimal analysis generally does not acknowledge that damage sustained through choice, sustained by the individual and by others, is loss. This brings me to the second point, which is that Pareto-optimal analysis generally has a narrow view as to evidence of loss. It takes acquiescence in a transaction as evidence of *non*-injury, as evidence of *non*-loss, as if the acquiescence purges the costs incurred or prices paid of their quality as a loss, which makes non-injury or non-loss tautological with choice.[89] That the individual chooses what is to him the lesser of two costs is considered to obviate the existence of costs. The Pareto-optimum treatment of loss thus tends to parallel the legal doctrine of *damnum absque injuria*, of damage without (legally recognized) injury, to the effect that only those losses are recognized as losses within the terms of the analysis which are deemed relevant. Yet all costs are costs, all losses are losses, and while the legal process cannot be tied up with the litigation of minutiae torts, what is minute to one person may be important to another, and may even change to a major matter over time—for welfare economics it is myopic to consider only certain costs and losses as Pareto-relevant (see Section IV). Not only does this fly in the face of the doctrine of the ubiquity of opportunity costs, but it considers losses only in terms of the *absence* of an individual's (subjectively-based) rejection of an alternative.

---

89. Thus Bator has acknowledged that "The liberal rule (J. S. Mill) that everyone should be allowed to pursue his own goals his own way save only that he not frustrate others is but a variant of the efficiency rule" of Pareto-optimality "applied to 'freedom.'" Bator, *The Question of Government Spending, op. cit.*, p. 120 (footnote). In a world of scarcity and interdependence the rule, either in the Stuart Mill or Pareto form, is impossible to enforce absolutely and is only applied selectively on the basis of seeing certain costs as reprehensible losses and others as inevitable or natural. (Again, I am not suggesting that we not choose, for indeed we have to; what I am suggesting is that welfare economics not be myopic in its theoretical construction, however inadequate cost-benefit analysis has to be in practice.)

Thus, if revolutionaries can convince owners of capital that the loss of certain of their apparent wealth is necessary for them to maximize their real wealth over time, there is no loss. Opportunity costs *are* subjective but they cannot be simply dismissed by failing to consider as losses the prices paid in the consummation of certain choices. The fact that an individual "accepts" an injury or loss as the necessary cost of avoiding what is to him a greater injury or loss does not keep the smaller loss from being a loss. If the hold-up man says to give him your money or your life, and you choose the former, it remains a loss. If the price of a commodity increases and the individual continues to buy, there is still a cost or loss, just as there was still a cost at the old price and just as there would still be a cost if the price fell part way. Economic actors sustain losses both when they choose and when they do not, i.e., through both their own choices and the choices of others. If we mean by loss any reduction or impairment in the position of the individual, then Pareto-optimal logic is simply incomplete when it treats as a "no-loss" situation any situation in which the individual makes a choice, for the opportunity costs of the alternative chosen are opportunity set losses also. Part of the problem is cost-identification and part, cost-calculation, yet much recent literature seems intent on salvaging the consensual character of the Pareto-criterion in the face of ever greater recognition of the ubiquity of what has come to be called external costs; but more on this in Section IV. Here I only urge that there are relevant losses far beyond what the Pareto-criterion has so far recognized.

We see, then, that *both* the normative and descriptive value of the ostensibly consensual, no-loss Pareto-criterion is greatly attenuated by the criterion's neglect of the fact of ubiquitous non-Pareto-optimal change. Although the Pareto-criterion would limit change by its consensual and no-loss requirements, much if not most economic change is through choices having impact upon others, impact which is both nonconsensual and loss (and benefit) imposing, both adversely and favorably affecting the structure of opportunity sets and their respective contents. Much if not all legal activity is nonconsensual; much non-Pareto-optimal change takes place within the market through mutual coercion as the inevitable direct and indirect result of the exercise of choice. Acceptance of Pareto-optimality *even on its own terms* is to neglect vast areas of non-Pareto-optimal change. Pareto-optimality thus accepts and even reenforces the consequences of power play outside of its own highly restricted domain. Consideration of only Pareto-optimal aspects of choice obscures the non-Pareto-optimal changes and thereby casts luster on certain change-producing activity.

casts denigration on certain other change-producing activity, and obscures still other change-producing activity. Among other things it
fails to acknowledge costs and losses and nonconsensual activity even
when they are the unintended consequences of otherwise purposive
and consensual activity and choice. In so doing it sidesteps critical
issues, issues which are critical on its own terms, not to mention issues
critical in terms of rules or criteria other than the Pareto-criterion.

2. *The Complex Ethical Character of the Pareto-Criterion*

The new welfare economics lauds the welfare superiority of the
Pareto-criterion, which, while remaining normative, is predicated only
upon the "one fundamental ethical postulate"[90] that individual preferences are to count, but involving the consensual and no-loss requirements. The ascendency of the new welfare economics, while rooted
to some unkown extent in an effort to make welfare economics safe
for the market system,[91] was also grounded in more technical concerns: the impossibility of making "correct" interpersonal utility comparisons; the inconclusiveness of such comparisons even if we could
make them with respect to individuals as they are, and the necessary
extension into an evaluation of the different capacities to derive
utility possessed by different people, and of the varying social conditions governing that capacity; and the general problems in making
acceptable ethical judgments the basis of social science research, particularly when they are explicitly and unambiguously made. Otherwise, if utility or ethical judgments could be proceeded upon, they
could be used as the substantive criterion of maximizing with which
to rank alternatives. Pareto-optimality is a minimum maximum seen
as obtained through avoiding interpersonal utility comparisons and
at the same time a maximum minimum seen as achieved through
consent. The Pareto-criterion is attractive in its apparent ability to
avoid making both interpersonal utility comparisons and deep value
judgments.

I am going to suggest, however, that the Pareto-criterion does *not*

---

90. Samuelson, *Foundations of Economic Analysis, op. cit.,* p. 223; Quirk and
Saposnik, *op. cit.,* p. 104; Bator *in* Breit and Hochman, *op. cit.,* p. 390 (footnote).

91. After all, the Pigovian welfare economics opened the door to all sorts of
tax-subsidy schemes and other tinkering under the legitimizing rubric of
bringing social and private costs and benefits into line, of correcting the
deficiencies of the marketplace, i.e., a powerful and open-minded rationale
for governmental activism; see below.

rest upon simply[92] the "one fundamental ethical postulate" that individual preferences are to count, but upon a much more complex and elaborate, if subtle, structure of value judgments; that so far from being "neutral" with regard to policy questions, the Pareto-criterion functions conservatively to reenforce the status quo decision-making process, its incidents and its results, whatever they are; and that its ethical character therefore resides in taking positions in precisely the areas of the larger paradigm of choice and power with respect to which Pareto-optimality has been seen deficient.

There is no question that the proposition that individual preferences are to count *is* a fundamental value judgment. But while it is fundamental, it is not simple, for, in the way it is used as the Pareto-criterion, it incorporates other subtle value judgments.[93] These value judgments include the following: that the individual is the best judge of his own wants, "the sole judge of his own welfare;"[94] "that individuals should have what they want;"[95] "that an individual is better off if he is in a chosen position;"[96] "that the welfare of the community depends on the welfare of the individuals comprising it, and on nothing else;"[97] and "that if at least one person is better off, and no one worse off, the community is better off."[98] These ethical propositions are considerably *more specific* than the general proposition that individual preferences are to count. Yet they are *not explicitly specific* as to *which* individuals or *whose* preferences are to count. Nevertheless we shall see below that there *is* a tacit or implicit value judgment as to who shall count.

---

92. "In the absence of elaborate value judgments concerning the desirability of alternative income distribution, a simple value judgment is to consider a reallocation to represent an improvement in welfare if it makes at least one person better off without making anybody worse off." Henderson and Quandt, *op. cit.*, p. 222.

93. The recognition that some of these uses are obviated when the Pareto-criterion is applied in the context of central planning—as will be seen below—only compromises the criterion itself. That recognition does point—when such application is juxtaposed to the uses noted in the following text—to the pro-market posture or use of the criterion in the West (as a substitute for consumer sovereignty as an assumption).

94. Mishan: Survey, p. 189.

95. Little, *op. cit.*, p. 258.

96. *Ibid*, p. 124. ". . . that anything which results from the voluntary agreements of uncoerced individuals must make them better (or best) off in some important sense." Samuelson, *Collected Scientific Papers, op. cit.*, vol. 2, p. 1409. ". . . that these individual preferences in turn are somehow related to the satisfaction or 'happiness' of consumers, an assumption that is at least somewhat debatable." Quirk and Saposnik, *op. cit.*, p. 105 (footnote).

97. Mishan: Survey, p. 156; cf. 189.

98. *Ibid*, p. 156.

The Paretian analysis is further ethically complex in its conception of optimality or goodness, "that it is a good thing to make one man better off if nobody else is made worse off."[99] The Pareto-criterion may be stipulated as either the *sole,* or *exclusive,* or the *minimum,* statement of goodness, but the typical advocate of the new welfare economics does postulate the "welfare superiority of any Paretian allocation over any non-Paretian one,"[100] that economics should not go beyond the Pareto-criterion.[101] In other words, it normatively assumes Pareto-optimality as *the* optimum for normative economics, e.g., in accepting the contract curve as representing welfare optima.[102] Also implicit is an ethical judgment of the propriety of *maximizing* per se. But while Koopmans is certainly correct that the descriptive and the normative theories of micro-welfare economics are two sides of one coin,[103] Stigler long ago pointed out that the Paretian analysis may conflict with elements of the traditional moral code.[104] Whose moral code, then? Since maximizing is recognized as always within the extant moral rules, to assume the propriety of maximizing regardless of moral code is an awkward ethical position. This is so except insofar as the notion of *constrained* maximization permits and carries detailed specification of the moral code—yet even this is often vitiated by the laissez faire animus of the Pareto analysis (though more usually directed against change of legal rather than non-legal working rules). The new welfare economics thus has "recommendatory force,"[105] but while it does posit a concept of the good, that concept is made ambiguous by its embodiment in a rule (the Pareto-criterion) which absolutely (too strong?) justifies maximizing per se independent of constraining moral rules yet also postulates that all maximizing is

99. Graaff, *op. cit.,* p. 10.

100. Writing about the neglect of welfare distribution effects, Thomas E. Borcherding wrote that, "Implicitly, this amounts to assuming the welfare superiority of any Paretian allocation over any non-Paretian one. This would also seem to imply the welfare indifference of one Paretian state to that of another. These assumptions are conspicuously common among applied welfare theorists." Borcherding, Liability in Law and Economics: Note, *Am. Econ. Rev.,* vol. 60, 1970, p. 946 (footnote).

101. Wallace E. Oates, Book Review, *Jour. of Econ. Lit.,* vol. 7, 1969, p. 104.

102. Henderson and Quandt, *op. cit.,* p. 208.

103. Koopmans, *op. cit.,* p. viii; see 64.

104. George J. Stigler, The New Welfare Economics, *Am. Econ. Rev.,* vol. 33, 1943; Mishan: Survey, p. 176 (footnote 5). Pareto optimal analysis also ethically abstracts from non-materialist value systems and, in addition, from distributional criteria which emphasize relative rank (on which see Mishan, *The Costs of Economic Growth, op. cit.,* p. 120.)

105. Little, *op. cit.,* p. 78.

undertaken within and indeed as a function of existing moral rules. This ambiguity (too weak?) enables the welfare economist to practice implicit ethicizing, perhaps even unbeknownst to himself. The Pareto-criterion thus posits itself as *the* optimum but its meaning and its recommendatory force are both substantively contingent upon *which (whose)* rules of morality are read into the Pareto analysis.

It would appear also that the Pareto-criterion rests upon, and may be considered as an extension of, a certain ethical system. This is the ethical system in which justice is what justice can get in the market, in which ethics is the ethics of bargaining, and in which values are the values of a middle class, bourgeois society; in short, in which everything is (at least potentially) up for sale, in which there is a (potential) market price on considerations of equity, all this albeit within, yet structured by, some vague limits imposed by assuming the status quo system of social control and working rules (as well as income, wealth, and power distributions). The Pareto-criterion represents the ethics of a business society and the economic theology of that society, an ethics of the market. The "simple" assumption is not only specific to a civilization but represents its ethical quintessence.

It may be objected, however, that the Pareto-criterion can be applied to central planning, that constrained maximization under planners or planners-cum-consumers preferences should follow (as in Lange-Lerner *et al.)* the price-equal-to-marginal-cost rule. That is correct.[106] But that is not the same thing as postulating that individual preferences are to count, or the consent and no-loss requirements, or the subtle ethical assumptions ensconced within the Pareto rule. The Pareto rule which carries those components is not the same Pareto rule which can be applied to individual adjustment and general equilibrium in a centrally planned economy. *Either* the Pareto-criterion is narrowly enough interpreted to apply to all economic systems *or* the criterion is system-specific, applicable to capitalism only. *Either* the Pareto-criterion is interpreted to cover gains from trade vis-a-vis both planned and market prices, to cover adjustments without the implicit moralizing of the consent and no-loss requirements; *or* the criterion is but a surrogate for consumer sovereignty (or consumers-cum-businessmens preferences). *Either* the Pareto-criterion is equally applicable to any power structure, to any economic system, a tool of dynamic-programming analysis as it were, so that the laissez-faire,

---

106. I here abstract from all marginal-cost and other pricing problems under central planning.

invisible-hand animus of the Pareto-criterion is excoriated; *or* the criterion is system-specific to capitalism, *or* system-specific to whatever institutional system is deemed functional for social control purposes, an admittedly normative but ostensibly innocuous working rule which encapsulates the fundamental ideological premises of the system, a doctrine of fundamentalist economic ideology. In *any* case, the Pareto-criterion will be limited vis-a-vis the broader considerations of the paradigm of choice and power developed earlier. In what follows, I shall abstract from the more limited specification of the Pareto-criterion and discuss it as it has been used in western economics. However, I would emphasize the potential utility of the Pareto-criterion as a more limited concept of a general, descriptive welfare economics, developed in terms of a broader paradigm of choice and power, applicable to a variety of actual economic systems with a minimum of ideological baggage.[107]

Continuing with the main discussion, it might be assumed that the ethical scope of the Pareto-criterion covers only Pareto-safe changes. This is false, for two major, albeit subtle, components of the Pareto-criterion are, first, the propriety of the status quo, and second, the propriety of non-Pareto-optimal changes outside the domain of the Pareto-criterion.

As to the first, not only does the Pareto-analysis assume the existing income and wealth distribution, working rules, power structure and so on, but it tends to assume their propriety. It does this either by silence (disregard) or by explicit stipulation. By ignoring the question of propriety, it accepts the status quo on its own terms, *accepting the status quo answer to the not-so-simple ethical question of "which" individuals count.* This can be expanded along three lines. The first line of expansion is that the Pareto-criterion assumes the propriety of past valuational choices, the propriety of the results of past mutual coercion and of past interpersonal utility comparisons; for the Pareto rule only applies to present consensual, no-loss changes from whatever substance the status quo has come to have through these routes. The second line of expansion is to argue that an assumption of the propriety of the status quo is required in order to give recommendatory force to the Pareto-rule itself and to all welfare implications drawn through its use. For to maintain that Pareto-optimal analysis can proceed unencumbered by further discussion of income distribution

---

107. "To derive from its postulation either a defense of competition or a categorical imperative for a socialist economy . . . has to be dismissed as obscurantism. Yet this has been a recurring theme of the professional literature and of long-drawn-out debate." Dobb, *op. cit.*, p. 253.

(etc.) considerations once we assume either a proper income distribution or state policy to bring about a desired primary redistribution,
which is a typical assumption, i.e., an ethically proper initial distribution,[108] is to assume that any Pareto-optimum analysis does presume an ethically proper initial distribution and that when Pareto-
optimum analysis is applied to the status quo it is in fact presuming
the status quo distribution to be ethically proper. The third line of
expansion is to argue that even when the marginal optimality rules
are silent on the question of distribution, Pareto-optimality accepts
the propriety of the status quo income distribution through its use of
status quo prices. As Baumol puts it:

> A statement that the marginal utility is the same for all con-
> sumers because it is measured by the same amount of money
> for everyone conceals a very strong and very questionable
> value judgment, which says that when any person, P, receives
> a unit of a commodity this adds to the utility of society as a
> whole an amount which is measured by the amount of money
> that P is willing and able to pay for it. In effect, this procedure
> tells us to determine the allocation of resources on the basis
> of an election in which some voters get to vote many times . . .
> so that the wealthy can exercise an influence proportional to
> the magnitude of their wealth.

Welfare economists "have not avoided committing ourselves on the
question of a good distribution of wealth—rather we have, by default,
decided to accept the status quo."[109] (Incidentally, Baumol makes
the same point in connection with the Kaldor and Scitovsky compensation criteria.)[110] The use of money prices is thus a proxy for the
income and wealth distribution under which the prices were generated, a proxy too for the power structure, working rules, and mutual
coercion out of which the prices were also generated. To accept the
prices and resource allocation of the marginal conditions is to accept
as proper the distributional factors giving rise to them.

The Pareto-criterion also assumes the propriety of non-Pareto-
optimal changes outside the domain of the Pareto-criterion, as surprising as it may seem. We have already seen that the Pareto-criterion
applies only to the limited domain of choice within the status quo

---

108. See, e.g., Samuelson, *Collected Scientific Papers, op. cit.,* vol. 2, p. 1410;
     and Tullock, *op. cit.,* p. 91.
109. Baumol, *Economic Theory and Operations Analysis, op. cit.,* p. 365.
110. *Ibid,* p. 379. See also Little, *op. cit.,* p. 120.

power structure and mutual coercion. In taking as given the domain of mutual coercion, and the non-Pareto-optimal changes in income distribution, wealth distribution, power structure, legal rules, etc., and limiting itself to Pareto-efficient or Pareto-safe adjustments *given* those changes, the Pareto-criterion assumes the propriety of those changes in order to give recommendatory force to *its* policy implications. (A more narrowly specified Pareto-rule would not assume such propriety, but then it would not have such recommendatory force or the evocative status which the rule now has.) Thus, in legitimizing Pareto-optimal marginal adjustments or solutions, in the event of changes in consumer tastes, in legal arrangements, and in the incidence of mutual coercion, the Pareto-criterion accepts those changes as proper.[111] The three lines of reasoning developed above concerning the status quo structure also apply to changes in that structure outside of the domain of the Pareto-criterion.

The fundamental ethical subtlety of the Pareto-criterion lies not alone in its assumption of the status quo and its assumption of the propriety of the status quo, but in that it also functions conservatively to reenforce the status quo. We have already seen that optimization in terms of the existing cost-price structure tends to reenforce the distributional institutions out of which that structure had been generated; that the Pareto-criterion accepts and reenforces the consequences of power play and non-Pareto-optimal change taking place outside of its domain; and that the basis of the standard compensation tests is the protection of status quo property rights.[112] What the Pareto-criterion does is to build in, cast luster upon, and support the status quo power structure, rights structure, opportunity set structure, and so on. Optimizing that is a function of the existing state of the law serves to reenforce that status quo law.[113] It serves to rationalize that part of the status quo brought within its scope. Its ultimate normative function is to limit change. It serves as an ideological limit to change, serving to admit or to exclude particular changes

---

111. "To ascribe ethical significance to the particular distribution of income effected by markets is to introduce a value judgment over and above the value of efficiently catering to consumers' tastes." Bator, *The Question of Government Spending, op. cit.*, p. 89 (footnote). It is ethical (an ethical assumption) *both* to accept the income distribution and mutual coercion base of resource allocation and to accept the resource allocation and mutual coercion base of income distribution.

112. Mishan: Survey, p. 157.

113. ". . . no output or set of outputs in the economy can be justified by the Pareto-criterion without implicit support of the existing law bearing on the question of compensation." Mishan, Pareto-Optimality and the Law, *op. cit.*, p. 276.

from taking place or even from being discussed.[114] It communicates
the economics of tranquility, of harmony, serving the function of
setting minds at rest.[115] More specifically, it tends to put the onus
on all deliberative change; to restrict deliberative change to only
Pareto-safe change, which is to reenforce the status quo power structure and to accept non-Pareto-optimal change arising out of mutual
coercion in the market. The instrumental function of the Pareto-criterion is thus to promote the market and to discourage legal change,
in a manner consonant with the historical ideological role of the gold
standard and laissez-faire philosophy in general. All this is widely
albeit sporadically evident in the literature. Thus, we find acknowledgement that "modern economics developed more or less as the
rationalization of the *laissez-faire* economy, hence its preoccupation
with the private sector and the operation of the market in the private
sector."[116] This is distinctively the case with the Pareto-criterion.
Mishan, for example, discusses how optimization in terms of the status
quo cost-price structure amounts to "rationalizing the *status quo . . .*
[in such a way as to bring] the economist perilously close to defending it."[117] And Samuelson, speaking of the unanimity or consent
principle, has written that "like standing friction it sticks you
where you are. It favors the status quo."[118] Samuelson has laid the
matter on the line: arguing that it has been used in connection with
a notion of justice which "is appealed to, not very successfully, to exercise veto power in extension of activities of government," he elabor-
ates thus:

> Not surprisingly, its spokesmen like to appeal to unanimity—
> or, to use an Irish Bull—to near-unanimity in social decision
> making. However, a unanimity requirement can, and usually
> does, lead to no way of deciding between two alternatives (and
> leads, at best, to a non-transitive ordering); and they hope
> either that this will be resolved by favouring the *status quo*,
> putting the burden of proof upon *all* change, or—and this will
> become an increasingly important strain in libertarian think-
> ing, the farther away recedes the laissez-faire conditions of
> Victorian capitalism—putting the burden of proof upon any

---

114. Robert L. Heilbroner, *The Limits of American Capitalism*, New York: Har-
     per and Row, 1965, pp. 65-66 and *passim;* and Joan Robinson, *Economic
     Philosophy, op. cit.,* ch. 1.
115. G. L. S. Schackle, *The Years of High Theory*, Cambridge University Press,
     1967, chs. 1, 2, 18.
116. *Readings in Welfare Economics, op. cit.,* General Introduction, p. 2.
117. Mishan, The Postwar Literature on Externalities: An Interpretive Essay, *op.
     cit.,* p. 17.
118. Samuelson, *Collected Scientific Papers, op. cit.,* vol. 2, p. 1414.

departure from their defined condition of inviolable natural rights and individual liberties (inclusive of property rights).[119]

Baumol, too, has called attention to the function of this veto power to prevent change.[120] Perhaps the crucial point lies in the tendency of the Pareto-criterion to disengage not all change but legal social policy and change. This thrust may be illustrated by comparing the argument of Mishan, that:

> In the last resort, if distribution does matter then it should be separately acknowledged as a judgment to be taken into account explicitly in any welfare function; certainly not left as a by-product of some single-minded pursuit in the hope that certain features in the real world would act to ensure that the resulting distribution would not be at variance with our ideas of fairness.[121]

with that of Haveman, who objecting to including in public policy decisions the externalities "inflicted by the market system adjustment process," takes issue with Schmid's Mishan-like emphasis on making clear the welfare implications of social judgements as to who is to count in society, Haveman arguing that:

> As Schmid, I am sure, recognizes, such a position indeed opens Pandora's box. Surely, if the box were to be opened all of the way, the situation would be intolerable—for example, few income changes due to the market system adjustment process would be free from the demands of compensation. However, if the box could be cracked without jeopardizing the adjustment process in the private sector, the Schmid position would be of merit.[122]

---

119. Samuelson, *in* Margolis and Guitton, *op. cit.*, p. 101 (footnote 2).

120. Baumol, *Welfare Economics and the Theory of the State, op. cit.*, pp. 43-44.

121. Mishan, The Recent Debate on Welfare Criteria, *op. cit.*, p. 226.

122. Robert H. Haveman, Economic Analysis of Water Resource Problems: Discussion, *Am. Econ. Rev., Papers and Proceedings*, vol. 57, 1967, p. 191. One does not have to disagree with Haveman's desire to not jeopardize the market in order to argue that the box can be opened without destroying the system. Those who have assumed the role of priestly function have long been anxious about public discussion of fundamental questions; this is characteristic of the role in every society. See Samuels, *The Classical Theory of Economic Policy, op. cit.*, p. 297 (footnote 80). As between tradition, command, and market economies, the choice is surely in favor of the market—with my own preferences running in favor of one with a wide diffusion of power rather than a narrow one. The point of much of this

Haveman would have policy decisions only include consideration of
"externalities imposed by public investment decisions," arguing that:

> For Schmid's argument to be taken seriously (as I believe it
> should), this distinction must be made. Indeed, without it one
> has no rationale for dealing with the entire bundle of such
> externalities and the market system becomes stripped of its
> resource allocating function.[123]

As with Hochman and Rodgers, a revision of primary redistribution,
of the pattern of exposure to others' coercive power, is deemed inconsistent with the viable functioning of the market; only the market is
allowed to make allocative decisions; allocation as a function of income distribution through mutual coercion in the market is a different matter than allocation as a function of legal revision of legal rights.
What clearer statement of the role of Pareto-optimum reasoning in reenforcing the status quo power structure could one want? It is one of a
genre that tends to presumptively accept change originating from the
mutual coercion of the market and presumptively reject social change
through legal change.

Yet the upshot of all this is gross ambiguity, for the Pareto-criterion,
which glorifies the consensual and no-loss requirements, also accepts
and indeed reenforces non-Pareto-optimal change originating outside
of its domain in the broad choice and power processes of mutual
coercion both in the market and elsewhere. *The Pareto-criterion is
used selectively to rationalize certain seemingly consensual, no-loss
activities and to oppose other activity.* Where the criterion is to apply
and where not is subjective and ambiguous, but where it is used to
apply, it functions conservatively in support of selected interests, in
support of individual acts of market coercion, in support of the market

---

paper is that the operation of the market is a function of the structure of
social power that works (in part) through market forces. Some will feel
that we injure the role of the market in checking social power if we acknowledge that social power operates through the market; others will feel
that the market cannot be left to the mercy of social powers. The problem
is a version of the more general problem of legitimizing powers when their
mutual function is to check each other. In the case of the market it is complicated by the fact that the market is given substance by the social powers
operating through it; which is a version of the more general problem that
social control institutions are also power players. Perhaps the most important point is that in a free or pluralist society no one institution should be
dominant, even the market, despite the fact that it is more pluralist in its
operation than most if not all other institutions.

123. *Ibid, loc. cit.*

and to limit change of the law. Such ambiguity is the nature of social myths which are always invoked selectively and subjectively.

The conclusion I urge from this consideration of the ethical character of the Pareto-criterion, is that the criterion carries with it very important, very complex, and very subtle, even if ambiguous, and subjective, ethical assumptions, consequences, and roles. Above all it defends and reenforces the position of certain established property rights, defending them against legal alteration while at the same time enabling them to participate in mutual coercion in the market exposed to non-consensual, loss-imposing mutual coercion. I also urge that the Pareto-criterion obscures the ethical problems of the distribution of power at the same time that it loads the ethical scales for or against certain changes or certain sources of change. As a ranking device the Pareto-criterion assumes the specific preferences of its users; as a general decisional rule it conveys ambivalent implications: it casts luster on the results of mutual coercion in the market and denigrates deliberate legal change. In all this the Pareto-criterion conservatively protects private power against legal alteration, if not against the exercise of other private powers; in so doing it neglects the conflict between the principle of the security of property and the principle that a capitalist society, if it is to work, has to be competitive and that concentrations of private power yield different Pareto-optima than do competitive conditions. The ethical complexity is enormous and so is the ambiguity; but so too is the flexibility of the Pareto-criterion: the same criterion which emphasizes that individuals' welfare is maximized if they are in a chosen position also accepts the coercion of the market and whatever power structure exists to operate through the market. The ethical defect of the Pareto-criterion is that it begs the problem of the structure of choice. It posits only a limited and ambivalent posture concerning the factors and forces governing the opportunity sets from which Pareto-optimum adjustments and solutions are worked out. It amounts to an ethical quagmire but the Pareto-criterion is thoroughly and distinctively ethical as well as skewed to the defense of the status quo structure of private power (including property rights) against legal alteration. At bottom it postulates that justice is what power can get in the market. It thus takes a particular, if complex and very ambiguous, ethical position with regard to the issues of the larger paradigm of choice and power.

IV.   Externalities and the Problem of Power

The foregoing analysis of Pareto-optimality in the context of a broader model of choice and power enables us to place in perspective both the meaning of externalities and the selective, restricted scope of externalities treated in welfare economics. In this section I argue for the meaning and scope of externalities considered in the total process of mutual coercion; that externalities are ubiquitous and inevitable, and that while their recognition and importance are both subjective such subjectivity should not obscure their ubiquity and the fundamental policy choices involved in externality solutions; that the existence and generation of externalities is a function of the structure of power and of changes in the structure of power; and that the critical policy issues involve the structure of power and the distribution of gains and losses both of which are often obscured by the intrusion of partial-equilibrium Pareto-criterion policy solutions.

A.   On the Definition and Scope of Externalities

The concept of externalities can be derived from the model in which the behavior and choices of each economic actor have an impact upon the choices open to other economic actors. With *coercion* defined as the impact of the behavior and choices of others upon the structure of one's opportunity set and relative cost of alternatives, *externalities* comprise the substance of coercion, namely, the injuries and benefits, the costs and gains, visited upon others through the exercise of choice by each economic actor and by the total number of economic actors. Given the conditions of scarcity and interdependence, included in the opportunity costs of any choice are the costs paid by or incurred by others; and similarly with benefits. These costs may be on others' consumption functions, production function, on the prices paid and received, on the opportunity to work and to earn a living at some level of real income, on the value of assets, and so on. Such phenomena as employer investment in workers' skills, research and development, innovation, linkage effects, competition, population growth, population density, air and/or water pollution, government manpower retraining programs, unemployment, inflation, education and so on, all involve the visitation of costs and gains upon others, externalities altering the scope of opportunity sets and the relative costs of alternatives therein for different individuals and subgroups. There may be activities undertaken to counter the activities of others through private or public action; which is to say that externality-solutions generate externalities in turn upon others. The system of mutual coercion is a system of the mutual visitation of inevitable and ubiquitous externalities, including the externalities generated through the market as well as through nonmarket institutions and forces, and including also externalities affecting production and prices, all of which affect opportunity sets. The economic decision-making process includes more than the market, and it generates both production and distribution consequences; the scope of externalities is coextensive with the total process of mutual coercion. A welfare economics which does not include the totality of the system of mutual coercion and the totality of externalities will not be adequate to the task of studying the forces making for the attainment and distribution of welfare. Those forces include the decision-making about which externalities to accept and which to attempt to counter, which is to say, who will bear costs and who will reap benefits, decisions truly crucial to the attainment and distribution of welfare.

Welfare economics, however, while recognizing the broader range of such a conception of externalities, has conventionally worked with a narrower (and narrowing) subset thereof.[124] Without attempting anything like a careful history,[125] the welfare-economic treatment of externalities generally has followed the conventions of microeconomic theory, so that "the bulk of recent literature has confined its investigations to inter-industry, inter-firm, and inter-person externalities," narrowly conceived, responding "to real world problems with a time lag, initially making use of more familiar, if less relevant, bits of apparatus."[126] No small amount of this usage has involved the confused[127] dichotomy of pecuniary and technological externalities, the terminology developed by Viner and Scitovsky. In this usage, regardless of the ambiguities, pecuniary externalities have not been considered "true" externalities.[128] Mishan has recently aptly summarized the reasoning followed:

> In popular expositions, an external effect is commonly defined in terms of the response of a firm's output, or a person's utility,

---

124. There are, of course, exceptions to the contrary, as in the work of Rosenstein-Rodan, Chenery, Hirschman, Schultz, and others, primarily in the field of economic development.

125. See, for example, the essays surveying welfare economics and recent developments in externality theory in Mishan, *Welfare Economics, op. cit.* chs. 1, 2, and his recent article on The Postwar Literature on Externalities: An Interpretive Essay, *op. cit.;* and the discussion in Baumol, *Welfare Economics and the Theory of the State, op. cit.,* pp. 24ff.

126. Mishan, The Postwar Literature on Externalities: An Interpretive Essay, *op. cit.,* p. 1.

127. See, *inter alia, ibid.,* pp. 6-7.

128. Mishan, *Welfare Economics, op. cit.,* p. 103; Baumol, *Welfare Economics and the Theory of the State, op. cit.,* p. 25.

to the activity of others. Insofar as the standard smoke and noise examples are cited, the correct impression is conveyed. This causal definition is unsatisfactory because the statement that a firm's output, or a person's utility, can be influenced by the activity of others, also holds true in the absence of external effects [as narrowly defined by welfare economists]. With the context of an interdependent system, e.g., the Walrasian general equilibrium system, an exogenous change in the behavior of individuals can alter the equilibrium set of product and factor prices and thereby alter the utility levels of persons and the output levels of firms and industries. In the presence of universally perfect competition, however, such exogenous changes entail equilibrium solutions that are all Pareto-optimal —and these solutions, therefore, cannot be ranked in the absence of a social welfare function.

In light of the above proposition, one is compelled to recognize the distinction between, on the one hand, instances where the influence upon the utility and outputs of others are exerted "indirectly," i.e., via relative prices only in a general interdependent system, and, on the other hand, those where such an influence is exerted on them "directly" i.e., via the arguments of their utility or production functions.[129]

One problem with this is that the Pareto-optimal character of the adjustments to price changes does not vitiate the coercion visited upon opportunity sets; the fact that the changes and the adjustments are worked out through market prices does not obviate the injuries and benefits to individuals' opportunity sets. Welfare economists have excluded such manifestations of mutual coercion here as well as in the development of the Pareto-criterion itself, even though the pricing system *is* a major conduit for the operation of mutual coercion and the visitation of externalities. But the attainment and distribution of welfare is partially a function of such changes and adjustments and welfare economics should so specify and study it. The

---

129. Mishan, The Postwar Literature on Externalities: An Interpretive Essay, *op. cit.*, p. 2. Mishan continues, still reflecting the orthodox position: ". . . an external effect arises wherever the value of a production function, or a consumption function, depends directly upon the activity of others . . . the essential feature of the concept of an external effect is that the effect produced is not a deliberate creation but an *unintended* or *incidental* by-product of some otherwise legitimate activity." There are, of course, many legitimate activities which intentionally and not always with incidental effects create externalities, e.g., pollution. But it is tradition, says Mishan, to treat "the subject within the context of partial equilibrium analysis: assuming, that is, that all optimal conditions are met in all sectors of the economy save in those under scrutiny." (p. 2) It is this latter assumption which the present analysis is challenging.

dichotomy of pecuniary and technological externalities, quite aside from both the ambiguities of standard usage and the advantages (for heuristic and other purposes) in certain uses, is false. The logic of technological and "merely pecuniary"[130] externalities is the same: they both involve mutual coercion. The fact that "most economists refuse to apply the concept of externality" to the "merely pecuniary" because "individual behavior in which individuals ignore some of the effects their behavior has on others is more desirable than compelling them to take these effects into account" and because some of our "own personal preferences point" in this way,[131] indicates that such a refusal is thoroughly subjective and ethical in nature, as would be any other treatment. In part it is to ignore that Pareto-optimality assumes the operation of moral rules, rules which govern the moral sentiments with which people view the effects of their behavior on others. The users of the Pareto-criterion, as we have seen, try to have it both ways: at times they acknowledge that the criterion is given substance by moral rules but then at other times they follow laissez-faire as if moral rules violated the ethics of the market. The relevant problem is not whether to compel individuals to consider the effects of their behavior on others (which may or may not be a good thing), but whether welfare economic theory will accurately study the forces governing the attainment and distribution of welfare. So much for the dismissal of pecuniary externalities.

Then there is the additional dismissal of certain other externalities as irrelevant. According to Buchanan and Stubblebine, an externality exists when "the utility of an individual . . . is dependent upon the 'activities' . . . that are exclusively under his own control or authority, but also upon another single activity . . . which is, by definition, under the control of a second individual . . . who is presumed to be a member of the same social group."[132] This view certainly accords with my own; but they differentiate *potentially* relevant and irrelevant, and *Pareto-relevant* and *Pareto-irrelevant*, externalities. "An externality is defined," they write, "as *potentially relevant* when the activity, to the extent that it is actually performed, generates *any* desire on the part of the externally benefited (damaged) party (A) to modify the behaviour of the party empowered to take action (B) through trade, persuasion, compromise, agreement, convention, collective action, etc. An externality which, to the extent that it is per-

---

130. Tullock, *op. cit.,* title of chapter seven.

131. *Ibid,* pp. 171-172.

132. James M. Buchanan and William Craig Stubblebine, Externality, *Economica* vol. 29, 1962, reprinted in Breit and Hochman, *op. cit.,* p. 478.

formed, exerts no such influence is defined as *irrelevant*."[133] Thus, "An externality is defined to be Pareto-relevant when the extent of the activity may be modified in such a way that the externally affected party, A, can be made better off without the acting party, B, being made worse off. That is to say, 'gains from trade' characterise the Pareto-relevant externality, trade that takes the form of some change in the activity of B as his part of the bargain,"[134] so that "What vanishes in Pareto-equilibrium are the Pareto-relevant externalities."[135] This *does* show that the existence of externalities is consistent with a Pareto-optimal equilibrium but *only by* neglecting the non-consensual aspects of opportunity set construction, despite, that is, the need of A to *have* to bargain for release from B's damage-producing activity; and by defining as irrelevant externalities existing where conditions are not propitious for market negotiation (say, because the distribution of wealth and income or the structure of legal rules e.g., legal standing does not permit certain individuals to have bargaining power). Market negotiation operates within the structure of mutual coercion, which structure governs which externalities will be relevant or irrelevant, whether some trades will be made and others not, in each case the matter being not a function of the damaged party's willingness to bargain but his market position. What the Pareto-relevant and -irrelevant distinction does is to salvage Pareto-optimality and the viability of market ideology from the onslaughts and intervention-stimulating thrusts of the Pigovian critique of harmonious market organization, to neutralize the threats[136] seen re-

---

133. *Ibid,* p. 479.

134. *Ibid,* p. 480.

135. *Ibid,* p. 481. On Demsetz's interpretation of Pareto-relevancy, see below, text at note 144. Both Buchanan-Stubblebine and Demsetz have definitions which only contingently identify externalities, i.e., which make (Pareto-relevant or -irrelevant) externalities contingent upon a cost factor.

136. Writing of public-goods externalities Samuelson has written: "This does, however, lead to an uncomfortable situation. If the experts remain nihilistic about algorithms to allocate public goods, and if all but a knife-edge of reality falls in that domain, nihilism about most of economics, rather than merely public finance, seems to be implied." One of his reactions to this is, "First, if worst came to worst and there were found to be no way out of the indictment, we should have to fact up to the disappointing truth. It would be ostrich-like to do otherwise." Samuelson, *in* Margolis and Guitton, *op. cit.,* pp. 109-110. In the first edition of his *Welfare Economics and the Theory of the State,* Cambridge: Harvard University Press, 1952, Baumol wrote of the problem of competing tautologies (pp. 12-13, 140-141) and of the threatened breakdown of economic theory (p. 165). There have been earlier perceptions of the threatened wreckage of the corpus of economic theory; on Harrod, see Dobb, *op. cit.,* p. 81; and on Hicks, see Schackle, *The Years of High Theory, op. cit.,* p. 27.

siding in the market-failure implications of externality theory, threats both to economic theory and to the ideology of individual productivity, harmonious equilibrium, and general beneficence. If Pareto-optimal equilibrium can exist with regard to Pareto-relevant externalities, forgetting those Pareto-*irrelevant* externalities, then the market and its ideology are salvaged. A grander, and more question-begging, tautology would be hard to find. The real issue should be the role of *all* externalities, the role of mutual-coercion produced externalities on the total structure of opportunity sets and the attainment and distribution of welfare. A welfare economics preoccupied with its priestly function cannot do this.[137]

Thus Haveman, in his strong reaction to Schmid, in which he articulated his fear of opening Pandora's box too far, lest the extent of market-adjudicated injury distribution be too well seen, maintained, with respect to "the three standard categories of external effects—(1) technological externalities which are Pareto-relevant, (2) technological externalities which are non-Pareto-relevant, and (3) pecuniary externalities," that "While standard externality theory holds that public intervention may be necessary to achieve a welfare maximum in the case of category 1 externalities (and then only if the Coase theorem is inoperative), it views both category 2 and 3 externalities as income redistribution and not real output effects."[138] Welfare economics cannot abstract from certain opportunity set effects of mutual coercion (e.g., externalities seen as income distribution) and include only real output effects; welfare economics, at least a welfare economics that discarded its social control function, would attempt to at least describe the process of opportunity set formation whether through production or prices, whether through market forces or not, and not necessarily attempt to rank alternatives. Calling certain externalities "income distribution" does not alter their character as externalities; nor does the treatment of income distribution as a dependent and independent variable require ethical assumptions—it does so only if we try to rank. I would go beyond the argument that real output changes have income distribution consequences that cannot be separated, and urge that externalities, seen as the coercive impact of the choices of others, cannot be dismissed as "merely pecuniary" and "Pareto-irrelevant" without welfare economics meriting the description of being either a monumental waste of resources or

---

137. See Joseph J. Spengler, Economics: Its History, Themes, Approaches, *Jour. of Econ. Issues*, vol. 2, 1968, pp. 14, 19.

138. Haveman, *op, cit.*, pp. 190-191.

out-and-out economic theology, a rationalization of a rationalization.[139] If that means making income distribution an explicit and
important variable, so be it: "As long as the marginal social value of
income to various citizens is not the same, acting as if it were[140] (i.e.,
worrying only about 'efficiency') represents a restrictive and dubious
ethical presumption. The crucial role of the professional in my view
is to clarify and make vivid the ethical implications of alternative
choices. If instead, he supresses or quietly ignores these issues, he
will only lead others to do likewise."[141] Welfare economics should
not embody obscurantism, either intentional or unintentional. It is
one thing to avoid making interpersonal utility comparisons and to
avoid ethical judgments, not that we have succeeded in welfare economics, as shown above; but it is quite another thing to fail to develop a comprehensive model of welfare attainment and distribution
with income distribution consequences, to treat income distribution
as if it were *absent from* (and not merely something to be ignored in)
the social decision making process. *All* externalities should be seen as
the substance of coercion in the generation of opportunity sets, and
neither the hold of traditional distinctions nor the demands of ideology
should interfere with the generation of new models, new concepts,
and new theorems. If there is a threat to economics and/or to the
market, it should be taken as a challenge to constructive and not defensive theoretical innovation. It is not a matter of making economics
relevant to practical problems, though that is not unjustifiable; it is
a matter of generating a complete general equilibrium theory of welfare economics, one which does not exclude certain phenomena and
thus yield only partial-equilibrium or biased and capricious conclusions. To exclude pecuniary and Pareto-irrelevant externalities is to
exclude behavior only because the coercion is conditional; but coercion is both conditionally and unconditionally imposed. Part of the
problem, therefore, certainly resides in the narrow scope of injury
recognized by Pareto-optimum analysis and welfare economics in
general, as shown in Section III. Externalities are the substantive im-

---

139. *Readings in Welfare Economics, op. cit.*, p. 2.
140. Thus, Haveman writes: "Accepting the proposition that the marginal utility
     of income is equal for all people, standard theory holds that no net welfare
     loss accrues from such externalities and, hence, they should be ignored in
     the social decision-making process." Haveman, *op. cit.*, p. 191, concerning
     Pareto-irrelevant technological externalities and pecuniary externalities
     (viewed as income redistribution). Such an assumption is obviously not the
     the same thing as ignoring distributional consequences.
141. Marc J. Roberts, Environmental Quality: Discussion, *Am. Econ. Rev., Papers
     and Proceedings*, vol. 61, 1971, p. 177.

pact of mutual coercion on opportunity sets and should be considered regardless of the transmission mechanism or type of injury or gain involved.

This analysis can be elaborated and extended by examining externality-solutions, anticipating somewhat the disscusion in Section V. Such solutions include internalization of external costs and benefits through taxes and subsidies, undertaking of collective action, and creation of markets for trade (markets in externalities, as it were) by legal investiture of new private property rights. There are several points, largely self-evident in the context of the foregoing analysis, which I want to make:

a. externality-solutions impose externalities of their own

b. externality-solutions involve the use of power, the restructuring of power, and the redirection of the use of power

c. externality-solutions involve the restructure of opportunity sets and the redistribution of costs and benefits

d. externality-solutions create a new decision making structure, giving effect to hitherto excluded interests and/or participants

These are intentionally somewhat redundant but they direct attention to the coercive character of externality-solutions and the non-Pareto-optimality of the acts instituting the solutions; however Pareto-optimal are the (expected) results reached by the solutions themselves.

Demsetz has stated the heart of the matter when he acknowledged that, "property rights convey the right to benefit or harm oneself or others. . . . It is clear, then, that property rights specify how persons may be benefited and harmed, and, therefore, who must pay whom to modify the actions taken by persons. The recognition of this leads easily to the close relationship between property rights and externalities."[142] The structure of property rights, in other words, governs the structure of mutual coercion and thereby the flow of payment, the income generated by charging prices to refrain from (other) coercive pressure upon others.[143] While Demsetz's definition of exter-

---

142. Harold Demsetz, Toward a Theory of Property Rights, *Am. Econ. Rev., Papers and Proceedings,* vol. 57, 1967, p. 347.

143. See Robert L. Hale: "The interest primarily promoted by the ownership of business property is . . . the interest . . . in collecting income from consumers by the threat to withhold from them the use of the fruits of it." Hale, Political and Economic Review, *American Bar Assoc. Jour.,* vol. 9, 1923, p. 107. ". . . all incomes are the result of coercion held in check by counter-

nalities becomes narrower than mine, he acknowledges the broader range and points to the role of property rights:

> Externality is an ambiguous concept. For the purposes of this paper, the concept includes external costs, external benefits, and pecuniary as well as nonpecuniary externalities. No harmful or beneficial effect is external to the world. Some person or persons always suffer or enjoy these effects. What converts a harmful or beneficial effect into an externality is that the cost of bringing the effect to bear on the decisions of one or more of the interacting persons is too high to make it worthwhile, and this is what the term shall mean here. "Internalizing" such effects refers to a process, usually a change in property rights, that enables these effects to bear (in greater degree) on all interacting persons.
>
> A primary function of property rights is that of guiding incentives to achieve a greater internalization of externalities. Every cost and benefit associated with social interdependencies is a potential externality.[144]

My first point is that his analysis builds in and thus obscures the critical role of income distribution in governing when the costs of bringing effects to bear are high or low and thus the existence of externalities by his definition. Externality analysis and policy has to tackle this question directly. My second point is that the very act of creating new property rights with which to internalize externalities amounts to a primary redistribution (in Musgrave's sense) and should be seen as such, for it takes power and opportunity set alternatives away from those vis-a-vis whom the new property right holder will have power. One cannot create new property rights without assigning them, and to assign them is to alter—without the consent of, and with loss to, some—the structure of opportunity sets and the pattern of mutual coercion. It is precisely here that the distributional limitation self-imposed by the new welfare economics breaks down: resource allocation is a function of wealth allocation and income distribution,

---

coercion." Hale Papers, New Canaan, Conn., Folder 62, item 1, p. 7. ". . . the income of each person in the community depends on the relative strength of his power of coercion, offensive and defensive." "The distribution of income . . . depends on the relative power of coercion which the different members of the community can exert against one another. Income is the price paid for not using one's coercive weapons." Hale, Coercion and Distribution in a Supposedly Non-Coercive State, *Pol. Sci. Quarterly*, vol. 38, 1923, pp. 477-478.

144. Demsetz, Toward a Theory of Property Rights, *op. cit.*, p. 348.

and both in turn are functions of the distribution of legal rights. Schmid's argument comes home: Pareto-relevant externalities describe "the existence of Pareto-better trading possibilities,"[145] but "One cannot talk of Pareto-better trades unless property rights are first established to say who counts. Depending on the property rights, there are all kinds of Pareto-better trades possible which would produce a whole range of price sets . . . and other performance results . . ."[146] We cannot justify externality-solutions in terms of results without knowing something and doing something about just "whose values shall count . . ."[147] As Schmid further puts it, ". . . externality theory, which is the logical extension of a given set of rights, is not useful for questions of the original vesture of the property right to a resource that becomes newly useful."[148] The creation of a property right in quest of conditions propitious to Pareto-optimal solutions functions to vest in certain individuals wealth and/or income-acquiring power whose justification it is beyond the capacity of the Pareto-criterion to provide. There are cases where the further right to trade will result in a Pareto-better situation. Still, property rights are decisional power; to create new property rights is to create new decisional power thereby altering the existing structure of decisional power. This is an externality, an act of power, a non-Pareto-optimal event, a phenomenon requiring ethical judgments in each case going far beyond the capacity of the Pareto-criterion. To defend a change as one which would enable the reaching of Pareto-optimal adjustments not achievable under the status quo property rights structure is to injure the interests of already-vested rights holders who will lose by the change and, further, to presume some Pareto-optimal solution when there is in fact no unique Pareto-optimum. It is to impose the analyst's notion of what is optimal. The Pareto-criterion cannot justify particular changes in property rights without an additional judgment or ethical assumption as to income and wealth distribution. There are many Pareto-optimal trading situations possible, no unique Pareto-optimum. To create one such situation is to choose from among many, to generate one income and wealth distribution (however inadvertently) rather than some other. Perhaps some rights holders and income recipients should lose, but the loss should be made clear and not obscured by the logic of Pareto-opti-

---

145. Schmid, *op. cit.*, p. 162.
146. *Ibid*, p. 164.
147. *Ibid*, *loc. cit.*
148. *Ibid*, p. 165.

mality and the language of internalizing externalities: one man's externality is another man's income, and all externality policy necessarily makes assumptions about income distribution either implicitly or explicitly. Change of the law of property is an exercise of mutual coercion that goes far beyond the self-imposed limits of welfare economics. It is inconsistent to support legal change in the interest of certain reforms yet ignore distributional consequences, while opposing other reforms under the rubric of avoiding interpersonal utility comparisons and distributional-ethical questions; it is inconsistent and it is obscurantist. Externalities do not exist in a vacuum; they are generated in a structure of mutual coercion and power. Despite the appealing logic of Pareto-optimality, since Pareto-optimal adjustments are possible within any number of power or rights structures, to argue for particular property rights' changes so as to produce conditions propitious to achieving some Pareto-optimal adjustment(s) is to beg the broader question of who will have what power to create which externalities and thereby engender which adjustments. Narrow recognition of the scope of externalities, or narrow recognition of the scope of injury, fails to get to the heart of this general-equilibrium question. Whatever the needs of legitimacy may require of policy makers, welfare economics can and must specify all relevant variables if it is to explain adequately and thoroughly the forces and factors governing the attainment and distribution of welfare.

B. *Externalities as a Function of Power*

While the process of generating externalities, such as pollution, is certainly more complex, we can state categorically that the *sine qua non* of externality generation is the structure of power. More precisely, our model of choice and power suggests that both the *existence* of any externality and the total *pattern* of externalities are functions of the structure of opportunity sets, *ergo* of mutual coercion, and ultimately of the structure of power. Externalities being the substance of coercion, coercion being the impact of behavior and choices from opportunity sets, and power being the means or wherewithall or capacity with which to exercise choice, it follows that externalities are generated by the interaction and exercise of relative power. This is the case with all externalities, however classified. I repeat: both the *existence* and *pattern* of externalities are functions of the changing structure of power. The economic meaning of an externality is specific to the power structure within which it is generated.

Such a view ties together many of the strands of earlier discussion. Some examples follow: (1) Since all choices involve opportunity costs, the power structure, in determining which costs are to be borne by whom, generates externalities; and the same with benefits. (2) Since the existence of an externality is a function of the power structure, a change of the power structure will tend to change the pattern of externalities and thereby possibly remove from existence any particular externality. This is the logic of internalization: since externalities are external to some locus (i) of decision making, internalization involves a restructuring of decision making, a restructuring of power. (3) The power structure not only determines which externalities will arise but also which externality-solutions will be worked out, and which new externalities thereby generated, i.e., which new distribution of costs and gains. One problem of public choice is thus the determination of which are the "important" externalities, the ones for which to construct externality-producing externality-solutions. This determination is a function of the structure of power. Thus, not only does the power structure govern the formation of the social welfare function but the degree of organizability (which is itself a function of the diffusion of externality-consequences and the importance of the damage or gain to each recipient),[149] which is a major determinant of power, will influence the capacity of recipients to organize to create externality-solutions. Similarly, legal rules (and other factors, such as unequal wealth distribution) govern the distribution of bargaining or transaction costs, the burden of negotiation, and thus the existence and substance of externality-solutions. (4) Since externalities are a function of the power structure, and since the power structure is partially governed by the structure of legal rights, it follows that the existence and pattern of externalities will be partially a function of the pattern of rights. The right of Alpha is indeed the capacity to visit coercion, i.e., externalities, upon Beta; or, as Demsetz has already been quoted to say, "property rights convey the right to benefit or harm oneself or others."[150] As Dolbear has put it, "The amount of externality that will tend to emerge depends on the extent of legal responsibility,"[151] which is to say, upon the structure of legal rights and obligations, upon the relative existence of rights to pollute (i.e., absence of protection against pollution) and rights against

149. Mancur Olson, *The Logic of Collective Action,* Cambridge: Harvard University Press, 1965.

150. Demsetz, Toward a Theory of Property Rights, *op. cit.,* p. 347. See also Schmid, *op. cit.,* pp. 162-165.

151. F. T. Dolbear, Jr., On the Theory of Optimum Externality, *Am. Econ. Rev.,* vol. 57, 1967, p. 102.

pollution, ultimately of legal standing in tort law, criminal law, or under the police power of the state, as well as the law of property. (5) The attainability and substance of Pareto-optimal solutions are partially a function of the power structure. Whether a Pareto-optimal solution is said to exist partially depends upon the scope of injury recognized, and thereby the determination of who is entitled to be considered. As Tullock puts it, with one inserted qualification of my own, "As long as one person who is affected is left out of the group whose consent is [considered] necessary, there is an externality."[152] I would suggest that the qualification, "considered," is crucial, for there always enters a subjective judgment as to who is affected and is to be acknowledged as within the power ambit. As we have seen, there is typically a wide range of coercive restrictions upon opportunity sets not covered by consensual arrangements (even when such arrangements are present, they do not necessarily include everyone affected nor every effect); and the mere fact that a consensual agreement does not exist (or cover such externalities) does not mean that there are no such externalities, only possibly that conditions (e.g., wealth distribution, transactions costs, legal rules, etc.) are not propitious to enable consensual agreement. To call such externalities Pareto-irrelevant is irrelevant to the fact of their existence; in any event, both Pareto-relevant and Pareto-irrelevant externalities are a function of the structure of power. (6) The existence of grants, in the recently designated grants economy, is a function of power structure; and the grants produce (intentionally and unintentionally) externalities. (7) Inequality of wealth, income, position, legal status, and so on, leads to inequality or asymmetry in the patterns of capacity to generate externalities and of exposure to the externalities generated by others. (8) It is possible for the production of externalities whose purpose is to elicit bribes to desist and become a business, a racket, at least a serious business consideration. As Rothenberg has so well put it:

> For if external diseconomies against others can be expected to lead to bribes by victims to desist, then the production of negative externalities becomes a valid by-product of primary production. Profitability is enhanced whenever any firm can select from among its input and/or output alternatives those which cause substantial damage to third parties. Resource use will tend to become specialized toward much-augmented third-party

---

152. Tullock, *op. cit.*, p. 71.

interference. The new legal industry of selling protection against disturbance will be highly profitable.[153]

(9) The greater the size of the decision-making unit required to internalize (really, redistribute) externalities, the more complex are the price and other calculations that must be made to conduct operations, e.g., benefit-cost calculations. There are efficiency gains possible from specialization or division of decision making (with externalities) and from coordinated or centralized or internalized decision making (with another set of externalities).

Externalities are not only a function of power *per se* but of changes in the structure of power; not only does change in the structure of power mean likely change in the relative capacity to generate externalities, but change in the structure of power generates an externality (ies) *per se*. The heart of the model of choice, mutual coercion and power, involves gains and losses in opportunity sets and thereby in choice, and the capacity to generate and/or withstand externalities. The most subtle and yet most important externality is the alteration in one's opportunity set consequent to the change in power of others. As Alpha gains the wherewithall of power, Beta, whose wherewithall (say) is unchanged, nevertheless suffers injury by virtue of his loss of relative power. While Tullock is certainly correct that "The prospects for reducing externalities by changing property laws are apparently almost infinite,"[154] it should be recognized that the very changing of property rights constitutes the generation of externalities in the form of both gains and losses of power. Once again the problem is not whether externality generating capacity will exist but which or whose capacity, a problem obscured by narrow recognition of in-

---

153. Jerome Rothenberg, The Economics of Congestion and Pollution: An Integrated View, *Am. Econ. Rev., Papers and Proceedings*, vol. 60, 1970, p. 115. See the earlier statement by Stanislaw Wellisz:

> Bargaining for the entire rent accruing to the opposite party does not, in itself, preclude the possibility of reaching a Pareto-optimum, for it is to the advantage of both parties to reach a level of joint maximum rent. Moreover, the process opens up magnificent business prospects: Any activity can be turned to profit as long as it is sufficiently annoying to someone else. As long as the activity absorbs no resources, i.e., as long as the blackmailers maintain amateur standing, the economist who refrains from social judgment can find no fault with the situation.

On External Diseconomies and the Government-Assisted Invisible Hand, *Economica*, vol. 31, 1964, p. 353. See also Mishan, The Postwar Literature on Externalities: An Interpretive Essay, *op. cit.*, p. 24.

154. Tullock, *op. cit.*, p. 145.

jury and of relevant externalities, for there are many possible changes in any property rights structure. The problem is a problem of continuity versus change, considered normatively or positively: the beneficiaries of existing institutions or arrangements have a vested interest in the benefit-cost distribution generated by existing institutions. Conflicts of interest are generated involving both the operation and change (or elimination) of those institutions,[155] which is to say, over one set of externalities or another, any change itself producing externalities. The notion of Madelyn Kafoglis, that "externalities ought to be defined as discrepancies between alternative legal and social arrangements,"[156] is fully consonant with the view developed here. Externalities are a function of power, and changing the structure of power signifies not only changed capacity to generate externalities but that the very change of the structure of power creates externalities.

C. *The Fundamental Problems and Context of Externality Policy*

Ronald Coase concluded his seminal essay on the problem of social cost with the injunction that "in choosing between social arrangements within the context of which individual decisions are made, we have to bear in mind that a change in the existing system which will lead to an improvement in some decisions may well lead to a worsening of others . . . . in devising and choosing between social arrangements we should have regard for the total effect. This, above all, is

---

155. "Existing institutions with their associated beneficiaries are jealous of their prerogatives and will resist new institutions that would share political and social and economic power. Existing institutions obviously have the advantage over any proposed institution with less certain benefits and beneficiaries and no existing bureaucracy to assure its birth and survival.

Usually compromises occur and only second-best institutional arrangements are feasible." Jack W. Carlson, Environmental Quality: Discussion, *Am. Econ, Rev., Papers and Proceedings,* vol. 61, 1971, p. 170. It has already been pointed out, in Section III, how the Pareto-criterion is inapplicable to situations in which there is both benefit to some and injury to others. The case of power is paradigmatic here, since the power of Alpha tends to be and generally is reciprocal to the power of Beta. The study by Buchanan and Tullock, *op. cit.,* is an ingenious attempt to come to grips with the latter case in matters of constitution making (e.g., fundamental allocations of power and rule making). For a perceptive review, see Baumol, *Welfare Economics and the Theory of the State,* second edition, *op. cit.,* pp. 43-45. Also relevant, *inter alia,* is the work of Anthony Downs, e.g., *An Economic Theory of Democracy,* New York: Harper, 1957, also reviewed in Baumol's second edition, pp. 39-41.

156. Madelyn L. Kafoglis, Marriage Customs and Opportunity Costs, *Jour. of Pol. Econ.,* vol. 78, 1970, p. 423.

the change in approach which I am advocating."[157] This point of view is nowhere more important than in the case of externalities considered in the framework developed in this paper. In this subsection I propose to examine the basic problems of externality policy and the larger problems of which they are but one facet.[158]

1. The basic problem of externality policy is: which externalities, or which social benefits to pursue and which social costs to inhibit? Closely tied thereto are the correlative problems of: which structure of power, which structure of opportunity sets, and which pattern of mutual coercion? The welfare economist cannot avoid the problem of power: with externalities a function of power and of change in power structure, to consider externalities is to consider power, to make externality policy is to make power-structure policy. Intertwined too is the problem of the distribution of gains and losses from externality solutions, injuries and benefits generated by the very act of effecting externality solutions and by the operation of the institutional arrangements thereby set in motion; in other words, the distribution of sacrifice, of who is sacrificed to whom. The elemental questions of policy are: whose interests, whose freedom, whose capacity to coerce, who may injure whom, whose rights, and who decides?[159] Nowhere are these problems more obvious and important than in the matter of externality solutions.

What dwarfs even the foregoing, however, is the fact that such externalities as water and air pollution may threaten the very basis and operation of civilization both in individual industrialized nations and on the planet as a whole. We may be dealing not with the subtle marginal conditions of a maximizing equilibrium, but the even more subtle total conditions of survival, a bounded consumption set, as it were, for the entire species. The threatened wreckage is far more than welfare economics.

2. I return to the basic problem of *which* externalities. The problem is one of social choice. Empirically the process of selection identi-

---

157. Ronald H. Coase, The Problem of Social Cost, *Jour. of Law and Econ.*, vol. 3, 1960, p. 44.

158. The problems of externalities are of course terribly more complicated than can be considered here, e.g., in terms of their technological aspects and their interactions. Also see Samuels, Externalities, Rate Structure, and the Theory of Public Utility Regulation, *in* Harry Trebing, ed., Essays in Public Utility Pricing and Regulation, East Lansing: Michigan State University, Public Utilities Institute, 1971; Public Utilities and Social Problems, *Public Utilities Fortnightly*, vol. 84, July 31, 1969, pp. 15-21; and Public Utilities, Social Order, and Housing, *ibid*, vol. 85, May 7, 1970, pp. 32-36.

159. Samuels, *The Classical Theory of Economic Policy, op. cit.*, pp. 282-286.

fies externalities for consideration and then selects which externalities
to promote and which to inhibit. This requires an additional, judgmental premise on which to base a determination to change the
situation from what would otherwise be the case. As other commentators have put the matter, ". . . to internalize an externality is not
something desirable in itself,"[160] ". . . there are many externalities
that we may wish to retain,"[161] ". . . the presence of externalities
does *not* automatically justify government intervention."[162] Some of
these commentators, perhaps all of them, were using a narrower
definition of externality than that used here. But the point remains
the same: in a world of ubiquitous externalities, in which externality-
solutions generate externalities, we have to choose between externalities. What makes the problem so complicated, irritating, and explo-
sive is that it involves changes in the structure of power and threats
to our images of what the economic system is all about.

Central to the social choice involved is the determination of what
is of "public importance." This is a matter of social valuation and
choice, in some sense the result of the aggregation of individual preferences, however learned. Part of the social process is the perception
of which—whose—injuries are to count, of which are to be considered
important and thereby suitable for inhibitory policy. Here is where
the power structure enters: the judgmental process is one in which
decisions are a function of the structure of power, in which decisions
are power-structure specific, and decisions based on the status quo
power structure are skewed toward the perceived interests of those
with more of "the say," whether power be based on wealth, property,
votes, position, rank, or force. Whoever is poor or weak by the criterion of the selection system used (which use itself is a function of
power play) will be sacrificed so long as their interests do not coincide
with the interests of the corresponding rich or strong:

> Optimal levels of the policy variables depend on how various
> losses are perceived. It is clear that these losses will be per-
> ceived differently among social and economic groups within
> any society. The political process will determine how the in-

---

160. Tibor Scitovsky, *Welfare and Competition*, Homewood: Irwin, revised ed.,
     1971, p. 271.
161. Tullock, *op. cit.*, p. 171.
162. Baumol, *Welfare Economics and the Theory of the State*, 2nd ed., *op. cit.*,
     p. 29.

terests of various groups will be reconciled or which groups will be able to impose their will on the rest of the society.[163]

If by "political" we mean the total decision making or power process, then that statement is precisely what I have in mind: perception of loss, of which losses are unacceptable, governs externality policy, and that is a function of social power—and social powers will tend *not to see or value as important* the injuries to others which they themselves have generated.

The selection of externality solutions, and thus the selection of which externalities to accept and promote and which to reject and inhibit, is a function, *inter alia*, of the limits imposed by ideology and the structure of power. In welfare economic terms it is a matter of the social welfare function, but that function depends upon the power structure or "institutional framework within which society decides upon such matters."[164] It thus helps to have consensus,[165] but that is relatively rare (which rarity, it will be recalled, accounts for the general irrelevance of the Pareto-criterion with regard to the crucial issues of policy). One of the limits within which this selection process operates is welfare economics.

3. I urge that these considerations are a part of the *problem of order*, the reconciliation of freedom and control, and continuity and change, of what Spengler calls autonomy, cooperation, and continuity.[166] Part of the problem, too, is that of hierarchy versus equality,[167] on which three comments: first, externalities may well be regressive in impact;[168] second, a hierarchical power structure will generate externality policy generally specific to itself; and third, inequality is the problem whose avoidance is one objective of the welfare-economic injunction against interpersonal utility comparisons and ethical assumptions, though we have seen that it works out rather differently in practice.

163. John R. Harris, On the Economics of Law and Order, *Jour. of Pol. Econ.*, vol. 78, 1970, p. 171.

164. Henderson and Quandt, *op. cit.*, p. 223.

165. The views of Tullock, *op. cit.*, p. 192, and Harold M. Groves, Toward a Theory of Progressive Taxation, *National Tax Jour.*, vol. 9, 1956, pp. 27-34, are remarkably similar on the role of consensus.

166. Joseph J. Spengler, The Problem of Order in Economic Affairs, *South. Econ. Jour.*, vol. 3, 1948, reprinted in Joseph J. Spengler and William R. Allen, eds., *Essays in Economic Thought*, Chicago: Rand McNally, 1960, p. 9.

167. Joseph J. Spengler, Hierarchy vs. Equality: Persisting Conflict, *Kyklos*, vol. 21, 1968.

168. *Inter alia*, see Mishan, *The Costs of Economic Growth*, *op. cit.*, p. 73.

Additional relevant questions of externality policy are:

a. not whether capitalism is or is not to be, but *whose* capitalism;

b. not whether a regime of free contract is or is not to exist, but *whose* choices will free contract give effect to;

c. not freedom or nonfreedom, but *whose* freedom;

d. not reform or no reform, but *which* reform;

e. not externality policy or no externality policy, but *which* externality policy;

f. not private property or not, but *whose* private property rights;

g. not democracy or no democracy, but *whose* democracy;

h. not government or no government, but *whose* government.

Considerations such as these are generally thought to be excluded from economic theory and welfare economics. But welfare economics cannot afford to exclude them as variables, for they are too important; nor does it exclude them even when silent about them, for they exist and welfare economists implicitly make assumptions about them. Thus, central to the problem of order is *conflict;* no accident, then, that Radomysler wrote that "the central economic problem is . . . conflict,"[169] or that Alchian began his essay on some economics of property rights with the statement that

> In *every* society, conflicts of interest among the members of that society must be resolved. The process by which that resolution (not elimination!) occurs is known as *competition*. Since, by definition, there is no way to eliminate competition, the relevant question is what kind of competition shall be used in the resolution of the conflicts of interest? In more dramatic words designed to arouse emotional interest, "What forms of discrimination among the members of that society shall be employed in deciding to what extent each person is able to achieve various levels of his goals?" Discrimination, competition, and scarcity are three inseparable concepts.[170]

There is indeed an ubiquitous struggle for control over the distribu-

---

169. *Readings in Welfare Economics, op. cit.,* p. 94.
170. Armen A. Alchian, Some Economics of Property Rights, *Il Politico,* vol. 30, 1965, p. 816.

tion of costs and benefits[171] and therefore over the structure of opportunity sets and of power. Welfare economists must come to grips with this; they treat it whether they want to or not.

4. One of the most profound analytical and practical problems of welfare economics is that optimal solutions are a function of and thus specific to the decision making structure or process generating them. There are no unique Pareto-optimal solutions; there are only solutions specific to the underlying power situation. Notwithstanding the insight that political and economic analysis can give about decisional structures and conditions of optimality, such structures cannot be conclusively justified in terms of the optimality solutions they yield, nor the optimality solutions conclusively justified in terms of the decisional structures, without smacking of circularity. There is potential conflict between the quality of decision-making structure and the quality of the resulting decisions: a criterion of one may be satisfied but not a criterion of the other, and trade-offs will have to be made. There is in addition the intractable problem of evaluating the status quo and potential changes of the status quo—potential externality solutions—in terms of the cost-price structure generated by the status quo. Costs are a partial function of the state of the law, and we cannot conclusively rationalize costs by reference to the law, nor the law by reference to the costs, nor changes in either costs or law by reference to the other. But we have no calculus with which to evaluate externalities and proposed externality-solutions independent of experience, and our experience is that of the status quo. We do have our imaginations; sometimes there must be a leap into the uncertain and unknown. But the hold of the status quo is formidable:

> In any historically given situation there is a social state which has a preferred status in social choice in that it will be adopted in the absence of a specific decision to the contrary. Politically, the status quo has this property, as is frequently all too obvious.[172]

Nowhere is this clearer, as we have seen, than in the case of the Pareto-criterion. Thus, writing about Buchanan and Tullock's *Calculus of Consent*, Arrow takes a position similar to that of Baumol:

> The asymmetry between action and inaction is closely related

---

171. Chandler Morse, New Dimensions in Natural Resources: Discussion, *Am. Econ. Rev., Papers and Proceedings*, vol. 60, 1970, p. 128.
172. Arrow, *op. cit.*, p. 119.

to their support of unanimity as the ideal criterion of choice; under such a rule, the status quo is a highly privileged alternative.[173]

At the very least, welfare economic analysis should make clear the strategic importance of the status quo or of equivalent alternative assumptions. It has not always, indeed rarely, done so. Thus, for example, it is certainly conventional to argue that we should "seek that combination of government and private action that optimizes the future discounted income stream of members of society."[174] But this raises the long-recognized but long-evaded problem of *whose* income. Since Alpha's income is Beta's cost, *which* cost-price structure, therefore *which* opportunity set structure and *which* power structure? This takes more than empirical information; but I share Tullock's enthusiasm that welfare economics can develop models with which to articulate what is involved.

5. There is another problem of enormous social importance which also requires social decision. I refer to the problem of concentration; that there may be a conflict between, on the one hand, the size of the decision making unit necessary to internalize externalities and enable participation in decision making of all those who are affected (and therefore consent), and, on the other, the desiderata of a pluralist power structure. There may have to be a trade-off between units large enough to enable consensual agreement between all affected parties and units sufficient in number to allow a diffusion of power.[175] The solution is not clear-cut in terms of freedom: large internalizing units provide freedom insofar as they make externality-generation responsible,[176] and a large number of units provide freedom insofar

---

173. *Ibid*, p. 120.
174. Tullock, *op. cit.*, pp. 53-54.
175. See Hollis B. Chenery, The Interdependence of Investment Decisions, *in* M. Abramovitz and others, *The Allocation of Economic Resources*, Stanford: Stanford University Press, 1959, reprinted in *Readings in Welfare Economics, op. cit.*, p. 366.
176. Thomas Gale Moore, An Economic Analysis of the Concept of Freedom, *Jour. of Pol. Econ.*, vol. 77, 1969, pp. 532-544. Moore's analysis is generally consistent with the model developed here. He argues the thesis "that freedom can be defined in terms of welfare. A change in the cost of action (or non-action) can be considered to be a movement toward freedom if it increases welfare." (pp. 532-533) The complication, of course, is that there is no independent test of welfare. Moore adopts a Pareto-optimal approach: "If the cost to the individual of performing some action is lowered without affecting the cost to others, then we will consider that a movement toward a freer society." (p. 533). He acknowledges that "Much of the problem with

as they diffuse power. Once again difficult, subtle judgments have to be made, including the valuation of injuries and of trade-offs between injuries and freedom. As Samuelson has written, "what is called 'freedom' is really a vector of almost infinite components rather than a one-dimensional thing that can be given a simple ordering."[177]

Somewhat related is a conflict of organizational efficiency: an organizational scope large enough to internalize relevant externalities may or may not be optimal in size in terms of economies and diseconomies of scale with respect to hierarchical organization and operation.[178] Once again externalities have to be traded against externalities.

6. A word about compensation. With externalities seen as ubiquitous, the demand for compensation (as Haveman perceived)[179] would also be rather ubiquitous. Society (or the legal process) cannot always compensate for injury, so the problem becomes one as to *when* and *to whom* should compensation be paid.[180] The problem underlying that is: who visits injury upon whom, for to argue in favor of compensation *or* to argue against compensation is to argue for one pattern of injury and/or one pattern of cost distribution rather than another. It is a matter of the distribution of cost and injury in a system of "creative destruction." Then, too, there are judgments as to the

---

the concept of freedom revolves around cases where externalities exist," (p. 533), so that "Free speech, freedom of religion, and so on, can only be justified if some restrictions are placed on the admissible set of externalities," (p. 536). After recognizing that whether something is an externality or not depends on the relevant unit, (p. 541), he concludes that "Since a free competitive market tends to internalize externalities, it suggests that such a market will result in a free society." (p. 543) The conclusion is in the right direction but too strong: first, freedom is relative and a matter of opportunity sets and not a "one-dimensional thing" (as Samuelson will be quoted in the text to say); second, the results of internalization are not unique but rather a function of the structure of power etc.; and third, even if we ignore the foregoing, the scope of decision-making units compatible with a wide diffusion of power (one notion of a free society) may conflict with Moore's notion (as internalization *per se*).

177. Samuelson, *Collected Scientific Papers, op. cit.*, vol. 2, p. 1414.

178. See Werner Z. Hirsch, *The Economics of State and Local Government,* New York: McGraw-Hill, 1970, p. 274.

179. Haveman, *op. cit.*, p. 191.

180. See Mishan, *The Costs of Economic Growth, op. cit.*, pp. 70-72; and Anthony Downs, Uncompensated Non-Construction Costs which Urban Highways and Urban Renewal Impose upon Residential Households, paper presented at Conference on Economics of Public Output, National Bureau of Economic Research, Princeton University, April 26-27, 1968, revised manuscript, summarized in Samuels, Externalities, Rate Structure, and the Theory of Public Utility Regulation, *op. cit.*, and cited to the same end in Tullock, *op. cit.*, p. 171.

propriety (and thus compensability for injury) of any particular
element of the status quo, and as to how much and what particular
injuries must be deemed accepted (and thus noncompensable) as part
of the burden of living in society. Taxes are not the only price we pay
for civilization: there are the externalities generated by our "neighbors"—the problem is *which* ones, and is complicated by inequality
of power. Compensation is also partially a function of injury or loss
perception, and that is partially a function of power structure.

7. The task of welfare economics, considered as a positivist attempt to comprehend the forces and factors governing the attainment
and distribution of welfare, should be to study externalities in a general equilibrium context, articulating models in terms of the foregoing
catalog of problems and variables, eschewing partial-equilibrium, *a
prioristic* lines of reasoning which build in normative positions concerning income and injury distribution. Welfare economists should
work out models of market and nonmarket decision-making and their
interrelation, with power and mutual coercion as critical explicit
variables.[181]

There are insoluble problems involved, but welfare economists
should attempt to study them as positive problems. The emphasis
should be on analytic description and explanation, and on neither
normative ranking nor the social control function of ideology. Neither
market nor government nor church (nor welfare economists' normative rankings) permit all values to be registered and counted in any
independently determinable "right" way; ". . . there is no single institutional technique, centralized or decentralized, which is ideal in the
management of externalities."[182] And where certain values are registered, both their registration and their weighting are a function,
skewed to be sure, of the structure of power: decisions, including
valuations, are a function of the decision making structure out of
which they develop. The problems of externality analysis are as follows: what should be the relation of the market to other valuation
and decision processes, what should be the power structure, and, as
a derivative thereof, what should be the pattern of sacrifice? I pose
these as essentially normative questions, which they are; and I acknowledge that there is a danger of overintellectualization, inasmuch
as the social processes involved have intellectual elements in them, but

---

181. Richard R. Nelson, New Dimensions in Natural Resources: Discussion, *Am.
Econ. Rev., Papers and Proceedings,* vol. 60, 1970, p. 128.

182. Emery N. Castle, The Market Mechanism, Externalities, and Land Economics, *Jour. of Farm Econ.,* vol. 47, 1965, p. 551.

they are primarly psychological and power-play in character;[183] I urge that they can be approached in a positive study. This should be the task of welfare economics.

---

183. See R. A. Bauer, Social Psychology and the Study of Policy Formation, *American Psychologist,* vol. 21, 1966, pp. 933-942.

2
PREDICTING THE PERFORMANCE OF ALTERNATIVE INSTITUTIONS
A. Allan Schmid

Those interested in a different performance with respect to the use of resources need two types of information. First, it is necessary to identify a number of alternatives which might be instrumental in changing performance, and second, it is necessary to be able to predict the broad range of consequences that might be expected from each. An institutional theory is presented here to achieve these objectives. it is illustrated with applications to natural resources policy, but it is generalizable to a wide variety of products and issues.

In some resource policy areas we have put all of our eggs in one policy basket. If we don't get results, the prescription is to intensify the selected approach. For example, if zoning has not achieved the desired pattern of land use, it is often suggested that zoning administration be improved, better officials be elected or move the zoning decision out of local control to higher levels of government. However, it might be useful to expand our list of institutional alternatives in a quite different direction. One purpose of this chapter is to develop a conceptual framework that might enlarge the list of institutional alternatives for a given resource area.

How many times has a group spent its political capital to get a new policy or rule adopted only to find that performance is unchanged or changed in an unanticipated direction? One suspects that sometimes there is agreement that current performance is unsatisfactory but little confidence that any of the suggested institutional changes would produce the desired output. There are some new approaches being tried in the various states and by different state and federal agencies. Are we learning all we can from these experiments? It is the character of social science experiments that we cannot run the world over again and again while changing the ingredients in the institutional mix one by one. We must have the capacity to learn from the experiments that do occur and to extend their implications into new areas. For example, if a new regulatory or jurisdictional approach is tried for one resource commodity, it would be useful if we could infer how it might work if applied to another commodity.

To accomplish the tasks outlined above, we need a theory to help us organize our experience, to suggest new institutional variables and to predict their performance. It is not in our power to predict with certainty. I believe our society must develop a more experimental attitude and be patient with government as it tries new things, rather than demanding that each new wave of politicians have all the answers for the promised land. It is in our power to aid this experimentation so that it can proceed in a less haphazard manner.

Institutional Theory

Each natural resource has a set of characteristics which shape human interdependence with respect to its use. Understanding the source of the interdependence and the resulting conflicts is essential to suggesting which rules of the game create opportunities for some of the conflicting interest groups and deny opportunities for others. Institutions shape opportunities and thus the resulting individual choices which can aggregatively be described in some terms of substantive performance—who gets what. In this paper, particular attention will be given to income and wealth distribution.

Several categories of sources of human interdependence will be outlined below and illustrated with natural resources issues that fit into each. The purpose is not just an exercise in filling empty boxes, but is designed to enlarge our capacity for learning from experience with institutional experiments. If we are to proceed less blindly, we must have the capacity to type the kind of interdependent situation presented by one kid of resource so that when a particular type of institutional variable (structure) is changed, we have some idea of its instrumentality in causing a certain result or performance. If this is understood, we may be able to predict that when the same type of institution is created for a different commodity in **name,** but presenting the same **type** of interdependence we will get similar performance to that already observed in the experiment. Or conversely, when an institution used in one interdependent situation is applied to a different type of resource representing a different source of interdependence, we might be able to predict how performance would differ. For example, Table 1 indicates that factor ownership is a structural variable instrumental in achieving a particular performance (use by a specified party) in the situation of an "incompatible use good" (line 1a; but factor ownership is not instrumental in the situation marked by "high exclusion cost" (line 2).

The essence of the model developed here then is comprised of varieties of **situation** (sources of interdependence), the types of institutional **structure** that control and direct each situation, and the resulting performance. [The model is developed in detail in Schmid, 1978.] Many resource commodities have multile attributes. If we can understand how these attributes interact with particular rules of the game, we can both suggest new institutional approaches and better predict their consequences. All any theory can do is suggest where to look.

Table 1. An Illustration of the Situation, Structure and Performance Paradigm.

Situation (Sources of Interdependence) Commodity and Interest Groups	Structure (Alternative Property Rights)	Performance (Who Gets What)
1. Incompatible Use:	Distribution of Factor Ownership:	
a. In land between farmer and hunter.	Land may be posted and trespassers sued.	Hunters are excluded.
b. In air between industry and breather.	Breather may sue polluters. Tradeable rights.	Industry is excluded. Industry makes bids to farmers to acquire air rights. If some rights are sold, air quality declines.
	or	
	Pollution prohibited by regulation, rights are not tradeable.	Air stays clean to benefit of non-owner third parties.
2. High Exclusion Cost Goods: In land (street) environment between litter-bug neatnik.	Factor ownership to neatnik	Litter-bug still uses because of ineffective exclusion.
	or	
	Regulation gives protection to neatnik.	Ditto
	or	
	Learned, internalized habits.	Clean landscape.
3. Economies of Scale: In electricity - Consumers in Region A vs. Region B. Both want to pay MC.	Consumers in Region A pay MC by administrative rule.	Consumers in Region A pay lower price than those in Region B.
	or	
	Average Cost Pricing	All consumers pay same price.

Situation: Sources of Human Interdependence

1. Incompatible Users or Uses

When one person's use of a resource means it is unavailable for use by another, there is conflict in the face of scarcity. One person's use is incompatible with that of another. If you don't keep your cattle fenced in, they will destroy the crop of your neighbor. This type of conflict is controlled by factor ownership. Ownership defines who gets to participate in resource use decisions and who is excluded whether implemented by so-called private property or governmental regulation.

One of the largest bodies of law which control physically incompatible land uses is the common law of trespass and nuisance. For example, it can prevent a hunter from walking across farm land, a funeral parlor from being built in a residential area, or a tall building from shading a neighboring swimming pool or solar energy collector. Some of these rights are so internalized into our habits and thoughts that we don't even think of them as rights when compared to the growing, explicit regulatory actions of government. But government is no less present when a hunter avoids posted land than when the Environmental Protection Agency (EPA) orders an industry to reduce its waste discharge.

The language of welfare economic theory has crept into popular speech. Everyone talks about externalities and the divergence of private and social costs. Some of this language is unfortunate and confuses public discussion and learning from experience with past resource controls. The term "externalities" is often selectively applied to certain situations where it suggests that market institutions are not appropriate and should be replaced with direct governmental action. For example, it is suggested that an industry putting pollution in the air beyond the absorptive capacity of the environment is a special case of creating externalities not properly accounted for. But how is it different from the interdependence between farmer and hunter which is controlled by ordinary factor ownership? Why does industry pay for **any** of its inputs? It wouldn't pay for labor if people did not own their labor power and could be enslaved. It doesn't pay for any of the air for waste disposal when it feels it already owns the air as it owns other resources.

If you want a different use of air resources, change factor ownership. Give the air rights to breathers and you will get a different use, or with trade at least a different set of beneficiaries of its use. It is no different structurally than if land ownership were altered to favor hunters in the rules of hunting trespass. It is factor ownership which controls access to incompatible use goods. It was noted above that a resource has multiple attributes and we will note below some of the features of air resources that are not related to incompatible use and thus not controlled by simple factor ownership.

When we want to change income distribution we can change resource ownership. The transfer payment can be seen as a new claim on the income from resources. By a curious evolution of ideas it seems easier in our country to pass a tax on income and transfer that income from the rich to the poor than to transfer ownership of the resources themselves. Via regulation we constantly change ownership of the air, forests, uses of public lands, land covering coal deposits (surface mines), land along highways which can be used for billboards, etc. These factor ownership shifts are not usually between groups that are seen simply as rich and poor. It seems by the prevailing ideology to be okay to transfer rights to land from farmers to car drivers, but not from a rich farmer to a poor farmer. If you want to do the latter, you must do it via taxes and not directly via land reform (as we sometimes recommend for other countries).

We do sometimes place limits on the size of factor ownership which can benefit from public spending. One of the hot issues in the West today is the 160 acre limit on farm units that can benefit from government irrigation projects. The limit on government price support payments to an individual farmer is similar in its design to limit the effects of size of factor ownership.

If we see factor ownership as the right to participate in resource use decisions with respect to incompatible use goods, it allows comparison of the effects of alternative ways to implement changed ownership. The commhanges slowly, but it does change. Further, some newly arising incompatibilities are often left to the courts for resolution (instead of seeking new statutory law). For example, the courts now seem to be evolving rights with respect to use of the atmosphere for rain making [Davis 1977a] and for hail suppression [Davis 1977b]. If a rainmaker ruins my picnic, can I sue for trespass?

While there is similarity between a so-called private right to use a resource and a right made available via government regulation, there can be important differences in the structure and thus performance. For example, a residential area is protected from certain incompatible uses in the common law of nuisance. The right to be free of a funeral home or a smokey factory is provided by common law as well as by statutory zoning. The first is backed up by the private right to sue in court while the second is administered by a government who can bring suit against a violator, or in some cases it may be a criminal matter. The nominal right of use via private ownership or regulation may be the same, but the location of initiative for redress and the cost of the protective transaction may produce a different *de facto* result.

Another potentially different result from government regulation versus a private property right stems from the saleability of the right. If the residences affected by a proposed funeral home can agree, they might sell their ownership to the funeral home developer. But in the case of zoning, the developer cannot buy the right since it is not for sale at any price (at least it is not supposed to be, though bribes to officials are in fact common).

Where resource use decisions are made by governmental administration, access to government works just like factor ownership in the private sector in determining participation. For example, take the case of the California Coastal Commissions [Healy 1977]. First, a public referendum declared that access and view of the beach was owned by all citizens and not the owner of other aspects of coastal lands. But, secondly, the actual exercise of this viewing right depends on decision of a commission. Who is a member of this commission then affects who gets to participate. The rules of commission membership are a type of factor ownership just as is stock ownership related to the management of a private corporation. a statewide constituency was obtained via a state referendum in 1973, but in 1976 the legislature shifted control back to local zoning bodies. A limited appeal to a state commission was retained, but the commission is one-half local officials [Grote 1978].

In summary, one can go a long way in understanding income distribution of the enjoyment of natural resources by looking at factor ownership which controls conflicts with respect to incompatible use goods. It leads to the question: Who owns America? In many cases, it is hard to tell. It is relatively easy to see if factories or breathers own the air, but it is harder to tell how much land is owned by any particular person. We do not keep ownership records in such a way that the holding of an individual can be summarized. For example, we have no Census data on the characteristics of nonoperator owned farm land. The application of the 160 acre limit to beneficiaries of public irrigation projects may be frustrated by the creation of dummy owners without revelation of the ultimate beneficiary. Even in states where people are uneasy about corporate ownership of farm land, there is little data on the characteristics of the corporate owners. For available data see [Rodefeld 1978]. The lack of data on the distribution of factor ownership relative to the distribution of money income may explain in part why we focus on income transfers rather than altering resource ownership.

1a. Bargaining Power

The size of one's factor ownership has additional meaning in an exchange economy. The right of exchange means that in addition to keeping other incompatible users away, you can bargain for a lot of what the other person owns without giving up much yourself. When you have many opportunities and the other person has few alternatives, you can extract a very favorable price for your factors. A prominent example in natural resources is the ability of the OPEC cartel to set high oil prices. Another item in current debate is the right of an owner of one energy source such as oil to own other sources such as coal. It is feared that ownership of multiple sources will prevent new firms from market entry. The market power of the big lumber companies has been much discussed [Mead 1966]. Sometimes government projects are used to compete with private firms to demonstrate the lowest possible cost of production. (This is an alternative or complement to government price regulation.) The Yardstick Principle was one of the selling points of the TVA, but has been used little since.

The institutional variables identified by neo-classical economic theory have now been discussed—namely, factor ownership and enforcement of competition. There is no question that they control an important source of interdependence with respect to natural resources. But, as we shall see below, there are other sources which are not controlled by these institutional variables. Knowledge of these other sources will help us suggest additional institutional alternatives and to interpret the results of new experiments.

2. High Exclusion Cost Goods

Factor ownership may give a person the right to exclude others from a resource, but if the actual cost of exclusion is high, it is an empty right. A hunter may purchase a license to hunt a managed herd of animals which would guarantee hunting success. But the animals are scattered over the landscape, and there are numerous opportunities for those who have not paid for the right to nevertheless harvest an animal. The government can always hire game wardens to prevent use by nonowners, but now the legitimate hunter pays not only for animal management, but also for policing. The cost of this policing may be infinite in some cases.

In the case of the air resource noted above, if the factor is owned by industry, it may be very difficult to organize a bid from the breathers. Each breather knows that if the air is made pure, no one can be excluded even if they did nothing to contribute to its creation. This is the familiar free rider problem. The temptation to be a free rider can prevent some who desire a product from organizing a bid to its owners. It is frustrating to own income but not be able to spend it to acquire certain resources because of the actions of the free riders. One way to curtail the opportunities of the free riders is to make them contribute to the provision of high exclusion cost goods via taxes. This solves one problem and creates another. A nonpayer may not be an opportunistic free rider, but simply a person who does not desire the product. If these people are forced to contribute, we create the "unwilling rider."

It is not enough to look at the distribution of money income. What that money will buy depends on the resolution of conflicts with respect to high exclusion cost goods. The person who pays while another rides free makes a transfer as much as in any negative income tax or other welfare program, as does the person who pays for something not wanted.

There are many environmental products which have high exclusion cost. Consider a litter-free environment, for example (see Table 1). The person who litters denies a resource to the person preferring a neat landscape. It is difficult for market incentives to work here. Even if the neatnik owns the resource, he can't charge those who litter when they drop something if it is costly to police. Likewise it is hard for administrative controls and fines to work for the same reason. This suggests a need for some new institutional variables. The only cheap form of exclusion is that internalized into the habits of people. If we grew up with neat behaviors, it would not occur to us to litter even when we knew the landscape owners or police were not looking. Neatness would not be the result of a calculation of advantage but simply the right thing to do. What do we know about how people learn these internalized standards of behavior? How, for example, do we learn to honor queues (first come, first served), and what are the factors which lead to breakdown of these practices? Can a nation which cares about its environment put all of its institutional marbles in the basket of market or administrative incentives? Where is the equivalent of the EPA for the maintenance and systematic change of these internalized standards?

3. Economies of Scale

Another source of human interdependence arises from the character of the cost function for production of certain products. The character of how costs per unit change with scale creates a situation where the choices of one person affect another. The production of electricity provides an example (see Table 1). In some cities the electric plant is not of a size to reach the low point in terms of unit cost. This encourages the management to seek new customers and expanded use by offering some groups of customers lower prices. This raises questions of equity as between groups of customers. Recently it has raised conflicts between utilities and those who want to restrict total electric use to save scarce oil and coal resources.

In the West where hydroelectric generation is available, it constitutes a cheaper source of power than that generated in thermal plants. The new units cost more than the old units supplied by hydro plants. Who gets to buy from the hydro plants and who from the thermal plants? The Bonneville Power Administration is in the middle of this controversy. It has been proposed that Bonneville market all power regardless of its source at the average cost of production. The rights conflict is over who gets to be regarded as the marginal consumer and entitled or required to pay the marginal cost.

Many urban public services have reached the point of increasing costs to scale (particularly on a geographical scale). Pricing at average cost encourages more growth and sprawl with implications for land use [Gaffney 1977 and Downing 1977]. Again, we can't understand wealth distribution by knowing only who owns the land or money income. We need to understand the rights inherent in pricing policies of both private and public firms in the situation of changing costs to scale.

3a. Peak Load Pricing

Interdependence also grows out of cyclical variations in demand. This situation is included here because the controlling property right is in pricing rules as is the case for economies of scale. People place great demands on highway systems during rush hours. If the system is built to meet the peak hours of demand, there is excess capacity at other times. The investment decision affects the amount of land needed for highways. The same situation exists with respect to electricity and water demand during the hot summer months. If people are charged the average price for these goods, they do not try to even out their rates of use. The person who finds other alternatives for cooling or uses hot water during the day rather than at night when everyone is home using hot water is not given any incentives by different rates. Yet those with few alternatives may feel that charging a higher price during peak periods is unfair. The rules for peak load pricing are part of the wealth of some people and a liability for others.

4. Joint-Impact Goods

The polar case of a good with declining cost to scale is the situation where the marginal cost of another use is zero (MC=0). This situation is in contrast to that of the incompatible use good. A new user can be added without subtracting from the utility of the former user. This might appear to be the best of all possible worlds, but alas there is interdependence. The conflict is over cost sharing. While MC=0, someone has to pay the fixed costs. The term "public goods" is sometimes used in the literature, but is not used here because the term presumptively includes a policy conclusion particularly when contrasted to "private goods."

A natural resource illustration of a joint-impact good is that of flood control. If a dam is built to protect a given area, it doesn't cost anything extra to protect one or a hundred homes in that area. That still leaves the question of who will pay for the dam. Sometimes, a particular resource has multiple characteristics. Flood control is both high exclusion cost and joint-impact. If any one is to have the protection, it will be hard to exclude others even if they did not help pay. But even if we could exclude those who did not pay, would we want to since their use adds nothing to cost? On the other hand, even if a user adds nothing to cost, is it fair to others if the cost is not shared? The same kind of issue arises with respect to multiple use projects. Once a reservoir is built, other uses such as recreation can be added with little or no extra cost. How should the fixed cost be split between flood control beneficiaries and boaters? These cost sharing practices are important property rights.

Use of the air waves for sound is a joint-impact good. When I pipe music to my backyard, you can hear it at no extra cost. I may be generous and be willing to bear the entire cost. But, you don't like my taste in music (neither type nor time of day). To people of similar tastes, the sound is a joint impact good, while to people of different tastes it is also an incompatible use of the air waves. The controlling institutional variable in the first case is cost sharing, but with respect to incompatible use, control is determined by factor ownership and the right to choose the existence of the good. In the latter case people do not care if they escape paying for an outdoor rock concert in the city park via entrance fees or taxes—they don't want the good created and consumed by anyone. so there can be two property rights arguments going on simultaneously with respect to the same resource but with different sources of the conflict. Those with complementary tastes are arguing over cost shares (they want the city to pay part of the cost of music with taxes or special assessment against the neighboring properties) while those with incompatible tastes are arguing over factor ownership and whether the good is to be allowed at all.

5.   Transaction Costs-Contractual

It is often costly to reach agreement with another party. Where these costs are inherent in the situation, institutions affect who bears these costs. In other cases, the institutions create transaction costs where there were none before. Regardless of who is designated as the original owner, if trade is allowed, the good can go to a new user. But, where transaction costs are high, the original owner may also be the ultimate user, since the higher bid of another user is overwhelmed by the costs of negotiation, etc.

Major changes in land use often require an area of land under one management. If the area is, however, owned by many individuals, there is a cost of assembling the total parcel. This is a problem for developers of new town sites. When word gets out that a large development is planned, the individual owners may ask exhorbitant prices. The same problem arises when an electric line, gas pipe line, or coal slurry line is to be built. The effect of these contracutal costs is reduced if the developer can use the power of condemnation and buy the land at the going market value rather than a price stemming from the superior bargaining position of the individual owners. Of course, those nonlandowners who do not like to see these utility lines on the landscape derive a benefit from high contractual costs which prevent land use change. One person's contractual cost is another's right to the *status quo*.

Getting any large group together for a common action is a costly undertaking. it is not enough for the public to be declared a factor owner if it is costly to make that right effective. For example, suppose that an individual feels that nonconsumptive public use of a natural resource has been foreclosed by a private developer. What are the individual's options?

A complaint can be made to some appropriate state or federal agency. But the agency may be slow to act and no court action is begun. In Michigan, a citizen has the right to bring a direct suit against a violator of the public rights in the environment [Sax and DiMento 1974]. But, court suits cost money. The individual gain if the wrong is righted may be less than the cost of bringing suit. Here we run onto the free rider problem again. When our citizen tries to get others to help pay for the suit, they may be tempted to be free riders. In any case the seeking out of the beneficiaries is costly. There are several rules that can shift the impact of contractual cost. One is to allow class action suits with lawyer's fees paid out of the court settlement. This gives an incentive to the lawyer to organize the suit and does not require explicit cooperation by all of the affected parties.

An earlier reference was made to the fact that many use rights are created by governmental administration, but that they seldom are saleable. For example, in the case of use of coastal areas, it is one thing to prevent private developments and another to trade part of the right to an unimpeded view of the beach for some improvements to make public access easier. The California Coastal Commissions are charged to grant permission to build in the coastal zone only if public use is not affected. A developer can not literally pay for any loss to the public uses. However, in practice the Commissions have obtained public use rights from developers in exchange for minor incursions on views, etc. [Healy 1977]. For example, a developer may agree to build an overlook for the public to view the beach or to build a walkway from the coastal road to the beach. In some cases, the developers actually pay a development fee which is accumulated to buy public parks, etc. In other words, the Commissions act as agent for the many public owners and trade some of the public's property for other things which it considers more valuable.

6. Transaction Costs-Information

Information is needed to make a good transaction. When the parties face different costs of acquiring information or different costs of being wrong, this is another source of interdependence which is controlled by institutional rules. Who has the cost of providing information on the effects of new resource uses—the developer or the persons impacted by the new use? The National Environmental Protection Act requires planners of certain developments to make available an environmental impact statement.

Higher units of government have been requiring lower units of government to plan and to hold public hearings on certain resource developments. Grants are made to hire professional staffs which can increase the availability of information. Thus, some of the costs of information are shifted to the developer and built into the cost of whatever product is created or shifted to government and financed by taxes.

One way to protect yourself against the specific occurance of unpredictable events is to buy insurance. A small certain annual payment is accepted to avoid an uncertain large loss. The ability of a person to have this opportunity depends on purchase by many others as well. In the case of flood insurance, private sellers have been unable to supply insurance because few buyers are interested. Part of this may be due to lack of information. Behavior might be different if home sellers had to make the past flood history of the area known or if past high water marks had to be painted on telephone poles. But, even when reasonably well-informed, people seem to discount heavily any large but improbable event. Insurance seems like a better investment for smaller and more frequent events [Kunreuther and Slovic 1978]. The freedom of some not to buy insurance means it is unavailable at reasonable cost to others. If flood insurance were made compulsory, this interdependence would be altered.

Asset mobility creates a special problem in the face of uncertainty. For example, when you make a large investment in capital equipment which is specialized as to use and has little salvage value, you would like to be sure that the resource being processed will be available over the lifetime of the equipment. This is a problem in water use under the reasonable use doctrine. A user is never sure of the available supply since it depends on the unpredictable and uncontrollable uses of others in the future.

Another example is provided by a number of states that have banned throw-away containers to reduce litter. All users bear a little extra cost in returning bottles, but investors and workers in glass bottle manufacture may face very high adjustment costs when the demand for their product drops. When the costs of change fall differentially on some groups, the potential losers often use their political capital to prevent the rule change. The prevailing ideology is that the costs of making mistakes is a useful incentive for prudent investment. Yet, was glass manufacturing investment imprudent? The point here is that the rules for the distribution of the losses to immobile assets can affect the realization of change. Note, for example, construction union opposition to ballot proposals banning nuclear power development.

Nuclear power development raises a host of uncertainties. Developers have been uncertain of the cost of possible future accidents and obtained legal limits on their liability [Price-Anderson Act]. This has shifted the cost of this uncertainty to those who might be harmed in the future. Federal courts have recently questioned this limit to liability [Lowenstein 1977].

Stock resources also present a special problem in the face of uncertainty. The supplies of oil, coal, wilderness and in certain arid regions, ground water are fixed. Many qualities of the ambient environment stock are also hard to reverse. Two uncertainties are a source of interdependence. The exact size of the stock is uncertain as is the future demand. it is therefore difficult for present prices to reflect future values. Ciriacy-Wantrup [1963] refers to the threshold beyond which reversability is technically or economically impossible as the "safe minimum standard." Kelso [1977] says the "ability to 'back up' and try something else in the succession of short runs is more important than is a constraining demand for optimizing..." (p. 820). One defense against uncertainty is to buy an option. This is a type of insurance policy where some present value is foregone to keep certain options open in the future to accomodate unforeseen demands. But, the organization of option demand via markets is difficult because of high transaction and exclusion costs.

The depletion of a stock resource creates great losses to immobile assets. Today's coal mining boom town may be tomorrow's ghost town. Some states such as Wyoming are collecting a tax on coal mined to accumulate money to make these future transitions. This is the essence of many people's fears of oil depletion. If we do not take steps now to alter our rates of use, exhaustion and rapidly increasing prices in the future may create huge transition costs. The economy may be able to adjust over time to different rates of use, but if it must do it quickly, the economy may collapse. But again, the present distribution of the costs of adjustment will affect whether the adjustments will be made or whether, for example, the unions will insist on maintaining current rates of use to protect current jobs. In the long run, less energy availability should mean more jobs as labor is substituted for energy, but in the short run, the holders of present jobs are not going to take unemployment lying down—as witness labor opposition to container recycling or nuclear power curtailment.

7. Surpluses

Different units of land have differential productivity. This is due both to inherent features such as fertility as well as locational features. This differential productivity means that as use is extended to the marginal unit, the intra-marginal units earn rents (returns above any cost of production). These rents, unlike profits, cannot be eliminated by enforcing competition since supply is fixed by nature and not by restraint of trade. Access to these surpluses or rents is an incompatible use good and factor ownership is controlling.

Land located near centers of population and economic activity appreciates in value without any effort on the part of its owners. Who owns these rents? If they are owned by the land owner, there is great incentive to obtain zoning allowing for maximum development even if the community would prefer open space at a particular site. Many local zoning efforts seem to cave in to the interests of developers. Some have suggested that adding state review would make the zoning more favorable to those who want controlled development. Adding new participants to zoning decisions is one way of creating new factor owners, but when the resource earns rent, we may have to change ownership of that feature since it interacts with the decision on allowable uses. If the appreciation goes to the landowners, they have great incentive to alter public land use plans regardless of the governmental decision level. A tax which would capture most of the appreciation gain would make zoning work better [Schmid 1968].

Land value appreciation is now shared by local government through property taxes. This often creates incentives for the local government to approve development to get the taxes. For example, a county may favor development in the coastal zone to get the taxes. But in Delaware, a county where a refinery was proposed did not oppose state control of the coastal area because under delaware tax law, the counties gain little tax revenue from such development [Healy 1976, p. 151].

Governmental action in zoning and in public investments such as road, navigation channels and reservoirs create rents for surrounding land [Harriss 1973]. Under prevailing current rights, this is captured by the land owner. At the same time other government action is causing losses to immobile assets [O'Hare and Sanderson 1977]. Don Hagman captures the essence in his words, "windfalls and wipeouts." It is hypothesized that a different performance would be obtained if the public were to capture some of the windfalls and use them to compensate some of the wipeouts [Hagman and Misczynski 1978].

The difference in average and marginal values also creates an interdependence in the context of preserving agricultural lands. The market places a value on the last parcel sold for nonfarm use substantially higher than the average value of land in the rural-urban fringe of cities. When property taxes are based on market values a farmer may face confiscatory taxation when sale for nonfarm use is not imminent. Those states with preferential agricultural land assessment remove this pressure for development. Still when the appreciation gets high enough, farmers will want to sell and the overall rate of conversion may be little effected by preferential assessment [Hansen and Schwartz 1974]. Thus, its primary justification depends on prevailing judgments on equity.

8. Inter-Generational Interdependence

The examples noted above primarily involve interdependence between living groups. The use of natural resources also raises problems between present and future generations. Perhaps this is a sub-class of incompatible use. Stock resources and flow resources used today beyond the threshold of irreversibility are denied to future people. What makes it a special case is that the future group can not speak for itself. If any options are exercised, it will be paid for and chosen by the now living.

Many current voices claim to speak for the unborn. Often it is merely a smokescreen for a current use which happens to be complementary with the asserted future interest. In any case, the assertions can't be tested. The current population chooses for the unborn, like it or not.

This is one of life's most basic moral issues. Primitive peoples had elaborate rituals which tied the living to the dead and the unborn in an unbroken chain of life. There is little of this left in our culture. Many find it quaint when an Indian tribe refuses to sell a burial ground or sacred lake. This is probably as much a birth right for those yet to come as a memorial for the dead.

The concept of "waste" can be found in the English common law, but is little discussed today [Harris 1974]. The concept refers to the idea that the current tenant is not free to exploit the resource if it means permanent damage to future interests. This was primarily applied to protect ultimate owners against the destructive acts of life tenants, but occasionally was applied directly against fee simple owners, such as limitations on tree cutting. The big problem is that the unborn owners are not around to sue.

There may be some stirrings of a new respect for the chain of life and the concept of stewardship in various counter-culture movements. This writer is no social historian and has no crystal ball to predict the future of these movements. From the perspective of institutional economics, we can ask what experiences contribute to learning of an identification with future peoples. The question will have to be answered by others. I would only add that the cost of keeping options open for the unborn may turn out to be lower than we think. It may well be that the "modest society" as opposed to the "great society" may be more humanely rewarding. Just as some have learned that driving 55 m.p.h. is safer and more relaxing, we may find that a society with less material throughput can be more fun—if we can learn to measure success in less material ways. I suspect this learning is made up of a lot of little things. It may be as subtle as giving high school letters for intellectual performance as well as athletics. Then again it may involve wholly new symbols and human relationships at a more tribal level. . . . But, can you imagine such things as part of the programs of the EPA or a state Department of Natural Resources?

Conclusions

It has been argued that most resources represent multiple sources of human interdependence. This has implications for policy design. When one institutional variable is changed, we hope for a changed performance. Often we are disappointed when no change occurs. This may occur because only one source of interdependence is altered, but total performance is overwhelmed by other opportunities of those favoring the status quo which remains unaffected. For example, we may change nominal factor ownership, but ignore exclusion cost, contractual and information costs and then be surprised that no change in performance occurs.

The ability to type sources of interdependence has implications also for learning from our experience with institutional experiments. I am troubled by our increasing specialization. I hear people say, I am interested in water policy, so I don't follow developments in land and energy. This is unfortunate for understanding probable effects of institutional change. There may be no chance to observe how a particular rule has behaved in water use since it has never been tried. But if we can find a resource that has similar sources of interdependence where the rule has been tried, we may be able to predict how it will function when applied in the case of water.

I believe that we can learn more than we have from recent institutional inovations. Yet, there are limits unless we develop a more deliberate policy of experimentation. Inter-state comparisons always raise threats to interpretation of causes because of noncontrolled variables. In some cases, the changed performance could be better attributed to specific institutional differences if part of a state could be subject to one set of rules and another part to another set. Is the public ready for this type of experimentation? They won't be if professionals and politicians can't admit that they don't have all the answers. Are we willing to say we don't know what rule changes will get a different performance, but we have some ideas and we would like to try them out on a limited scale and see what happens? Or, do we lack even the ideas in some cases?

Those analysts who are hard pressed by demands for authoritative analysis of institutional alternatives have found little help here. No typology of resource attributes has been developed which suggests that welfare is maximized when a certain attribute is matched to a certain policy. Rather it is suggested that in the face of conflicts growing out of human interdependence, the political process must choose whose interests count. Analysts can then use systematic observation organized by the theory outlined here to implement these value choices by linking sturcture to performance.

Note: Page 80, line 25, should read "common law changes slowly, . . ."

Bibliography

Bardach, Eugene et al. 1976. *The California Coastal Plan.* San Francisco: Institute for Contemporary Studies.

Bosselman, Fred and David Callies. 1972. *The Quiet Revoluation in Land Use Control.* Washington: G.P.O.

Ciriacy-Wantrup, S.V. 1963. *Resource Conservation.* Berkeley: University of California, Agricultural Experiment Station, Ch. 18.

Congressional Record. 1977. "Bidding Practices in National Forest Timber Sales." Sept. 14, p. S14825 ff.

Costonis, John J. 1974. *Space Adrift.* Urbana: University of Illinois Press.

Davis, Ray Jay. 1977a. "Legal Uncertainties of Weather Modification" in W.A. Thomas, ed. *Legal and Scientific Uncertainties of Weather Modification.* Durham: Duke University Press, pp. 32-64.

Davis, Ray Jay. 1977b. "The Law and Hail Suppression" in *Hail Suppression, Impacts and Issues.* Urbana: Illinois State Water Survey, pp. 138-1975.

DiMento, Joseph. 1977. "Citizen Environmental Litigation and the Administrative Process:

Empirical Findings, Remaining Issues and a Direction for Future Research," *Duke Law Journal*, No. 2, pp. 409-48.

Downing, Paul B., ed. 1977. *Local Service Pricing Policies and Their Effect on Urban Spatial Structure*. Vancouver: University of British Columbia Press.

Gaffney, Mason. 1977. "The Synergistic City: Its Potentials, Hindrances and Fulfillment." To be published in Judith deNeufville, ed. *Colloquium on Land Policy*, Cambridge, Mass: The Lincoln Institute.

Grote, Lenard. 1978. "Coastal Conservation and Development: Balancing Local and State-wide Interests," *Public Affairs Report*, Berkeley: University of California Institute of Governmental Studies, Vol. 19, No. 1, February.

Hagman, Donald G. and Dean J. Misczynski, eds. 1978. *Windfalls for Wipeouts: Land Value, Capture and Compensation*. Chicago: ASPO Press.

Hansen, David E. and S.J. Schwartz. 1975. "Landowner Behavior at the Rural-Urban Fringe in Response to Preferential Property Taxation." *Land Economics*, November, 341-54.

Harriss, C. Lowell, ed. 1973. *Government Spending and Land Values*. Madison: University of Wisconsin Press.

Harris, Marshall. 1974. *Legal-Economic Aspects of Waste Law*. Iowa City: Agricultural Law Center, University of Iowa, Monograph 13.

Healy, Robert G. 1976. *Land Use and the States*. Baltimore: Johns Hopkins University Press.

Healy, Robert G. 1977. *An Economic Interpretation of the California Coastal Commissions*. Washington: The Conservation Foundation.

Ingram, Helen. 1972. *The New England River Basins Commission—A Case Study*. Washington: National Water Commission (NTIS Accession No. PB 204 375).

Kelso, M.M. 1977. "Natural Resource Economics: The Upsetting Discipline." *American Journal of Agricultural Economics*. Vol. 59, No. 5 (December), pp. 814-23.

Kunreuther, Howard and Paul Slovic. 1978. "Economics, Psychology and Protective Behavior," *American Economic Review*, May.

Lowenstein, Robert. 1977. "The Price-Anderson Act: An Imaginative Approach to Public Liability Concerns," *The Forum*, (Section of Insurance, Negligence and Compensation Law, American Bar Association) Vol. XII, No. 2, Winter, pp. 594-628.

Mead, Walter J. 1966. *Competition and Oligopsony in the Douglas Fir Lumber Industry*. Berkeley: University of California Press.

_____ 1977. "Pricing Policy for Timber Products from Forest Lands: Resource Allocation and Income Distribution Effects" in Marion Clawson, ed. *Research in Forest Economics and Forest Policy*. Baltimore: John Hopkins University Press.

O'Hare, Michael and Debra Sanderson. 1977. "Not On My Block You Don't—Facilities Siting and the Strategic Importance of Compensation," *Public Policy*, Vol. 24, No. 4.

Rodefeld, Richard D., et al., eds. 1978. *Change in Rural America: Causes, Consequences and Alternatives*. St. Louis: C.V. Mosby Co.

Sax, Joseph and Joseph DiMento. 1974. "Environmental Citizen Suits: Three Years Experience Under the Michigan Environmental Protection Act," *Ecology Law Quarterly*, Vol. 4, No. 1.

Schmid A. Allan. 1968. *Converting Land From Rural to Urban Use*. Baltimore: Johns Hopkins Press.

_____ 1978. *Property, Power and Public Choice*. New York: Praeger.

INTERRELATIONS BETWEEN LEGAL AND
ECONOMIC PROCESSES
Warren J. Samuels

T HE purpose of this paper is to extend the analysis of the interrelations between legal and economic processes through an identification of certain basic legal-economic interrelationships hitherto given inadequate expression and attention. Such an identification should correct or preclude the attachment of simplistic nuances to the analysis of legal-economic processes, in part by establishing the greater complexity and intricacy of both the policies and policy-making processes involved.

It should be made clear that the thrust of the paper does not depend on a broad definition of either the scope of economics or of welfare economics, however appropriate or inappropriate such a broader-than-conventional definition may be. Given the primacy of relevance of voluntary market exchange as the focal point of analysis (that is, methodological individualism), it nevertheless remains necessary, it is suggested, to examine certain legal-economic processes with respect to which it is true both (a) that voluntary market exchange is a partial emanation or dependent variable and (b) that voluntary market exchange is an independent and determining or conditioning variable.[1]

The vehicle for this attempt will be a 40-year-old court case which (a) is possessed of the constituent elements of most if not all legal-economic problems, cases, or situations; (b) is beautifully illustrative of the interrelations of legal and economic processes, and, what is more, of the basic social forces and patterns in terms of which legal and economic processes and their interrelations ultimately have meaning and may be interpreted; and (c) is not a

The analysis in this paper relies heavily on the writings of John R. Commons, Robert L. Hale, Frank H. Knight, and Edwin E. Witte, as well as the recent discussions of externalities and public goods by such writers as James M. Buchanan and R.H. Coase. I wish to thank Walter Adams, Milton Z. Kafoglis, and Henry M. Oliver for their advice and insight in reacting to an earlier draft.

[1] For references and related discussion, see Warren J. Samuels, Legal-Economic Policy: A Bibliographical Survey, 58 L. Library J. 230 (1965).

case with which one can get readily emotionally or ideologically involved, thereby adversely affecting one's powers of perception and analysis; in short, a case which accords deep and positivist insight into the difficult subject in question.

II

Miller et al. v. Schoene[2] is a case which involves red cedar and apple trees and their respective owners; and cedar rust, a plant disease whose first phase is spent while the fungus resides upon its host, the chiefly ornamental red cedar tree, which is not harmed by the cedar rust. The fungus does have a severely adverse effect upon the apple tree during a second phase, attacking its leaves and fruit. The legislature of the state of Virginia in 1914 passed a statute which empowered the state entomologist to investigate and, if necessary, condemn and destroy without compensation certain red cedar trees within a two-mile radius of an apple orchard.

More specifically, the statute provided that "upon the request in writing of ten or more reputable free-holders of any county or magisterial district,"[3] the state entomologist was to investigate "to ascertain if any cedar tree or trees . . . are the source of, harbor or constitute the host plant for the said disease . . . and constitute a menace to the health of any apple orchard in said locality . . . within a radius of two miles. . . ."[4] In the event of an affirmative finding, such tree or trees were declared by the statute to be a public nuisance, subject to destruction. Accordingly, the state entomologist was to communicate to the owner or owners of such trees the nature of his findings and to instruct them to destroy said trees. If the owner, upon notification, failed to destroy the trees, the statute empowered the state entomologist to destroy them. No compensation would be given the owners although they could retain possession and make use of the cut trees.[5] The statute also provided for a prior appeal procedure to the county circuit court which was authorized to "hear the objections" and "pass upon all questions involved."[6]

Miller et al., plaintiffs in error in the instant case, unsuccessfully brought suit in state courts, and sued to reverse the decision of the Supreme Court of Appeals in Virginia. The arguments for the plaintiffs in error were basically simple and direct, as well as of profound heuristic value. Their main contention was that the legislature was, unconstitutionally in their view, attempt-

[2] Miller et al. v. Schoene, 276 U.S. 272 (1928).
[3] *Id.* at 277-78.
[4] *Id.* at 278.
[5] *Id.* at 277.
[6] *Id.* at 278.

ing to take or destroy their property to the advantage of the apple orchard owners. Their pleadings, summarized for the decision, amplified that theme:

The statute is invalid in that it provides for the taking of private property, not for public use, but for the benefit of other private persons.

It seems a wholly untenable view that of two species of valuable property, one may be selected for destruction for the protection of the other from the effects of a disease for whose existence and continuance they are interchangeably responsible.

In no case can property be taken for private use; and the taking of private property for *public* use without due process of law and proper compensation cannot be justified under the guise of the exercise of the police power.

. . . The alleged injury to the apple orchardist "will not justify his shifting the damage to his neighbor's shoulders."

We submit that there is not, in the American theory of government, any room for the view that one man's property may be taken or destroyed, either directly by eminent domain or indirectly, under the guise of taxation, or of the police power, in order to enhance the property values or the financial prosperity of another.[7]

The plaintiffs further argued that the statute placed control over their property in the hands of "other owners of property,"[8] *viz.*, the initial petitioning freeholders; that "the red cedar trees denounced by the Cedar Rust statute are not nuisances at common law"; and that the "statute is void for vagueness and uncertainty," specifying the absence of (a) any criterion of eligible freeholders, (b) a technical meaning to "locality"; and (c) a definition of "orchard." The thrust of their argument as a whole was that the statute was an unconstitutional exercise of the state police power by virtue of its violation of the due process clause of the Fourteenth Amendment.

The Supreme Court affirmed the judgment of the lower state courts, denying the challenge to the statute on the grounds of unconstitutionality under the due process clause of the Fourteenth Amendment. In an opinion delivered by Mr. Justic Stone, the Court held that:

On the evidence we may accept the conclusion of the Supreme Court of Appeals that the state was under the necessity of making a choice between the preservation of one class of property and that of the other wherever both existed in dangerous proximity. It would have been none the less a choice if, instead of enacting the present statute, the state, by doing nothing, had permitted serious injury to the apple orchards within its borders to go on unchecked. When forced to such a choice

[7] *Id.* at 273-75.
[8] *Id.* at 276.

the state does not exceed its constitutional powers by deciding upon the destruction of one class of property in order to save another which, in the judgment of the legislature, is of greater value to the public. It will not do to say that the case is merely one of a conflict of two private interests and that the misfortune of apple growers may not be shifted to cedar owners by ordering the destruction of their property; for it is obvious that there may be, and that here there is, a preponderant public concern in the preservation of the one interest over the other. And where the public interest is involved preferment of that interest over the property interest of the individual, to the extent even of its destruction, is one of the distinguishing characteristics of every exercise of the police power which affects property."[9]

With respect to the additional arguments by plaintiffs, the Court held that:

We need not weigh with nicety the question whether the infected cedars constitute a nuisance according to the common law; or whether they may be so declared by statute. For where, as here, the choice is unavoidable, we cannot say that its exercise, controlled by considerations of social policy which are not unreasonable, involves any denial of due process.[10]

that the freeholders bringing the petition

. . . do not determine the action of the state entomologist. They merely request him to conduct an investigation. In him is vested the discretion to decide, after investigation whether or not conditions are such that the other provisions of the statute shall be brought into action; and his determination is subjected to judicial review. The property of plaintiffs is not subjected to the possibly arbitrary and irresponsible action of a group of private citizens.[11]

and that,

The objection of plaintiffs in error to the vagueness of the statute is without weight. The state court has held it to be applicable, and that is enough when, by the statute, no penalty can be incurred or disadvantage suffered in advance of the judicial ascertainment of its applicability.[12]

III

What *Miller et al. v. Schoene* illustrates first of all, indeed what the Court so clearly perceived, is the ineluctable necessity of choice on the part of government. The state had to make a choice as to which property owner was to be made not only formally secure but practically viable in his legal rights. The Court, as part of the state, had to make a judgment as to which owner

---

[9] *Id.* at 279-80 (citations deleted).
[10] *Id.* at 280 (citations deleted).
[11] *Id.* at 281.
[12] *Id.* at 281.

would be visited with injury and which protected. The state, ultimately the Court, had to decide which party would have what capacity to coerce the other, meaning by coercion the impact upon one party of the actions of the other. There was a direct conflict between two private interests (between two private rights' claimants) which required choice, and choice on the basis of some (rational) criterion, in the instant case involving the criterion(ia) which the legislature and the courts embodied or read into the concept of the public interest, public value, or the public welfare, ultimately through the vehicle of the police power.

In the absence of the statute in question (the *Cedar Rust* statute), that is to say, under the pre-existing state law of property (which the statute in question would have, in effect, altered or amended), the supposedly equal rights position of the red cedar owners and apple orchard owners would have, under the circumstances, operated to place the apple orchard owner at a disadvantage: his rights, his security, his protection, presumably of equal standing with those of the red cedar owner, in fact would have been prejudiced and for practical purposes weakened if not destroyed as the working of the law of property—to repeat, under the circumstances—effectively favored the red cedar owners. Albeit at random, so far as any original legislative design or intent may be presumed, the working of the existing law of property would have allowed the visitation of injury upon the apple orchard owner. Moreover, it would have put the red cedar owner in a coercively advantageous position so far as the market value of his rights were concerned. Under the pre-existing law, the burden of reaching an optimal arrangement[13] was put on the apple orchard owner, for the apple orchard owner would have had to bargain with the red cedar owner, to overcome the latter's capacity to withhold or exercise his reservation demand. The existing law, in other words, put the coercive advantage in the hands of the red cedar owner, which meant that the flow of payment to withhold injury ran from the apple orchard owner to the red cedar owner.

Under the *Cedar Rust* statute, however, it is the rights of the apple orchard owner which are given effective legal protection and economic viability; it is the red cedar owner upon whom the injury is visited; and it is the apple orchard owner who is given coercive advantage. Under the effective new law of property, the burden would be upon the red cedar owner to attempt to buy off the apple orchard owner in the face of the destruction of his red cedar trees. In other words, the new law put the coercive advantage in the hands of the apple orchard owner, which meant that the flow of payment to withhold injury now ran from the red cedar owner to the apple orchard owner.

[13] E.J. Mishan, Pareto Optimality and the Law, 19 Oxford Econ. Papers 255 (n.s., 1967).

Miller et al. v. Schoene therefore suggests that there is an ineluctable set of choices with which government—the state, law, the legal process—is inextricably bound up: choices as to relative rights (whose rights are to be effectively paramount to whose?), choices as the visitation of injury (who will be allowed to injure whom, or who will be sacrificed to whom; and when is an injury, that is, to be recognized as such in law), and choices as to who will be exposed to whose coercive power. In all these matters the state must and does choose: there exists scarcity in the sense that conflicting interests and claims cannot each be secured at the same time (under existing technology), giving rise to conflict (for example, court litigation or legislative enactment of a change) and the necessity of choice.

What the immediate foregoing suggests, moreover, is that the fundamental processes involved—in which nominally economic and legal processes participate as interacting subsystems or subprocesses—center on an ubiquitous economic decision-making process, specifically a system or structure of power or of participation which is at the same time a pattern of freedom and of exposure to the freedom of others and therefore a pattern of mutual coercion. Market forces emerge and take on shape and slope only within the pattern of, *inter alia*, legal choices as to relative rights, relative exposure to injury, and relative coercive advantage or disadvantage. Private rights, for example, property rights, are in effect capacities to participate in the economic decision-making process as a coercive force; they define and delineate loci and conditions of power, or participation. That means, then, that since relative effective rights are a partial function of law, the pattern of mutual coercion (relative withholding power) is a partial function of law, and, moreover, that the distribution of relative risk, business costs, and resource allocation, income distribution and general level of income are a partial function of law. In the case of apple orchard and red cedar owners, these inferences are obvious. They apply also, *mutatis mutandis*, to the decision-making process of the economy as a whole. The economy is a system of power, of mutual coercion, of reciprocal capacity to receive income and/or to shift injury—whose pattern or structure and consequences are at least partially a function of law.

This may be articulated in terms of the light which *Miller et al. v. Schoene* throws on the meaning of freedom in a situation of general interdependence. If we define as *volitional freedom* the opportunity or capacity to choose between alternatives, and if we define as *voluntary freedom* the opportunity or capacity to determine the alternatives themselves between which one may choose, then it appears that the difference between voluntary and volitional freedom is very largely for present purposes the impact of the operation of choice by others, as manifest and embodied in, for example, particular legal arrangements, which is simply another way of saying that one economic actor is limited or constrained to bear the costs in various forms imposed by other economic actors jointly and severally either through market forces or the legal process. The impact of others' decisions and choices is transmitted to the one actor whose range of alternatives is thus circumscribed so that his freedom is volitional and not voluntary. As Bentham argued, every law both increases and decreases freedom, though typically for different people; consequently, it is a matter of whose volitional freedom will be reduced from voluntary freedom and in what particulars by the granting of volitional freedom to others. The statute in question in *Miller et al. v. Schoene* altered the respective pattern of volitional and voluntary freedom for both red cedar and apple orchard owners.

It will be noticed, furthermore, that *Miller et al. v. Schoene* is *not* a case in which the issue is government or no government, or of laissez-faire or intervention. Government is present in either case: it is present with respect to the already existing law of property working as it turned out to the advantage of the red cedar tree owner, and it is present under the new, altered law of property working by legislative intent (and court acquiescence) to the advantage of the apple orchard owner. Damned if it did and damned if it didn't, government had to choose between the effective promotion of one group or the other: government is in both cases a participant in the economic decision making process. In neither case can one be simply "against" government. The issue is not government or no government but, rather, the old law or the new law, or, to say the same thing in different words, the one interest or the other. Both laws are a function of the state, so the issue is one of which law, ergo of continuity versus change; which is to say, an issue of which interests, or whose interest is law to protect and give effective substance. Law will protect, under the circumstances, one vis-a-vis the other; the issue is which one: the one substantially protected by the pre-existing law of property or the other one. What the enactment of the statute in question accomplished was not the intrusion of government into a situation in which it had hitherto been absent, but rather a change of the interests to which effective legal support would be given. (The situation would be reversed but not analytically different if the fungus had spent its first phase on the host apple tree and wreaked its damage later on the red cedar: the legislature would have to choose which interest to support, the apple (by leaving the law unchanged) or the red cedar (by changing the law).) It is a matter neither of intervention into a new situation nor of "socialism"; it is a matter of which interest government will be used to support, ergo a matter of continuity versus change with respect to the pattern of freedom and exposure to freedom or distribution of power or structure of mutual coercion. Should the effect of the fungus have been the reverse (as examined parenthetically earlier in this paragraph), the necessary choice there too would have been neither intervention nor socialism: as between the two cases, the one which did exist and the hypothetical reverse case, it was a pure random situation that the fungus was in fact a menace to the apple orchards. What is involved in either case is the role of the state as an instrument of change, altering the effective substance of rights which the law will enforce.

Looking back, the analysis thus far has revealed some very important facets of the interrelations between legal and economic processes and the basic social forces and problems in terms of which they have meaning. There is, first of all, an existential necessity of choice over relative rights, relative capacity to visit injury or costs, and mutual coercive power (or claims to income). The economy, in which the legal process is so obviously involved, is a system of relative rights, of exposure to costs shifted by others, and of coercive impact of others. In choosing between conflicting rights' claimants, furthermore, the choice is between one interest or another. The choice is over capacities to participate in the economic decision-making process—over seats at Spencer's banquet table. These choices are a function of rights which are a function of law; so that, *inter alia*, income distribution—through relative claims to income—is a partial function of law. It is ineluctable, then, that government is involved in the fundamental character, structure, and results of the private sector. Policy issues thus become which or whose rights will government operate to effectively secure, which rights will government no longer operate to effectively secure and which new rights, that is, the use of government to change the effective pattern of rights or realization of interests.

So interpreted, *Miller et al. v. Schoene* elicits still further insights. If the issue is one as to which interest government will be used to support, part of the character of the legal process is clarified. The legal system (government, law) is not something given and external to the economic decision-making process. Rather, since government is a mode through which relative rights and therefore relative market (income securing) status is given effect, the critical question is *who* uses government for *what* ends.

This may be approached from the perspective of the question, who decides? First, with respect to who within government decides, in *Miller et al. v. Schoene* the decision making structure is a complex one. With respect to the condemnation of red cedar trees, the freeholders have an initiating but not conclusive role. The state entomologist is himself checked by the possibility, indeed the reality, of judicial review. In a word, who decides depends on the permissiveness with which the entomologist is treated by the courts, given the propensity of red cedar tree owners to petition; or, the literalness with which the statute is interpreted. With respect to the determination of whether there will even be such a condemnation process altering the pre-existing law of property and the coercive pattern established in effect thereunder between apple orchard and red cedar owners, this is a matter for the legislature and the courts, in sum, government, presumably operating in the public interest or for the net welfare of the public. Both decide one way or the other, upon a pattern of reasons; the court may substitute its constitutional judgment for legislative wisdom. As it turned out, the courts recognized the ineluctable choice of determining the marginal public welfare. To repeat,

. . . It would have been none the less a choice if, instead of enacting the present statute, the state, by doing nothing, had permitted serious injury to the apple orchards within its borders to go on unchecked. When forced to such a choice the state does not exceed its constitutional powers by deciding upon the destruction of one class of property in order to save another which, in the judgment of the legislature, is of greater value to the public.[14]

In any case, the question is, who decides: legislature or judiciary, and in the American system, state legislature and/or state judiciary or federal judiciary. The holding in *Miller et al. v. Schoene* could have been the opposite—including in the legislature, in which case the litigation may never have materialized.

But the question of who decides goes deeper. The question also takes the form of who will influence government, that is, the legislature which enacted the statute. Apple orchards, as both the plaintiffs in error and the court recognized, are a major industry in Virginia. Red cedar trees are of primarily ornamental use, with some use and value as lumber. The apple growers were organized and influential and the red cedar owners were not; the prestige and influence and possibly the membership of apple orchard owners in the legislature in an apple growing state was of great significance. But transcending these considerations, yet running through them too, is the question, who will use government? The Virginia legislature was not insensitive—nor should it have been—to the pattern of interests and pressures at stake. Apple interests were able to use government—in a non-pejorative sense—in support of their interests. Government, in supporting the one against the other, was the instrument or vehicle for the realization of the interests of the one against the other. Government as a government responsive to the people—a government, that is, of, by and for the people—must in such cases as *Miller et al. v. Schoene* be more responsive to one party than the other. Max Weber argued that "political capitalism" was a system or situation in which profit opportunities accrue to those with political prerogative.[15] This can be generalized: with government as an instrument or vehicle available to whomever can con-

---

[14] Miller et al. v. Schoene, 276 U.S. 272, 279 (1928).

[15] H.H. Gerth & C. Wright Mills, (eds.), From Max Weber: Essays in Sociology 66 (1946).

trol or use it, opportunities for gain, whether pecuniary profit or political or other advantage, accrue to those who can use government. This proposition makes of government an object both to and with which economic activity can be directed one way or another. If income distribution and risk allocation is a partial function of law, then the law is an object of control for economic or other gain, an instrument for economic objectives by both those outside and those inside official government positions. This is neither sordid nor the exception; rather it is part of how government operates and for what it is used: that is the way the legal-economic world is, whether the instance be tariff protection, oil subsidies, real estate agents' attempts to ban "for sale" signs on private homes, or protection to red cedar or apple orchard owners (as the effect of the fungus *vis-a-vis* the existing law tends to evoke). Adam Smith wrote in the *Moral Sentiments*, "The great secret of education is to direct vanity to proper objects."[16] He would also have agreed, I think, that legislative activity is directed to provide legal support to proper objects, and that in both cases it is not a matter of whether or not but rather *which* objects are proper and government becomes an instrument for the realization of such objects as deemed proper by those in control of or with influence in government. *Miller et al. v. Schoene* suggests that given the legal participation in the economic decision making process established above, it can be no other way. It may be added that this conclusion holds for Republican and Democratic administrations, and for market and non-market (for example, socialist or planned or command) economies: the issue is not government or no government but which interests, that is, whose interests the state is used to effectuate.

This raises still another matter involved in the interrelation of legal and economic processes, the issue of temporal priority, that is, of specificity and sequence. Specifically, *Miller et al. v. Schoene* may be interpreted to have in effect opted for pecuniary (or economic) over aesthetic values, interests or considerations. This is a matter of choice, of necessary choice as the court comprehended. The court had to come up with a specific solution as did the legislature by action or inaction, to wit: allowing the pre-existing law of property and its consequences to remain in force, or not. In effect, the combination of legislature *cum* court did choose the economic over the aesthetic interest. The ultimate quality of choice is the determination of *when* competing general rules or, as in this case, competing general values (positive goods) are to be given specific application or allowed specific fruition. It is not enough to talk of general laws or general rules; the nub of each policy situation (policy choice, court case) is the necessity for specific content, for a specific application of conflicting interests or general rules to a particular

---

[16] Quoted in W.J. Samuels, The Classical Theory of Economic Policy 67 (1966).

instance. The specificity will devolve to one power player or another, however ignored or nondeliberately it is legislatively treated. Specific content must be given in response to the question, given competing affirmative values, what (temporary) marginal priority is to be given which one in each instance. And, what is more, assuming for purposes of argument that there is encountered either diminishing returns or diminishing marginal rate of substitution as one value is continually sacrificed to the other, when does the temporal marginal priority get reversed? Consider a production possibility curve with respect to the realization of two values. Society, *viz.*, those whose values are given weight therein, for example, in the legal process—or, simply, those who control government—must and will determine the proportions of realization of the respective values and the specificity of their realization in particular cases or situations. It is their preference function which will have to be made tangent to the production possibility curve for them to determine the aggregate relative realization of the two values and, in each particular situation, their respective application.

Simply put, the question of whose interests the state will be used to effectuate reduces in part to the question of which specific interests or values will dominate in a particular case. This ultimate specificity of choice is the existential burden of man, which no reference to general or neutral principles or choices will avoid. The choices have their specificity coefficients whether intended or realized or not. The same point applies to the adoption of constitutional rules, however ambiguous.

But the foregoing, regardless of how corrupt and sordid interest seeking may get, really is part of another still larger process of which both economic and legal processes are subprocesses or subsystems. What I have in mind is that society is not only a pattern of rights and a structure of power, a system of mutual coercion, but that society is also, and no less analytically importantly, a process of the identification, classification, juxtaposition, confrontation, and selection of values in all aspects of living, individual and collective. What the economy produces is not only goods but men, and in producing men it produces values and interests also. The critical values, in the context of this paper, are those embodied in the intermediate working rules through which conflicts and choices such as existed in *Miller et al. v. Schoene* became resolved. The operation and interrelation of legal and economic processes must also be comprehended in this respect as well as in the others noted.

One further matter that must be discussed, even summarily, is the question of compensation. In *Miller et al. v. Schoene*, the Virginia Statute did provide for retention of the cut red cedar trees by their owners. It did not provide for "compensation for the value of the standing cedars or the decrease in the market value of the realty caused by their destruction whether considered as ornamental trees or otherwise."[17] The circuit court did allow to *Miller et al.* "$100 to cover the expense of removal of the cedars."[18] The obvious question is: compensation or no compensation? But is it really the central question? Looked at directly, the answer (to compensation or no compensation) turns in part on whether taxpayers generally should socialize the risk of loss in (a) situations where the operation of the law of property visits injury and/or (b) situations where the change of the interest to which the law gives effect visits injury. In the case of (a), the bill would be huge; in the case of (b), rather large also, unless no change in the law of property could ever be allowed. Or, perhaps more realistically, the question is, *when* should compensation be paid? One is reminded of the thrust of the compensation analogy from eminent domain which some in the 1890's tried to bring to bear on public utility regulation: regulate the utility to eliminate the monopoly profits but pay compensation equivalent to the loss sustained, in effect guaranteeing such profits. (Some, of course, believe that that is precisely what public utility regulation has in effect if not intent actually accomplished, *vis-a-vis* promoting the advantages of a competitive market.) One is reminded also of the semantic device of denying the earlier (and potentially compensable) right ever existed. In *United States v. Causby*, the Court acknowledged that,

It is ancient doctrine that a common-law ownership of the land extended to the periphery of the universe—*Cujus est solum ejus est usque ad coelum.*

"But," the Court immediately went on to say,

. . . that doctrine has no place in the modern world. The air is a public highway, as Congress has declared. Were that not true, every transcontinental flight would subject the operator to countless trespass suits. Common sense revolts at the idea. To recognize such private claims to the airspace would clog these highways, seriously interfere with their control and development in the public interest, and transfer into private ownership that to which only the public has a just claim.[19]

It "is" ancient doctrine that the rights of property to land included domain over the airspace to the periphery of the universe; but "To recognize such private claims to the airspace" would "transfer into private ownership that to which only the public has a just claim." "Transfer into private ownership"? "Transfer into private ownership" what is *already in* private ownership, according to "ancient doctrine"? Treat as "claims" what had been established rights? Such is the semantics of private property and policy generally. What

---

[17] Miller et al. v. Schoene, 276 U.S. 272, 277 (1928).

[18] *Id.*

[19] Nevertheless the Court held that "that general principle does not control the present case." United States v. Causby, 328 U.S. 256, 261 (1946).

the compensation issue touched upon (really incidentally) in *Miller et al. v. Schoene* really involves is this: who visits injury on whom. To argue in favor of compensation *or* to argue against compensation, is to argue for one pattern of injury and/or one pattern of cost distribution as opposed to another (whether the fungus attacks the apple tree or the red cedar tree, to again refer to the hypothetical alternative example posed earlier). The question of compensation always arises in terms of the actual pre-existing law *vis-a-vis* the new one (which could be reversed in chronological sequence) and is thus only part of the larger issue of the distribution of gain and injury in which the legal process is an important variable.

Some of the latter is underscored by reference to two possible working definitions of the police power: (a) the power to regulate in the interest of public health, welfare, safety, and morals, and (b) the power to modify rights of property and contract through due process of law for a public purpose but without compensation. The law does not deal with minutiae, but what is minutiae to one person is major or crucial to another: does the legislature compensate for the loss of possible (and perhaps actually antecedent but now destroyed) rights in cases of stop signs, devaluations, health codes, building codes, tariffs, tariff changes, and so on? Compensation is part of a larger problem. The matter, complicated enough, is made further complex when the following is considered. The law of property in Virginia and elsewhere protects an individual's property against theft. But when is a theft a theft, and when is it competition? The hold-up man may be prosecuted and convicted but if one firm enters and competes away the customers of another, pre-existing firm, the former may destroy the value of the latter's business as surely as if it had been destroyed physically and possibly even more irretrievably. Here again compensation is part of a larger problem. One of the subjects with respect to which, then, the interrelations of legal and economic processes relates is the question when is a taking competition and when is it theft. But this too is a problem of legal determination of the distribution of cost and injury in a system of "creative destruction."

The point is, of course, this: the necessity for specific answers to specific cases is part of the social valuation and interest-realization process. But part of the picture is also the ineluctable necessity of legal choice: of the structure and restructuring of patterns of rights, injury visitation, and mutual coercion; of the impact of legal resolutions of the foregoing upon the basic economic problems; and, *inter alia*, the jockeying for position to use government.

Finally, the picture is increased exponentially when it is recognized that private property the contract rights are but one way in which decision-making participation and interests are secured in a market economy. There are private property equivalents which accomplish the same function: tenure, corporation law, unfair labor practice provisions, moral rules, interests protected by statute under the police and commerce powers and by constitutional provision, managerial-position rules (rights of office), seniority provisions, and so on. Most of the controversial cases in constitutional history of an economic character involved conflicts and necessity of choice between property and/or contract rights on the one hand and non-property-contract rights on the other, for example, child labor, often taking the emotional form of property versus human rights. But the underlying issues, basic social processes, and interrelations of legal and economic processes in those cases are essentially if not precisely the same as in *Miller et al. v. Schoene*. To argue for the passage of a statute altering a property right *vis-a-vis* some non-property right is to argue for a change in the interests to which legal support is to be given, just as in *Miller et al. v. Schoene* it was a question of which property-right interest would be given legal support. In every case the logical and substantive nexus of the matter is the role of law in the restructuring of private power, which is to say, the response by or use of government to and by those who would use government to restructure the distribution of private power, or use government for some other purpose.

IV

The interrelations between legal and economic revealed in *Miller et al. v. Schoene* are not exceptional phenomena. Rather, they reflect to correspond to fundamental social processes and problems. These may be approached and examined under the heading of "theory of economic policy," or, as I have relied upon in several other writings, Joseph Spengler's identification of what he has called the *problem of order*. As Spengler defines the problem of order, it is that posed by the need to reconcile "three somewhat incompatible conditions," namely, autonomy, coordination, and continuity.[20]

In general, it may be said that the problem of economic order is solved in proportion as the three objectives, autonomy, cooperation, and continuity, are achieved and reconciled both with one another and with the force of secular and random change.[21]

As an alternative formulation I have specified the problem of order in terms of the necessity to continually resolve the dual basic social problems of freedom and control, and continuity and change, particularly with respect to the structure of power or decision-making. Spengler has given a further con-

[20] Joseph J. Spengler, The Problem of Order in Economic Affairs, 15 So. Econ. J. 1 (1949), reprinted in Joseph J. Spengler & William R. Allen (eds.), Essays in Economic Thought 9 (1960).

[21] Joseph J. Spengler & William R. Allen, *supra* note 20, at 10.

struction to one dimension of the problem of order, penetrating both freedom and control, and continuity and change, namely, the problem of hierarchy versus equality.[22] It is the contention here that the ultimate meaning of the legal and economic processes and of their interrelation is in terms of their functioning toward the resolution of the problem(s) of order.

Indeed, the genesis and history of the modern state and modern economy over the last two to four centuries are aptly characterized by reference to the continuing conflict over whether control over the state and control over the economy—participation in state and participation in economy—would be narrowly or widely diffused, that is, hierarchy versus equality (not necessarily strict equality: wide, or wider, participation), including competition between elites. Most of the great episodes of political and economic-policy history (not entirely excluding international wars both great and small) are constructed of the power plays with and through which various groups attempted to gain or repel entree or domination in either or both of the two systems. The key questions always were: whose state (for example, whose democracy) and whose economy (for example, whose capitalism)? There has always been the "question *which* is really to be maximized, the number or percentage of (more or less) happy people, or the intensity of the happiness of those most largely benefited."[23] Jeremy Bentham was thus both the father of English individualism: he sanctioned the greater responsiveness of the state to the masses, insisting upon their participation in the franchise and thereby in government affairs, that is, the important matter is the individual, meaning all individuals; and the father also of the English collectivism: once the masses received the franchise and government (read: politicians) became responsive to their interests and votes, the interests which government was to be used to support became more extensive, socialized some would say—with respect to which most modern conflict over the role of government has developed.

In the context of the problem of order, the aforementioned may be interpreted in terms of the pattern of freedom and of exposure to the freedom of others (not freedom *per se*, except on the ideological and emotional level, but the structure of freedom); the forces of social control in the form of either power players and their interactions[24] or regulatory systems and their interactions[25] as well as overall interaction and interpretation; and the forces (partially encompassed in the foregoing) making for selective and random

---

[22] Joseph J. Spengler, Hierarchy vs. Equality: Persisting Conflict, 21 Kyklos 217 (1968).

[23] Overton H. Taylor, A History of Economic Thought: Social Ideals and Economic Theories from Quesnay to Keynes 134 (1960).

[24] Businessmen, labor leaders, *rentier*, church, government officials, *et al.*

[25] For example, such institutions as market, plan, money, religion, private property, law of business organization, law of contract, and so on.

continuity and selective and random change in society, in the foregoing and in the resolution of the basic economic problems.

What is true on the level of general history is also true on the level of particular cases. Thus the concepts and categories developed in the preceding paragraphs with respect to order in general may also be used in analyzing *Miller et al. v. Schoene*. As indicated in section III, the issues in *Miller et al. v. Schoene*, from the necessity of choice to the question of who decides (that is, who uses government), are precisely the issues encompassed in the problem of order generally considered. What was examined in section III, in terms of the structure of power, the capacity to visit injury, and the system of mutual coercion, are merely alternative ways of formulating the concepts and incidence of freedom and control, and continuity and change. The interrelation of legal and economic processes on the level of *Miller et al. v. Schoene* is a microcosm of the larger level on which these same processes also interact and interpenetrate.

V

In the foregoing pages I have endeavored to identify some of the major forces, concepts, and categories involved in understanding the enormously complex yet important subject of the economic role of the state, trying particularly to establish the respects in which fundamental-level interaction, interpenetration, and interdependence exists between them, bearing on otherwise voluntary exchange activity. Analysis of the interrelations between legal and economic processes must be grounded in recognition and analysis of (1) the system of mutual coercion or system of power; (2) the impact of private interests on state action; (3) the broader range of forces (including changes in income distribution) affecting the allocation of resources; (4) the problem of order; and, *inter alia*, (5) the problem of choice with respect to the structure of power or decision-making. The economy must be seen as an object of legal control and the law as a means of seeking private economic gain or advantage. Legal impact upon the private economic sphere and the economic use of government have not been the exception; rather, they have been the fundamental and the regular, perhaps daily, pattern. Both the market mechanism and the legal system, as well as the system of moral rules, are modes of social control and social change. The economic character of the politico-legal process must be conjoined with the political character of the economic process.

4
ECOSYSTEM POLICY AND THE PROBLEM OF POWER

Warren J. Samuels*

The purpose of ecological policy is to introduce environmental considerations into human decision making so as to protect the environment, which is really to say, so as to protect mankind against environmental disasters and to enable man to live in a comfortable symbiotic relation with his metabolic and physical environment. The thrust of ecological concern is that man has abused and damaged his environment in ways and to an extent that can only further redound to damage man's own well-being. Man should instead think out the ecological implications of his behavior and adjust his activities so as to reflect environmental considerations and to inflict the minimum damage, especially the minimum irreversible damage, on his environment. The result of this current position has been a widespread call for the design and management of environmental protection systems. Such suggested solutions have varied extensively, and include the mandatory imposition of waste disposal, the creation of pollution rights as a new subset of property rights, the creation of new organizations and institutions, citizen education, and so on.

The purpose of this article is to suggest that there are certain analytical problems involved in the coupling or integration of ecological and social factors and therefore in the design and management of environmental or ecological systems. These are problems which have beset the social sciences *qua* sciences and the application of social science to questions of social policy (whether or not ecological problems were considered, and whether or not the social scientist was aware of them), and which severely constrain the ecologist both in his analysis and in his policy recommendations. These are problems consequent to the ultimate *choice* character of social and ecological life.

I. Preliminary Considerations

1. The making of social policy and the solution of social, and now ecological, problems involves the process of making choices from a smaller or larger set of alternatives. In this decision making process there is a quest for definitive and authoritative answers and solutions. But these answers and solutions, whatever else one can say about them, are adopted primarily because they are acceptable to whomever is in a decision making position. Absolute and conclusive answers and solutions are hard to come by, although we may try to convince ourselves differently. Actually there exists a process of value articulation, juxtaposition, confrontation, and selection on an on-going basis with each participant in the decision making process looking at his own thoughts and feelings and at the findings of others. Thus, for example, private labor and commercial arbitrators—and ombudsmen of all kinds—look to the courts for precedents, rules of procedure, formulas for composing conflicts, and leads in the substantive balancing or relative equities and hardships; and the courts similarly look to commercial and labor arbitrators for similar insight into conflict resolution. Both groups are chasing their own tails, so to speak, in the process of hammering out the working rules and choices by which we live. The quest for definitive and authoritative answers and solutions, important from the points of view of motivation and legislation, is deceptive. Decisions, answers, and solutions are worked out in the process of living, in and through interaction.

2. In one respect the argument of this article centers upon and emphasizes the complexity of choice and decision making in the real world and its relevance to ecosystem policy and the design and management of ecological systems. I therefore have the dilemma of having to choose between analysis and argument that overdoes the complexity and thereby burdens communication and the reader, and analysis and argument which oversimplifies the complexity and thereby defeats my purpose. I can only caution the reader that the construction of the paper involves an imperfect balance between these two considerations.

3. The reader, if I may anticipate some reactions to the article, may respond that the coupling of ecological and social factors in the design and management of environmental systems is either not as complicated or more complicated than I make it out to be.

I can only assert here that the coupling of ecological and social factors is as complicated as I suggest and even more so. In partial elaboration, let me say that there are answers and solutions to ecological problems which can and do "work," but the fact that they do "work" does not obviate the complexity that is avoided or short-circuited by particular answers and solutions. Each answer or solution to a particular problem of environmental protection in effect involves a choice from among a set of alternatives. This set has to be understood within a very large and typically open-ended matrix of social variables (discussed in Part II); it presumes some position on the fundamental analytical problems to be posed in this article. A similar situation exists, for example, in the analysis of ideology: almost any ideology can serve as a source of "efficient" answers to particular policy issues, i.e., a source of solutions to problems that "work." (Actually the "efficiency" is misleading: no ideology provides a complete and conclusive calculus by which to generate solutions, each solution rather being in fact a result of an act of choice or imagination *within* the ideology—as is partially evidenced by the fact that different true believers often come up with different solutions while each profess to apply the same ideology. Ideologies are frameworks channeling but also accommodating different chains of reasoning. But while an ideology is seemingly able to provide a "ready made" solution, that solution has meaning only insofar as the ideology (or the particular chain of reasoning on which the solution rests) resolves or takes a position on a complex matrix of social variables and values as well as on the fundamental analytical problems developed below. Moreover, ideology may provide efficiently forthcoming answers but not efficiently functioning or conclusively desirable solutions to problems. The same point applies to schools of thought, say, in economics: each tends to provide insight and direction to solutions to problems only on its own terms, within, that is, the terms of its own paradigm, thereby avoiding the complexity represented by the terms of rival paradigms.

4. Most discussions of ecological or environmental policy are partial in that they are limited to only a subset of the total number of variables actually relevant, and normative in that they are premised upon particular operative values and aim at particular policy solutions to problems to the exclusion of other values and solutions. I will discuss partial versus general interdependence in Part II; here I wish to stress the importance of positive analysis. The

position of most environmentalists, for example, as to the Alaskan North Shore depends in part upon insight which they have as ecologists, zoologists, etc., and in part upon particular value choices they make or value positions they hold as to the priority of considerations that should govern the use of the region. I do not in the least denigrate these normative approaches: they are a necessary and important part of the process of value articulation, juxtaposition, confrontation and selection that is central to social life and which embodies man's quest for the meaning of human dignity, subsuming considerations of justice, ethics, and the place of man in his natural environment and his relation to other creatures. I do insist, however, that the coupling of ecological and social factors *is* normative and involves normative considerations. Some environmentalists tend to state their case in such a way as if ecological facts eschew the opportunity for social choice. This is not typically the case: usually there is both the opportunity and the burden of social choice. (The environmentalist who so states his case is most likely functioning to have the social choice be his implicit choice. Environmentalists, like economists, disagree.) Paradoxically, however, I urge, and premise this article upon, the importance of an objective or positivist approach to what is a normative (choices of values as to alternative uses of the environment) and positive (determination of objective sceintific data concerning the environment) matter. I suggest, broadly speaking, the importance of a positive approach which will: first, provide hard scientific knowledge as a basis for social choice; second, unveil the policy alternatives between which trade-offs exist; and third, identify the fundamental problems with respect to which each normative solution is but one approach. In this article I attempt a contribution to the third area, the identification of fundamental problems. I stress that the ultimate problem in the design and management of environmental protection systems involves determining the normative matter of what should be done; but here I want to treat that in a positive way. Society will reach and work out solutions to ecological problems; here I want to explore what is involved as society works out its solutions and the fundamental analytical problems involved—in a positive, objective manner. Nothing developed here will necessarily apply for or against any particular environmental policy or reform; but the fundamental problems on which all environmental policies must take some position will be developed. Those policies will be better informed if we understand the fundamental problems involved.

II. General Interdependence

The primary fact of all social life is the interdependence of all variables. The interdependencies are not homogeneous but all social variables are in one way or another interdependent. All schools of economic, political, and sociological thought recognize this general interdependence, but just as economic, political and sociological thought each takes for its domain a more or less ambiguous subset of partial interdependencies, each school within each discipline tends to emphasize a particular set of variables or a particular set of (partial) interdependencies.[1] General interdependence is acknowledged but inter- and intra-disciplinary specialization tends to result in partial-interdependence models; one reason for this is the limited capacity of the human brain and the need for the reduction of variables to a manageable number.

Given social life as a system of general interdependence, the fundamental problem is that of order, defined as the reconciling of freedom and control, or autonomy and coordination including hierarchy and equality, with continuity and change. This is the dual problem of organizing and reorganizing the human decision making process and of making and remaking and effectuating decisions.

The continuing social resolution of the problem of order has to be understood as taking place in a dynamic general-interdependence system and with general-interdependence characteristics. Let me elaborate first by identifying several dual sets of representative and important partial relationships:

  a. the working rules of law and morals govern the distribution and exercise of power *and* the distribution and exercise of power governs the development of the working rules;
  b. values depend upon the decision making process *and* the decision making process depends upon values;
  c. tastes and preferences depend upon the institutional structure *and* the institutional structure depends upon tastes and preferences;
  d. the opportunity set of an individual depends upon the total structure of power *and* the total structure of power depends upon the decisions made by individuals from within their opportunity sets at any point in time and over time; and
  e. the distribution of income and wealth depends upon the use made of government *and* the use made of government depends upon income and wealth distribution.

Second, let me enumerate some of the variables which are part of the system of general interdependence: individual choice, power structure, opportunity set structure, working rules, allocation of resources, distribution of income, government, value system, preference structures, and so on. Third, let me baldly state that social policy may be understood and analyzed as the result of the interaction of the three dimensions of power, knowledge, and psychology; and that running through all three are the forces of technology, power play, material and ideal preferences functions, and, *inter alia,* the combination of choice, choice processes, and power structure. Finally, let me say that society involves a number of sometimes competing and conflicting and sometimes reenforcing social control systems, such as the market, religion, law, and custom; and, moreover, that one critical characteristic of social control institutions is that they are also power players, e.g., church versus state, business versus state.

The foregoing paragraphs constitute an abbreviated overview of what is involved in the problem of order under the condition of general interdependence. Even this cursory overview indicates the difficulty of a limited grasp of a system characterized by an infinite open-ended complexity and general interdependence. The dilemma of systems-analytic approaches vis-à-vis marginal- or incremental-analytic approaches resides in the tendency of the former to neglect important partial-interdependencies and of the latter to neglect the burden of general-interdependencies. Even though I am stressing here the importance of a general-interdependence approach, I must acknowledge that partial-interdependence approaches, despite the fact that they are always incomplete, possessed of tautological elements, and often excessively presumptuous, are nevertheless inescapable and useful. We do not yet and perhaps never will have a completely specified theory of general interdependence—but we must bear in mind, more than we have in the past, the general interdependence nature of our problems.

This means that any positive analysis of ecological *cum* social systems must differentiate between models which prescribe or proscribe particular policies, these being normative models, and positive models which identify critical variables, identify critical alternatives and tradeoffs, and study how society chooses between alternatives. Specifically, this latter means that the ecologist who is interested in introducing environmental considerations into human decision making must be concerned with how society does handle ecologically "sensible" considerations, with how society does form working rules and rights concerning the adoption of ecologically "sensible" considerations, and most especially with the role of social structure and economic-interest groups (power structure *in toto*) in determining just what substantive content is to be accorded "sensible," and, as discussed in Part III, just what costs are to be recognized as costs.

A systems-analytic ecology concerned with the design and management of environmental systems is both a science and a policy discipline. As a policy discipline it necessarily confronts what I shall call the dilemma of design and evaluation: the design (and management) of environmental systems depends upon evaluation, yet evaluation depends upon the (decisional) system designed. One question is, where does the analyst start; another question, upon which I shall concentrate here, is, whose evaluation and whose design? The analyst is a participant-observer and his partial-independence models and theories are themselves part of a general-interdependence system. In everything he does, the analyst will be taking some position on evaluation and design. The problem is: whose choices are to be made operational either in design or in evaluation; or, which costs are to count; or, who is to count and for how much? The actual social solutions to these equivalent queries depend upon the complex general-interdependence system (including the interplay of power players and psychic states within the market, between the market and other institutions, and in regard to institutional development). General interdependence ultimately, however, is a grand process of choice, and the critical questions are the three equivalent queries just posed. When the ecologist wants the consideration of environmental factors to be conjoined with other aspects of social choice, when he wants to foster the design and management of ecological systems, he is ineluctably getting involved in the problem of whose choices are to count, a problem which in actuality is only worked out through the complex and dynamic processes of social choice and whose solution cannot readily be taken for granted without begging the question of ecological optimality which is ultimately a result of general-interdependence interaction. Ecological optimality, like economic optimality, substantively depends upon whose choices are to count, that is, who is to count and for how much. The design of environmental systems, the evaluation of environmental systems, and the selection of ecological alternatives and tradeoffs all depend upon some antecedent determination of who is to count. The following two sections discuss the two most important types of cases in which this problem arises in ecosystem policy.[2]

III. THE PROBLEM OF COSTS

All persons concerned with ecosystem policy appreciate the need to consider costs in designing and managing as well as evaluating environmental systems. Economists, for example, have long insisted that the ecological issue is not pollution versus no pollution but the efficient or optimal amount of pollution given consideration of all cost factors, and that "excess" pollution is the result of using the waste disposal capacity of the environment too often free of charge, that is, without adequate attribution of costs to polluters. But what is the nature and origin of the "costs" so contemplated? I argue in this section that with prices dependent upon demand and supply, and with the seller's price being the buyer's cost, that the structure of costs is the obverse of the structure of prices; that with prices (and therefore costs) being dependent upon demand and supply, prices (and therefore costs) depend upon the forces and institutions operating through demand and supply; that there is thus no such thing as "absolute" costs (or prices) but only the costs which happen to be registered in the market through equilibrium or other prices; that costs (and prices) are partially dependent upon the structure of rights giving effect to the extant solution to the question of who is to count (as a cost factor to others) and how much, such that costs (and prices) are specific to a given structure of power (based, in part, on legal rights), among other factors.

What are normally considered as "costs" are in fact a commingling of several different things, and none of them is substantively an "absolute" either in economic relevance or magnitude. The closest one can come to an example of an absolute cost is the use of a nonrenewable natural resource. But even here the short run (and to an extent even the long run) market price associated herewith depends upon numerous demand and supply factors, such as substitutability; furthermore, some of them do not carry prices at all—this is one of the causes of overuse of many bodies of water and the air space for waste disposal.

One type of "cost" certainly includes real or physical input costs of production, given by technology and related factors. It takes steel to make an automobile and the steel is a cost factor. Waste disposal from steel manufacture and electricity production, both used in the production of automobiles, is likewise a conventional cost factor, though it has some of the characteristics of an output or joint product.

Another type of "cost" involves the property and other rights which partially govern whose values and interests are to be made a cost to others and how much, which is to say, the weighting of persons and interests as to who has to be bought off (paid for) so that production can proceed. If persons do not have a right to something that others want for use in production, then their interests will not count as a cost to the others; if they do have something that has to be paid for (i.e., a claim to income based on the right to have their consent secured in order that their something be used in production, or their consent as a prerequisite to production), then they will enter as a cost factor. This is the case with owners of land and natural resources generally, with owners of copyrighted material, and with owners of property that cannot be freely polluted without their consent. The converse is true in the absence of rights-holders to navigable streams and the air space.

Costs (prices) generated in the market reflect the commingling of both types of factors—real input costs and rights—as both influence the opportunity-set array of alternatives available at any point in time and over time to producers or potential producers. Those organizing production select, from the opportunity set of factor-combination possibilities given by their technical production functions, on the basis of alternative unit costs of production. One of the factors governing unit costs of production is technology, including economies of scale and so on. Another factor is the cost-price structure in the market with regard to those things which producers must pay for (the price of those things which they do not have to pay for is nonetheless subject to the following discussion). This cost-price structure (even when the price or cost is zero because someone else's interests are not given effect in the price-costing process) depends upon the usual array of demand and supply factors, but specifically upon the requirements of physical costs imposed by technology *and* the structure of rights in the market. The structure of rights in the market in turn is partially dependent upon the structure of power, in a system of general interdependence in which it is true both that rights are a function of power and that power is a function of rights (see above). This is to say that those who have greater power can get legal identification, assignment and protection of their interests, now called rights, as opposed to those with lesser power. If copyright owners can require (because of legal rights given them) a fee for permission to copy, then users of copying machines will face a cost of their production which would not otherwise (or not otherwise directly) accrue to them. Similarly, the distribution of wealth and income, together with other factors, governs relative costs in the market, and the cost-price structure would tend to be different if redistribution took place or were assumed. (More generally, income and wealth distribution partially depends upon the cost-price structure and the cost-price structure partially depends upon income and wealth distribution—another facet of the general interdependence system.) Thus cost-benefit calculations using the existing cost-price structure give effect to and reenforce the existing power structure which generates the cost-price structure, valuing highly those interests accommodated by the power and rights structures and valuing lowly those not so accommodated.

The point is that there is no such thing as absolute costs. Actual market costs are specific to the pattern of demand and supply in which they originate or have market-clearing and resource-allocation meaning, including the pattern of preferences, technological substitution, cross-elasticities of substitution, structure of rights, and so on, all of which are subject to change so that all prices and costs are only temporary magnitudes along an ongoing path of pricing. The costs involved in the actual economy are highly contingent costs; they are both dependent and independent variables in a system of general interdependence and, moreover, are subject to many lag and other effects. Costs, like prices, only reflect the constellation of factors which happen to be given effect at that time or through time. There is no more intrinsic meaning to costs than to the prices which are their obverse. Costs and prices are only the result of episodic real-world algorithms.

Costs, then, must be seen as having a general interdependence character. They are dependent upon tastes, power structure, technology (itself a range of alternatives in each instance), and rights structure. At any point of time only some of the possible acknowledged "costs" may be registered in the market (or on cost-benefit worksheets): not all social costs are accrued by the imposers as private costs of production (the traditional Pigovian case of market failure); and not all costs are perceived and become institutionalized (the Federal Reserve System has long been more sensitive to the "costs" of inflation rather than the "costs" of unemployment). The range of "costs," meaning adverse impact upon someone's opportunity set or interests, of most if not all acts of production are very great, though often with different degrees of proximity to the situs and time of production—this latter having a bearing upon the differential perception of such adverse impact as "costs."

The economy involves an ubiquitous incidence of costs and also an ubiquitous shifting (or attempts at shifting) of costs and acquisition of benefits. The critical problem is who is to bear costs, or whose interests are to count as costs to others—this is the distributive problem, over time, both within and between societies. Ecological analysis, and ecosystem design and management, involve the devising of pricing systems to register environmental costs and of reward systems to protect the environment; but the critical issues are: which reward system, which pattern of environmental costs and benefits, and which pattern of ecological tradeoffs? Given that there are typically varying patterns of environmental use, and therefore complex sets of ecological tradeoffs, not only does ecosystem policy confront a cost-price structure generated in the rest of the economy that provides only system- or situation-specific contingent prices and costs, but the very selection of particular patterns of environmental use, of particular tradeoffs, will affect the particular costs involved and affect them typically in very complex and different ways, that is, generate very different cost patterns. If "costs" are used as a partial-interdependence substitute for direct choice in ecosystem policy making, it should be remembered that they themselves are only existentially contingent and episodic phenomena; "costs" are a partial product of and therefore surrogate for the rights structure and other variables that enter into their making and which thereby indirectly but no less importantly govern the choices made by using those "costs." One way or another, choices between alternative environmental uses are being made. Ecological policy is an interacting part of a generally interdependence system, both a dependent and independent variable; and "costs" reflect specific patterns of interdependence which are themselves contingent and neither permanent nor absolute.

I should make clear that there are at least two important relevant psychological aspects of costs. First, psychological values are costs when they are adversely affected by, say, production. The policy problem is: whose psychological values are to be protected? Second, social action—including remedial and preventive environmental protection policy—depends upon complex processes of perception of costs, which is itself partially dependent upon power (and thus also upon class and economic interest group) structure.

While we wish to consider costs in designing and managing ecological systems, costs are thus no simple matter. Costs—whose interests are to count as costs—are themselves a critical variable in a system of general interdependence, a proxy for temporary solutions to choice problems reached in a dynamic system. Costs —for example, actual market prices—are used in a partial inter-dependence manner only with several implicit qualifications; the fact that it is easier or only possible to use them in partial inter-dependence ways does not alter their highly constrained significance nor does it obviate the implicit policy making involved through their use.

IV. The Problem of Structure Versus Results

Most discussions of environmental policy jump from considera-tion of decision making or control systems to consideration of specific policies or results. In a general interdependence context it is undoubtedly necessary to be concerned with both, but it is difficult to work with or to specify at the same time; hence discus-sions shift from one to the other, making analysis difficult to handle, communicate, and conclude. In any case, the treatment of one requires the making of assumptions about the other, something which has not always been clear.

What is the relationship(s) between designed structure and operating results? In the design of environmental systems are we interested in erecting decisional structures or in the decisional results? Is the ecologist satisfied with a system that will consider environmental factors or does he insist upon certain ecological results?

The problem of design and management is to set up control systems to effectuate ecological policy. The control systems can be designed to effectuate certain particular ecological ends or they can be designed to themselves select the ecological ends. The ends which each designed system tends to produce will be different. Is the structure to be designed to produce particular results, and if so then what (whose) results, that is, who chooses ecological trade-offs? Or is the structure to be designed in terms of principles of (or-ganizational) design independent of ecological tradeoffs with the understanding that whatever results are produced by the designed structure are presumptively optimal, and if so, then by what (whose) principles of (organizational) design? Is structure to be evaluated by results or by structural criteria; or, are results to be evaluated by structural criteria or by criteria of results? The problem is analogous to this the following: given that decisions are a product of decision-making structure and process, are decisions to be evaluated in terms of criteria independent of decisional structure and process or are decisional structure and process to be evaluated in terms of criteria independent of decisional results; or, does structure justify results or do results justify structure? These and related questions can be asked *ex ante* (with regard to design) and *ex post* (with regard to evaluation of operation).

The actual social solution to particular instances of this problem is a result in each case of the operation of the system of general interdependence as outlined above. The ecologist or other environmentalist usually is interested in both structure and results but typically does not have control or influence in regard to both and typically also is preoccupied with one or the other. What is at stake is the substance to be given to ecological optimality: ecological optimally involves the making of a complex set of decisions about environmental use patterns and associated tradeoffs, but decisions depend upon decision-making structure and environmental limits. Any particular ecologist, in specifying desirable or needed environmental results, is making certain tradeoffs and not others, and any decisional structure and process will make certain tradeoffs and not others; whichever are optimal will depend upon the weighting and choices made by the decision-making process subject to environmental limits. The environmentalist is probably only rarely able to predict how the larger society will choose as between ecological alternatives; more typically, the environmentalist has his own particular alternative in mind, whatever his set of allegiances to various interests. Should policy and policy recommendations be directed to structure or to results; is ecosystem results—particular ecological policies—the goal, or is ecosystem control systems—and whatever ecological tradeoffs they make—the goal? This is the fundamental problem typically begged in ecosystem policy discussions.

An important subsidiary problem involves the question of absolute versus relative environmental limits. How absolute are the ecosystem mass-energy, metabolic, physical-chemical, and other parameters? Is there only one optimal environmental policy in each case and that one given by ecological theory and fact alone? Or is there an opportunity-set array of possible alternative environmental policies with optimality depending upon the tradeoffs made by the extant decision-making structure; and if so, which if any alternatives are ruled out by environmental limits—and what is the meaning of "ruled out?" Is the expertise of the ecologist or other specialist going to make or govern ecological policy, because of the absolute limits which their skills enable them to discern; or is the decision making process or structure—such as politics, market, or other collective decision or social choice institutions— going to have the opportunity and the burden of making and selecting environmental tradeoffs? Is the use of the Alaskan North Shore determined by environmental limits or by the expertise of the ecologist, solely or in part and if so which part? Or is that use going to require the balancing of the relative merits of ecological and other considerations (and therefore choosing between alternative cost configurations and distributions), with the expertise of the ecologist and others serving as one input to identify critical variables and alternatives and tradeoffs, with the ultimate decision depending upon the structure of power governing whose interests are to be counted and given effect? Somewhere, somehow, such questions have to be answered, and will be answered as part of a general interdependence system. What is the balance between ecological optimality being dependent upon the power structure and being dependent upon environmental or ecological limits? And who is to say?

The problem is which ecological tradeoffs are to be made. The actual social solution will be forthcoming from and as a product of the general interdependence system. The environmentalist wants to develop regulatory systems and to make them responsive to ecological needs. But which needs and whose needs, insofar as mankind has a choice? Whose values are to be counted in making choices between ecological tradeoffs and use-alternatives? Whose interests are to be counted as costs in evaluating alternatives? All this is complicated by the fact that the cost-price structure and power structure are constantly changing, that is, they are themselves dependent variables; not only is the environment undergoing a continuing complex organic evolution but so also is society. The ecosystem policy maker, accordingly, has to be seen as a participant in a complex process of choice, as one factor in a system of general interdependence. More important, ecological ends are themselves to no small degree dependent upon the same system of general interdependence. The complex sets of causal chains and symbiotic relations found in the ecosystem or biosphere must be juxtaposed to the complex structure and process of social choice and its open-endedness. To existential scarcity (not always honored by those who have treated the environment as a free good to mankind) must be added not only the data of the existential environment but also existential choice.

V. THE LIMITS OF ECONOMIC ANALYSIS

As an economist interested in the analysis of environmental and decision-making problems, I am personally desirous of neither defending nor criticizing the work of either economists or ecologists. If I have pointed to the limits of ecological analysis, I have also pointed to the limits of economic analysis. In both cases, knowledge of the limits of disciplinary analysis in the real world of policy making would inform and improve that analysis.

So far as economic analysis is concerned, it is clear, first, that market valuation of costs and benefits is specific to the *status quo* distribution of power, including legal rights and wealth. It is the structure of power, broadly considered, which governs whose interests are to count in the dollar voting of the market. Similar statements could be made of political decision making. Second, the usual view by the economist, and it is very important as far as it goes, is that negative externalities, such as pollution, arise because the waste disposal capacity of the environment is allowed to be used without any or without adequate attribution of costs. But the deeper questions are: which costing, whose costs are to count, whose interests are to count as others' costs? Externalities, properly understood, are ubiquitous. It is impossible to eliminate all externalities; rather it is necessary to evaluate and choose between externalities, which choice will itself involve externalities. The problem is ultimately a distributional one: whose interests are to count, whose to be sacrificed, and who is to decide? Concentration upon allocative efficiency typically tends to beg these questions. Economic analysis can identify the critical variables and alternatives and can study how society chooses but economists can no more properly than ecologists preempt the decisional process by introducing their own norms and goals.

VI. CONCLUSION

Ecosystem design and management must be seen as entering into a system of general interdependence in which the very existence and magnitude of basic variables depend upon the interplay of a changing host of factors and are ultimately problematic and stochastic in the sense of being made rather than comprising something to be discovered and applied. They are made in the very process of our trying to apprehend them.

This is conspicuously the case with "costs." Costs are no less relative and artifactual than the ecological alternatives chosen by social institutions such as market and government. When we consider the problem of structure versus results we perceive that the quintessence of the process in which both structure and results are produced in our attempts to apprehend them is ultimately choice. The environmentalist is making choices even when he is passively and unknowingly adopting and effectuating the choices embodied in the cost-price structure. Social policy is choice with regard to society's opportunity set of alternatives and tradeoffs, however the choosing process is disaggregated and structured. The ecologist, not unlike the economist, has important and distinctive inputs for that choosing process, but his role will be but one among many, even with respect to specifically ecological issues—for not all ecologists (any more than economists) agree and even when they agree they are not the only ones relevant to the selection between environmental tradeoffs. When the ecologist attempts to specify ecosystem policy he is attempting to invoke his preference function alone, and, regardless of what we think of that, he is making very important but inconclusive assumptions about whose interests are to count as costs to others and about the problem of structure versus results. All discussion of ecosystem policy must come to grips with the problems of costs and structure versus results; choices are made with respect to them even when they are not recognized as such.

Ultimately, then, ecosystem policy, or the design and management of environmental systems, is involved with the formation and use of power in society, for it is power which distinctively determines costs and the choice of environmental alternatives and the choice of environmental alternatives and the corresponding distribution of costs will influence the distribution of power in society. Ecosystem policy recommendations make or carry assumptions—explicit or implicit—about the structure and use of power, ultimately with respect to who will make what fundamental decisions or choices. A systems-analytic ecology must comprehend the impact of the problem of power if it is to understand what it itself is all about, both as science and as policy discipline.

FOOTNOTES

* Professor of Economics, Michigan State University. I want to acknowledge my enormous debts to William Cooper, Herman Koenig, Allan Schmid, and John Taylor for uncountable insights not only into the design and management of ecological systems but into the problems of social choice generally, and to absolve them of all responsibility for their failure to extricate me from errors which I may continue to harbor.

[1] These differences are partly a matter of the scope of variables considered relevant and partly a matter of the central problem(s) taken as the object of study.

[2] The analysis of this and the following section depends in part on Samuels, W. J., *Interrelations Between Legal and Economic Processes,* 14 JOURNAL OF LAW AND ECONOMICS 435–50 (1971), and Samuels, W. J., *Welfare Economics, Power and Property,* in PERSPECTIVES OF PROPERTY, G. Wunderlich and W. L. Gibson, ed. (Institute for Research on Land and Water Resources, Pennsylvania State University, 1972).

5
NORMATIVE PREMISES IN REGULATORY THEORY
Warren J. Samuels

Economics has developed important concepts of policy analysis that are widely applied to problems of regulation: cost-benefit analysis, the economics of property rights, and techniques of constrained maximization. They encompass such lines of reasoning as: (1) the view that the property right should be assigned to the party to whom it is the most valuable; (2) the view that the burden should be placed on the party best situated to solve the problem at the lowest cost; (3) the view — regulation *ipso facto* creates inefficiencies and distortions; and (4) the view that law should promote efficiency.

The concern of this article is to identify a ubiquitous problem (with a multiplicity of manifestations) inevitably encountered in the art of regulatory analysis. The problem is one of circularity; the analyst assumes something about the object to be determined that governs the determination.[1] Thus the first steps in analysis often carry commitments that significantly prefigure the decisional results. Typically the assumption takes the form of an implicit antecedent normative premise[2] embedded in a tool or concept. While normative premises are necessary and inevitable, the argument here is that they should be made as explicit as possible.

This article attempts to answer two questions: What are we really doing when we use certain techniques of regulatory analysis? In what ways do normative premises condition the conclusions reached?

The author is Professor of Economics at Michigan State University. Allan Schmid and Nicholas Mercuro provided invaluable consultation during the course of the work on which this article is based. I am also indebted to Ken Boyer, Martin Bronfenbrenner, Charles Cnudde, Dan Hamermesh, Leland Yeager, James Shaffer, and Sidney Weintraub for comments, and to the writings of C. Edwin Baker, Thomas C. Heller, Arthur Leff, and Mitchell Polinsky cited below.

[1]Thus, the use of price-earnings (P/E) ratios in cost-of-capital calculations in public utility rate setting, because it makes assumptions with regard to investor expectations, assumes something about past and future rates of return when the latter is the object of determination.

[2]Normative premises concern values and/or definitions of reality, in both respects bearing on whose interests count. See Samuels (1977). This article does not deal with the often intractable problem of precisely defining "interests."

SOME RECOGNIZED PROBLEMS

Let me list some well-recognized problems of cost-benefit regulatory analysis: the choice of a discount rate, measurement difficulties (data subjectivity and nonmeasurability), boundaries of analysis, and the hazards of unique optimal solutions. The point which I want to make is that judgment involves the inevitable exercise of normative choice, ultimately with regard to whose interests are to count. Selection of a discount rate involves inter- and intragenerational choice. Measurement difficulties lead to practices implying preferences as to whose interests are to be given most weight. The choice of a starting point, which must be called presumptive, tends to promote certain interests and not others. For example, the proper measurement of competing benefits, and the specification of the status quo, require an antecedent determination of entitlements (the assignment of rights governing both allocative and distributive results).

The point is clear with regard to the boundaries of analysis. The very definition of community governs whose interests are to be considered, and how much they are to count. The optimal solution likewise is a function of the decision locus (the power to regulate), as well as the regulatory behavior, of the jurisdictional decision makers. Different specifications of community and jurisdiction lead to diverse solutions. Moreover, the allocation of political power is economically indeterminate without an antecedent premise specifying whose interests are to count: the identification of community *and* jurisdiction governs the "neutral" efficient solution.[3]

Conventional analysis neglects the positional character of costs and benefits and thereby adopts one set of magnitudes instead of another. To do so, however, is to give effect to one set of interests rather than another. The point arises in two connections. First, the identification of costs and benefits *is* a function of perspective: what is a cost and what a benefit is a function of selective perception. Cost-benefit identifications are made from one decision maker's point of view, they would not necessarily be the same when made from another decision maker's perspective. Second, since there is no overarching, independent calculus, the problem arises as to whose valuation to use.[4] The use of any valuation is equivalent to making interpersonal utility comparisons that favor certain interests and govern both the analysis and policy conclusions, as well as carry inevitable allocative and distributive consequences.

[3]Many of the points in the preceding paragraphs are made by Heller (1976, pp. 438, 466 ff., 489, 500, and passim).

[4]"The ethical question is closely tied up with, though it is not the same as, the question of who is competent to decide that some change in resource use would benefit some people more than it harms others" (Michelman, 1967, p. 1176). "Should equal weight be attached to welfare benefits felt by the rich and costs maintained by the poor in the creation of policy regarding income distribution? And should we weight equally benefits accruing to wrongdoers and costs incurred by their victims in writing the criminal

Selective perception is especially important in governing: (1) the definition of output; (2) problem identification; and (3) the definition of productivity. In each case, the definition assumes something about the objective and programs the conclusion.

A key point is that the definition of output is inherently *normative*; it gives effect to certain interests and not others and foreshadows the conduct and results of efficiency analysis. Output refers to a wide range of possible performance categories and may be defined from a number of different points of view — say, social, consumptive, and productive (or, alternatively, from the viewpoint of the national treasury, the national income accounts, and various immediate participants). A well-known example is the mechanical tomato harvester. This device was a product of private and public sector decision making which decreased labor costs to growers, increased unemployment among migrant pickers, and led to the cultivation of a tough-skinned tomato. Not only is the identification and valuation of costs and benefits a matter of selective perception but the definition of output depends upon point of view (Randall, 1974, pp. 227-34). The relocation and unemployment costs of the migrant workers were not included in the benefit-cost calculations encouraging mechanization.

Another example involves the appointment versus election of state attorneys general, a conflict that turns in large part upon the definition of desired output (or intended goal performance). As a third example, what is the output of the automobile industry? Cars, workers, profits, or, *inter alia*, all three? With economists as diverse as John R. Commons and Frank H. Knight insisting that the chief output of the economy is the type of persons produced, surely the definition is affected by the systemic structure of the economy producing certain complex types of persons rather than others (Baker, 1975, pp. 37-38). In the tomato harvester and automobile examples, there is arguable (hence normative) neglect of the social value aspects of goods, work as a character-forming experience, participation in collective decision making, and qualitative interpersonal relations (Baker, 1975, pp. 34-35).[5]

---

law?"("Just Compensation and the Assassin's Bequest: A Utilitarian Approach," p. 1022). "Although the damage to plaintiff may be slight as compared with defendant's expense of abating the condition, that is not a good reason for refusing the injunction. Neither courts of equity nor law can be guided by such a rule, for if followed to its logical conclusion it would deprive the poor litigant of his little property by giving it to those already rich." *Whalen v. Union Bag & Paper Co.*, 208 N.Y. 1, 5, 101 N.E. 805, 806 (1913), quoted in Large (1973, p. 1046 n. 29).

[5]Emphasis on consumption-oriented physical qualities (and quantities) of goods may neglect worker interests in the definition of output; see Roosevelt (1969, pp. 3-20) and Mishan (1975, pp. 714 ff). Similarly, consumer interests may be neglected in industry definitions of output; thus courts have held that the existence of administrative costs is no excuse for the failure of a public utility to provide hearing procedures on matters of importance to the individual. See *Stanley v. Illinois*, 405 U.S. 645, 656-657 (1972); *Reed v. Reed*, 404 U.S. 71, 76 (1971); and "Constitutional Safeguards for Public Utility Customers: Power to the People," pp. 493-521.

Second, the protection of interests, or rights, governs the definition of output and the meaning of economic welfare (Leff, 1974, pp. 464 ff.). The composition of output is an endogenous variable and is not independent of distribution. Different rights systems produce different behavioral and performance results, including different definitions of output. Welfare performance is specific to the structure of rights (Dales, 1975, pp. 486, 499, 502). Right-assigning rules promote different values, purposes and, therefore, outputs (Baker, 1975, p. 8). As the tomato harvester and automobile examples suggest, different conceptions of output rationalize different definitions of cost. Finally, the actual definition of output is a function, in part, of the legal system, the social power structure, and the power structure internal to the firm.[6]

Third, the use of any definition of output tends to imply some assignment of rights. Performance evaluation is a function of output definition, giving priority to certain rights and becoming a proxy for the choice of rights. Performance-oriented decision making amounts to the negating of possible rights, say, by the analyst, corporate decision maker, economic planner, or consumer. Effective rights are asserted by legal decisions, statutes, planning decisions, and pricing systems (Samuels and Mercuro, 1976, pp. 44-82); each gives effect to and protects interests in the name of output-oriented performance goals.

The definition of output thus is one of the most subtle ways through which an analyst or policymaker assumes something about the object to be determined which governs the determination and which becomes the subject of profound controversy. Productivity itself is a partial function of the legal-economic status given to respective property right claimants (Michelman, 1967, p. 1204). Rights-based definitions of productivity, in part through the definition of output, are at the basis of the productivity theory of production and distribution. They give effect to both legal and market forces in determining who gets whatever is produced: productivity is a partial function of whose interests are allowed to count, in part as embodied in output definitions.

A subtle intrusion of values also occurs in identification of the "problem." Different definitions of the farm problem, for example, convey associated but different solutions, fostering certain interests and not others.

A common contemporary example is the identification of externalities. Externalities are reciprocal in nature. Alpha may be seen as visiting an impact on Beta, or Beta on Alpha; restraining Alpha's impact upon Beta inevitably ignores the reciprocal state.[7] The externality can be specified in opposite ways (Sax, 1971, pp. 150-54, 165). Different definitions of prop-

[6]See Goldberg (1974, pp. 555-579), Williamson (1975, ch. 3 and passim), and Galbraith (1967, chs. 11-13 and passim).

[7]"The real question that has to be decided is: should A be allowed to harm B or should B be allowed to harm A?" (Coase, 1960, p. 2).

erty rights clearly generate diverse interpretations of externality problems: for example, granting the right to the cigarette smoker implies for him an externality in the form of pollution control, whereas assignment to the nonsmoker (to clean air) implies for him an externality in the form of pollution; recognizing preservationist rights implies an externality in the form of polluting second homes, whereas assignment of the right to development interests implies for them an externality in collective preservation services (Heller, 1976, pp. 451-52). Conversely, different definitions of externality problems presume different definitions of outputs and rights, thus giving effect to different normative interests. One cannot identify the intruding or causing party without presuming a certain definition of the problem and thereby protecting certain rights and interests and not others (Heller, 1976, p. 457). All regulatory solutions require normative specifications of interests, including assignment of rights, output definitions, and identification of externalities (Heller, 1976, p. 489).[8]

It is well recognized, of course, that the specification and use of utility (or "objective") and social welfare functions of the Bergson-Samuelson type are normative per se, in part because they weight certain implicit rights and not others. Too frequently the mere mathematical expression is presumed to have an objectivity that exists only in the symbolism, and not in the facts that are covered or to which they are applied. The economic analysis of law, for example, requires the selection of a utility function to be maximized and a distribution within which to work, both of which are normative.[9]

REGULATION AND RIGHTS

Our concern here is with regulatory law and theory. The literature of the economics of regulation contains frequent evaluative assertions to the effect that this or that regulation — indeed, regulation per se — produces inefficiency or distortions. While the matter of efficiency is deferred, at this point I want to indicate that regulation *is a functional equivalent of rights in protecting interests*.

Many, if not most, rights are a function of past regulatory actions of government. In order to assess the inefficiency of any regulation, one has to reject normatively the regulation at issue and accept normatively — as rights— all other (including substitute) regulation (Samuels, 1972; Polin-

[8]The conventional distinctions between pecuniary and technological and between Pareto-relevant and -irrelevant externalities are important avenues through which normative premises enter analyses and channel conclusions. See Samuels (1972, pp. 61-148).

[9]One mode through which implicit normative premises channel conclusions is in the use of existing market (or proxy) prices. This embeds the existing distributions of income and wealth and selectively reinforces certain interests and not others. The use of cost-benefit analysis in conjunction with the existing cost-price structure (for example, to assign rights to the party whose use is more valuable; see Posner, 1972, p. 18) gives selective effect to certain *other* rights.

sky, 1974, p. 1668). Concentration of attack upon a given regulation imparts differential normative status to all other law. The issue tends to be the relative desirability of a regulation; the rule can be shown efficient or inefficient only by rejecting or accepting the law, and behavior, which it is the putative purpose of the regulation to change. Those who advance what is sometimes called "the" *economic* case against regulation do so by building in implicit antecedent normative premises that reject the interest protection provided, while accepting other protections provided by other laws left standing.

One mode of introducing implicit normative premises that channel policy conclusions involves the definition of the police power vis-à-vis property rights. Property rights may be defined so as to build in future exercise of the police power *or* to prohibit future police power actions (which then amount to a taking under the Fifth Amendment). The police power, of course, is a mode of giving effect to interests beyond the interest regulated under the given rule; private versus public conflicts are often translatable into private versus private conflicts.

"Optimal regulation" — another "innocuous" and "scientific" term found in the literature of the economics of regulation — entails an antecedent normative specification of the interests to be protected. Any analysis purporting to yield rules for optimal regulation renders judgments preferential to certain selected interests and not others.

Whether or not an interest is to be protected as a property right, a perceptive court recognized, "is really the question to be answered."[10] The answer is channeled normatively by the view which holds that regulation is a priori inefficient: by assuming something about regulation (or the police power), the analyst predestines his findings. Yet there is no basis in economics for choosing between alternative rights systems (Dales, 1975, pp. 486, 502). Regulation involves choices between alternative rules of the game and between alternative assignments of rights that are logically prior to economic analysis. Economics can no more tell us what rules and rights structures should be than what technology and tastes should exist. Thus, for the economist to assert the substance of "optimal" regulation, or the regulatory policy that will result in the optimal level or direction of control (which is distinct from predicting the behavioral and performance consequences of alternative regulatory systems), is to assert covertly the rules and rights structures and to reach beyond economic analysis to antecedent normative premises as to whose interests should count. The point applies to both regulation and deregulation.

To conceive of legal regulation as a technical operation alone only makes implicit the choices that inform and channel regulatory analysis. If rights assignments preceded legal regulation, welfare maximization could in

---

[10]*U.S. v. Willow River Co.*, 324 U.S. 499, 503 (1945).

theory be a purely technical matter. But regulation is a functional equivalent of rights; regulation is one mode of the ongoing process of rights articulation and (re)definition; and rights determination is normative both per se and with regard to distributive considerations. Regulation necessarily makes distributive choices that compel allocative solutions. With no unique optimal use of resources and opportunities independent of rights identification and assignment, the legal system must select the result to be pursued: *the definition of the efficient solution is both the object and the subject of the legal system.* It is ironic that much conventional analysis assumes fully defined rights and a principle mandating compensation. The reality of the ongoing rights redetermination process is implicitly evident through the selective acceptance and rejection of interests (rights) by the analyst. These amount to changes in rights (say, rationalized by granting the right to the party to whom it is most valuable, placing liability on the party best able to solve the problem at lowest cost, or differentiating regulation from rights) that necessarily correlate with uncompensated losses.

An example of: (1) the reciprocal character of externalities and its significance for both rights and the normative character of regulatory theory; (2) the normative influence of definitions of problem and output; and (3) the relation of property rights to the police power and regulation, is provided by the fact that the taking party, in Fifth Amendment cases, may be specified alternatively. A pollution externality, legal control of the polluter (through regulation), or inaction or lack of government control each may be defined to be the taking.[11] As additional examples, the developer may be seen as imposing costs upon the municipality, or the local government, by not providing municipal services, may be seen as imposing costs upon the developer (Van Alstyne, 1971, p. 58; Tabb, 1973, p. 84); freedom granted to slaves may be seen as a taking from the slaveowner or as a legal correction of the slaves' past loss of freedom.[12] In each case, the definition of the problem and the solution reached by analysis is a function of the identification of the interest to be protected as a right, involving both an ascription and a denial of entitlement, stabilizing and giving effect to different values and interests. Each decision defines what is an illicit taking and what is a licit keeping, typically changing the past structure of rights in material respects (Leff, 1974, p. 480; Samuels, 1971, 1972). When courts and legislatures do this they are participating in the process of rights redefinition; when economic analysts do this they are joining the courts and legislatures in the social valuation process; in each case, the court, legislature, and/or analyst inevitably articulates antecedent implicit normative premises as to whose interests should count.

[11]Michelman (1967, p. 1236), Large (1973, pp. 1062, 1069-70, 1077, 1083), Kramon (1971, pp. 149, 158, 160), and Smith (1917, p. 394).
[12]Rothbard (1973, p. 37), Sax and Hiestand (1967, pp. 872, 884 n. 68).

PRIVATE AND PUBLIC, FREEDOM AND CONTROL

Two further ways in which the analyst tends to assume something normative involve the distinctions between private and public, and between
freedom and control. The distinction between private and public is at
bottom ambiguous and always selective. There are private elements in
public phenomena and public elements in private phenomena. Property is
both a private and a public thing. Specification of something as private or
as public is a mode of introducing subtle and selective normative premises
as to whose interests are to count. If the police power represents private
interests other than the one regulated, the rhetoric of rights enables certain
interests to be identified as private (however much they are a function of
public action) and others as public. The distinction between private and
public may intrude into policy analysis a false aura of autonomous individual behavior as the object of collective or government action; it always
tends to promote certain individual interests rather than others.

Labeling economic growth and/or smoke abatement as a public interest
or as a private interest (when in fact they may be both) is a semantic device
used to introduce, as appropriate to circumstances, implicit normative
premises by which to direct discussion and preprogram conclusions (Laitos, 1975, pp. 449, 450-51; Large, 1973).

Similarly, the differential specification of something as freedom or as
control tends to prejudge and channel analysis and policy recommendations. Reality, however, is much more complex. First, freedom and control
are positional and subject to selective perception. Rights may be seen as the
equivalent of freedom, and regulation as control; security may guarantee
access to, or protection from; and so on. In each case, subsequent analysis
is prefigured by the selective, normative specification given the terms.

Second, in every economic system there is a structure of control necessary for the relevant system of freedom. The problem is, who is to be
controlled for, and by, other persons' interests (say, through rights regulation)? Each individual tends to have an ambivalent attitude toward government and law; these both enhance and limit the individual's interests. By
identifying government and law with one's interests and conducting an
appropriate analysis, one can preprogram the results of legal policy: what
enhances one's interest is designated as freedom, all else is control. Law is a
mode of organizing and controlling the economy. As such, it is a method of
creating a sense and reality of orderliness, coherence, and permanence, but
with variable content that is relatively open in the long run as well as an
object of control in both the short and long runs. Each theory of the
economic role of government gives effect to some conception of freedom
and implies the system of control necessary for the postulated content of
freedom. In doing so, it assumes something about the object to be deter-

mined by analysis which governs the conclusions of analysis, thereby sustaining certain interests and not others.

CONSTRAINED MAXIMIZATION

Many of the relevant concepts used by economists represent our preoccupation with techniques of constrained maximization. Indeed, to many economists constrained maximization is the very logic of economic analysis. Within the present context, several points can be made. First, constrained maximization per se is a tautology with regard to the content of the objective function by which maximization is reckoned. Second, what is irrational by one calculation may become rational with a change in objective function (or circumstances). Third, the content of the preferences ensconced within an objective function is either provided by the economic actors themselves (inferred empirically by the analyst) or adduced presumptively (adopted or said to exist as a given by the analyst).

Economic analysis of law requires a utility (or objective) function. It is remarkably easy to manipulate the substance of analysis by adopting an appropriate objective function to produce the conclusion that such and such a legal action is optimal or suboptimal. The goals residing in the utility function are often empirical in form but almost wholly nonfalsifiable by facts. In the face of contrary evidence, the analyst can always say that the objective function has changed, or that circumstances have changed, or that the decision making was irrational. In all cases, the analyst's assumption with regard to the objective function governs the analytical conclusions on optimality. Constrained maximization clearly is positional: it depends on whose objective function, definition of output, and capacity to decide are dominant.

EFFICIENCY ANALYSIS

Efficiency

Economists stress efficiency, often without consciousness of the distributive-equity premises and consequences of their analysis. One connotation of efficiency defines "better off" as a position chosen voluntarily; that is, a function of private choice and adjustment. But such private voluntary choice always is within the law, and typically the law is the very thing to be determined. Selective implicit normative premises as to "the law" (that is, rights) govern the conduct of efficiency analysis, specifying who is in what position to make choices. Another connotation of efficiency is Pareto optimality, the notion of perfect adjustment that precludes further gains from trade within market and endowment constraints. The point here is the same: legal constraints are typically at issue, and the normative assumptions implicitly made frequently govern analysis and conclusions.

It also must be noted that optimal solutions are formal and nonoperational (nonobservational) by nature. Not only is inefficiency meaningless without an adequate definition and measure of output (Dales, 1975, p. 494; Leff, 1974, p. 456), while there are limitations in amount of data available and means of collecting it, but efficiency is a *relative* condition. It is relative to circumstances (for example, specification of objective function and all other prices) and is not a function of any intrinsic substance or relation per se. Nonobservational efficiency solutions can be given seeming precision only through the adoption of premises as to whose interests should count, so that the judgment is in substance tautological. Some social welfare function is implicit in all such work.

Efficiency and rights

Efficiency is a function of rights and not the other way around (Schmid, 1967, pp. 162-64). There is no unique structure of rights; thus there is no unique efficient solution. Efficiency is rights-structure specific and is a partial function of law.[13] To evaluate rights on the basis of efficiency is to adopt the antecedent implicit rights premised in the specification of "efficiency" used in the analysis (say, through different perceptions of externality). Economic efficiency is both an inadequate and presumptive basis for making law; it is circular to seek an external specification of efficiency with which to determine rights (Heller, 1976, pp. 441, 445, 447). Insofar as voluntary private adjustments are concerned, there can be "efficient" adjustment to any law or legal change, but efficiency cannot be the criterion of the law or legal change itself without presuming whose interests are to count in the efficient solution.

Efficiency (or optimality) is a function of rights, typically the very point at issue.[14] The choice of rights for analysis determines results that are efficient only on the basis of the presumed rights. As noted above, it is ironical that changing rights to produce ostensibly "efficient" results — efficient by some criterion — is non-Pareto optimal: loss accrues to some former holders of rights. A subtle and largely nonobserved transformation in the meaning of "efficiency" occurs in such works: from voluntary private adjustment to comportment with the analyst's criterion. Thus, granting a right to the party for whom it is presumed to be the most valuable embodies a distributive principle: someone receives the right and someone else does

[13]Polinsky (1974, pp. 1657, 1658, 1663) and Dales (1975, pp. 486, 499).
[14]"Just Compensation and the Assassin's Bequest: A Utilitarian Approach," p. 1016.

not, and often the decision reinforces the prevailing distribution of wealth with regard to "most valuable" (Baker, 1975, pp. 7-8).

It is because of the role of implicit normative premises that most, if not all, optimality reasoning in applied economics is presumptive. A verdict of efficient or inefficient is a function of the presumption of some antecedent rights structure or criterion of advantage. Efficiency cannot be judged without first determining the aim of the activity, and this is normative. Economists concerned, for example, with the efficiency of criminal law reach their conclusions in part because of their interpretation of case law and in part because of their specification of the end of law — deterrence, conduct of trials, regulatory content, and so on.[15]

One can denigrate any law or legal change as inefficient because: (1) law is not voluntary adjustment (unless one sees it as the product of a political market); and (2) a presumptive propriety is adduced to antecedent law with regard to which the new law produces distortion. The income tax is frequently said to establish distortions because it leads to a greater demand for leisure, but this assumes as proper the operation of all other law that also governs the relative demand for leisure. One can judge something as "inefficient" only by assuming an aim or basis other than the one putatively achieved by it. The issue always begged is: whose interests count, those promoted by the old (all other law) or the new law?

Value-of-output maximization as a function of rights

In the marketplace, the maximum social valuation that occurs is a function of demand and supply conditions which are in part a function of rights. A change in rights leads to a change in wealth distribution, which leads to new relative prices, resulting in turn in a new maximum valuation and new efficient allocations.

The legal system itself can be seen as maximizing value only in accordance with the rights actually supported; different rights specifications lead to different and (economically) noncomparable maximum valuations. Courts can be said to maximize value only in terms of the rights they declare, ex post. The value-maximizing rights assignment "depends on what initial distribution is assumed while the content of the initial distribution is the precise issue in dispute" (Baker, 1975, p. 11).[16] As Baker has observed, the initial assignment of a right affects the parties' wealth, and can affect each's valuation of the right and its valuation by a court. Moreover, the person favored in a previous case is more likely to survive the next case because the previous grant of a right makes the person richer and the claim in the next case is likely to be perceived by a court to be more

[15]Leff (1974, pp. 464-67) and Heller (1976, pp. 445, 493).
[16]See Sax (1971, pp. 158, 171-73, 186).

valuable to him. This is in part because he is more likely to claim the right for productive use, and his past gain of a right will tend to make his labor more valuable to him (Baker, 1975, pp. 10, 12-14).

Maximization of the value of output requires an antecedent premise as to the rights governing that maximization. Maximization is a function of rights; it is circular to assert rights on the basis of their money value. The crucial decision is that of the rights themselves.

IN CONCLUSION

The central argument of this article is a caution against the inevitably conclusionary and tautological character of certain uses of regulatory policy analysis. Too often, policy conclusions are tautological, with implicit normative premises that assume something about the object to be determined which prefigures the determination — typically, of whose interest is to count.

Rights determination is a necessary process. It is an important normative activity with distributional consequences. Decision making with regard to whose interests are to count (for example, as rights endowments) is necessary and inevitable in determining efficient solutions.

There is no value-free or procedural theory of social justice offered by legal economics or the economics of regulation. Economic analysis alone is unable to provide determinate answers for policy. This requires antecedent normative determinations that govern the recommendation (Heller, 1976, pp. 468, 387, 499). To conceive of legal-economic analysis as a technical operation alone only makes implicit the determining choices. Often economists either assume the problem away or channel its solution by the premises they make (Seitz and Headley, 1975, p. 641). There is "no refuge from discretionary value choices" (Heller, 1976, p. 502); the economic analysis of regulation tends to codify the analyst's biases. (Microeconomic theory, as applied to the economics of regulation, has become a conservatives' refuge largely because, improperly used, it can sanction certain themes and implicit normative premises congenial to conservatives.) Conclusions follow from implicit value premises; they are not inherent in the techniques of analysis.

In optimality reasoning, the analyst makes a determination as to value premises that transforms his role from that of observer to that of participant. His is a form of social engineering: in making normative assumptions, he inevitably becomes a normative decision maker, participating as a legislator or judge.

Unless we are to sanction the role of high priest, in which economists manipulate values and interests outside of immediate inspection, the solution must be to make all normative premises as explicit as possible.[17] The

[17]On the problems of making value premises explicit, see Samuels (1977).

decision-making role of the analyst — the role that involves his participation as a legislator-judge — should be specified by making both the fact thereof and the normative premises explicit. Regulatory efficiency theory is a set of procedures and modes of reasoning with which to acquire factual insights, reveal effective premises, and draw likely consequences of alternative lines of action, and not to provide a litmus test or calculus of decision making nor a vehicle for the subtle intrusion of political and normative premises. The value premise on which *this* argument rests is the desirability of public discussion of fundamental issues (such as whose interests are to count). Economists should and do participate in the social valuational process, despite disclaimers to the contrary. Higher standards of value-premise specification should be expected of economists than of interested parties.

Not only should normative premises be made explicit, but an array of studies should be conducted on the basis of *alternative* normative (and factual) assumptions. To do only one study is to give effect to only one perception and specification of outputs, costs, benefits, and rights. Alternative studies call attention to the subtle intrusion of ideology and partisanship, emphasize the necessary and inevitable critical choice of underlying values, highlight the fundamental distributional consequences that depend on the political determination of output definitions, and so forth.

Such alternative studies also test the degree of dependence of the conclusions on the specifics of the normative premises themselves. In addition, they elicit a more informed discussion within the policymaking process.

The problems of how property rights ought to be assigned in, say, novel cases of interactions, must be confronted explicitly. Such a strategy would open the door to a more careful and elaborate reexamination of the rights system and to more knowledgeable decision making.

So far, I have stressed the conclusionary and tautological character of regulatory theory; rights determination as the critical choice problem; the inevitable participant role of the analyst; and the desirability of making explicit the normative premises which channel policy recommendations as well as the merit of alternative studies. The foregoing discussion also permits us to see the rival utilitarian and Kantian approaches as much less disjointed. The utilitarian approach asserts the desirability of making cost-benefit-type judgments concerning rights. The Kantian approach emphasizes the importance of rights as categorical imperatives. In the Kantian view, rights are so preeminent as to rule out utility maximization "as inconsistent with a structure of agreed-upon obligations" (Tribe, 1975, p. 552).[18] The point I wish to make is that there is an inescapable Kantian element in utilitarian analysis, which reaches its conclusions only by pre-

---

[18]See Baker (1975, pp. 39, 40, 43, 46). I refrain from citing examples of improper conduct of regulatory efficiency theory. See, however, Samuels and Schmid (1976, pp. 99-105).

suming certain implicit rights, and not others, through its antecedent implicit normative premises. A properly conducted Kantian or utilitarian study would make explicit the fundamental choice of rights. To take rights as given and categorical (Kantian) or as implicit (utilitarian) is to beg the question at issue. In practice, both utilitarians and Kantians make assumptions as to whose interests will count as rights.

One concern that clearly emerges from the argument is whether a functional nihilism is necessary to avoid building in either the status quo or the analyst's private prejudices or ideology. My answer is in the affirmative. To proceed otherwise is to convert analysis as an exploration in search of knowledge and understanding to casuistic manipulation in the guise of science. Much work in the area of applied microeconomic regulatory theory is flawed by ambiguous premises as to whose interests are to count. I grant that, as Frank Knight argued, to make certain premises explicit is to hold them open for scrutiny. But that is the procedure most likely to let us know what we are doing (what are the consequences of our actions and choices) in a free and open society. To conceal premises is to allow ourselves to be manipulated. Nihilism does not mean that we cannot analyze. My argument is not against analysis. Rather, analysis should make values as explicit as possible, perhaps most effectively by making alternative value premises. The economist's work is important (not least when it is used by policymakers); we should proceed carefully and overtly, not carelessly and covertly.

REFERENCES

Baker, Edwin C. "The Ideology of the Economic Analysis of Law." *Philosophy and Public Affairs*, Fall 1975, *5*.

Coase, R. H. "The Problem of Social Cost." *Journal of Law and Economics*, October 1960, *3*.

"Constitutional Safeguards for Public Utility Customers: Power to the People." *New York University Law Review*, 1973, *48*.

Dales, J. H. "Beyond the Marketplace." *Canadian Journal of Economics*, November 1975, *8*.

Galbraith, John Kenneth. *The New Industrial State*. Boston: Houghton Mifflin, 1967.

Goldberg, Victor P. "Public Choice-Property Rights." *Journal of Economic Issues*, September 1974, *8*.

Heller, Thomas C. "The Importance of Normative Decisionmaking: The Limitations of Legal Economics as a Basis for a Liberal Jurisprudence — as Illustrated by the Regulation of Vacation Home Development." *Wisconsin Law Review*, 1976.

"Just Compensation and the Assassin's Bequest: A Utilitarian Approach." *University of Pennsylvania Law Review*, 1973, *122*.

Kramon, James M. "Inverse Condemnation and Air Pollution." *Natural Resources Journal*, January 1971, *11*.

Laitos, Jan G. "Legal Institutions and Pollution: Some Intersections Between Law and History." *Natural Resources Journal*, July 1975, *15*.

Large, Donald W. "This Land Is Whose Land? Changing Concepts of Land as Property." *Wisconsin Law Review*, 1973.

Leff, Arthur Allen. "Economic Analysis of Law: Some Realism About Nominalism." *Virginia Law Review*, March 1974, *60*.

Michelman, Frank I. "Property, Utility, and Fairness: Comments on the Ethical Foundations of 'Just Compensation' Law." *Harvard Law Review*, April 1967, *80*.

Mishan, Ezra J. "The Folklore of the Market: An Inquiry into the Economic Doctrines of the Chicago School." *Journal of Economic Issues*, December 1975, *9*.

Polinsky, A. Mitchell. "Economic Analysis as a Potentially Defective Product: A Buyer's Guide to Posner's *Economic Analysis of Law*." *Harvard Law Review*, June 1974, *87*.

Posner, Richard A. *Economic Analysis of Law*. Boston: Little, Brown, 1972.

Randall, Alan. "Information, Power and Academic Responsibility." *American Journal of Agricultural Economics*, May 1974, *56*.

Roosevelt, Frank. "Market Socialism: A Humane Economy?" *Journal of Economic Issues*, December 1969, *3*.

Rothbard, Murray N. "Value Implications of Economic Theory." *American Economist*, 1973, *17*.

Samuels, Warren J. "Interrelations Between Legal and Economic Processes." *Journal of Law and Economics*, October 1971, *14*.

Samuels, Warren J. "Welfare Economics, Power and Property." In G. Wunderlich and W. L. Gibson, Jr., eds., *Perspectives of Property*. University Park: Institute for Research on Land and Water Resources, Pennsylvania State University, 1972.

Samuels, Warren J. "Ideology in Economics." In Sidney Weintraub, ed., *Modern Economic Thought*. Philadelphia: University of Pennsylvania Press, 1977.

Samuels, Warren J., and Mercuro, Nicholas. "Property Rights, Equity, and Public Utility Pricing." In Harry M. Trebing, ed., *New Dimensions in Public Utility Pricing*. East Lansing: Division of Research, Graduate School of Business Administration, Michigan State University, 1976.

Samuels, Warren J., and Schmid, A. Allan. "Polluters' Profit and Political Response: The Dynamics of Rights Creation." *Public Choice*, Winter 1976, *28*.

Sax, Joseph L. "Takings, Private Property and Public Rights." *Yale Law Journal*, December 1971, *81*.

Sax, Joseph L., and Hiestand, Fred J. "Slumlordism as a Tort." *Michigan Law Review*, March 1967, *65*.

Schmid, A. Allan. "Nonmarket Values and Efficiency of Public Investments in Water Resources." *American Economic Review*, Supplement, 1967, *57*.

Seitz, W. D., and Headley, J. C. "Changing Natural Resource Property Rights: An Overview." *Natural Resources Journal*, October 1975, *15*.

Smith, Jeremiah. "Reasonable Use of One's Own Property as a Justification for Damage to a Neighbor." *Columbia Law Review*, 1917, *17*.

Tabb, William K. "Book Review." *Journal of Economic Issues*, March 1973, *7*.

Tribe, Laurence H. "From Environmental Foundations to Constitutional Structures: Learning from Nature's Future." *Yale Law Journal*, 1975, *84*.

Van Alstyne, Arvo. "Taking or Damaging by Police Power: The Search for Inverse Condemnation Criteria." *Southern California Law Review*, 1971, *44*.

Williamson, Oliver E. *Markets and Hierarchies*. New York: Free Press, 1975.

II
APPLICATIONS: FUNDAMENTAL PROCESSES AND INSTITUTIONAL IMPACTS

The articles in this section apply the mode and paradigm of the analysis presented in Part I to specific problems of research and policy.

Chapter 6 applies the general model of interdependence to public administration, particularly in the context of determining the mix of inputs from the different government agencies that define the content and objectives of complex economic development programs. In contrast to classical theory, which focuses on jurisdictional boundaries and command hierarchy, this article emphasizes the institutional variables that affect the bargaining power and ability of a given agency to elicit the cooperation of other agencies.

Chapter 7 illustrates further the rules that affect who can use government and the outcomes of power play in the context of the lower courts. The empirical results suggest the performance effects of several reforms that have been suggested in the method of judge selection and in the level of government that finances the lowest courts.

The next chapter employs neo-institutional economic theory to formulate and empirically test hypotheses related to the effect of alternative rules for consumer participation in controlling health care costs. The results suggest that formal membership on health-facility planning bodies, which is equivalent to a redistribution of factor ownership, is not instrumental in furthering consumer interests. Rather, the relevant institutional rules are those that affect transaction costs and overcome the free-rider problem.

Chapters 9 and 10 present an extended analysis of a major problem of policy—namely, the application of the requirement of just compensation. The first of these chapters applies the analysis of Part I to an identification of the compensation problem in terms of a theory of rights, which takes into consideration the ultimate necessity of choice about whose interests are to be sacrificed and the inevitability of ubiquitous uncompensated losses, notwithstanding the compensation principle in constitutional law. It uses the concepts of power, interdependence, and choice to transcend the simplistic conceptions and forlorn hopes typically found in the area. Chapter 10 develops a theory of the legal process in order to identify the complex roles of the compensation principle in society—roles that penetrate to the foundations of the existing order and that vary markedly from the mythology of the compensation principle.

The final chapter explores the ways in which regulatory reform and deregulation are, contrary to their usual interpretations, analytically equivalent to regulation. It, too, represents an application of the theories of rights, power, and legal-economic interrelationships. Its conclusions regarding freedom versus control, interest protection, and the relation of regulation to inflation are considerably at variance with the conventional wisdom.

6

A RESEARCH APPROACH TO INSTITUTIONAL ALTERNATIVES IN THE ADMINISTRATION OF AGRARIAN DEVELOPMENT PROGRAMMES

A. Allan Schmid and Ronald C. Faas

Large-scale development project implementation requires the delivery and co-ordination of several inputs. Often, these inputs are under the control of separate agencies. A model to guide empirical testing of alternative institutional structures is developed and applied to a case study. Alternatives include a co-ordinating forum, a planning agency and versions of a consolidated, centralised super agency. The model emphasises variables which affect the bargaining power of a project initiator in obtaining the co-operation of other parties.

INTRODUCTION

Any agricultural development programme or project is a complex thing with many ingredients. For example, an irrigation project involves not only the engineering structures for water management, but also fertiliser, seeds, insecticides and knowledge of their productive combination. In addition, once the crop is made, it requires storage, transport and processing. Further, the project is embedded in a series of rules and policies related to tenure, pricing, international trade, etc. If some of these are missing or the mix or timing is wrong, the project may fail.

There is a great deal of debate over what the optimum combination of inputs and of policies is for a given problem situation. In fact, there may be little agreement on what the problem is or on the specific objectives of development. The success of a project, then, is not only a function of good advice on the most productive 'recipe' for development, but also depends on the institutional co-ordination of the various 'cooks' and suppliers. How, then, should each of the specific suppliers of goods, services and policies in a developing country be related to each other to achieve a given performance?

This question is relevant to both: (1) outside donors who try to influence not only the recipe but also the structure of its administration as a condition for grants and loans and (2) host agencies who must ultimately design the relationships between the parties involved in a project's administration. The purpose of this paper is to develop a model of alternative relationships between the various public suppliers of project inputs which might be useful in guiding empirical research. (The model developed here is in terms of relationships between governmental units, but could be extended to include private firms as well.) Donor agencies, such as USAID, have been known to withdraw aid for certain kinds of projects when a host country refuses to set up a new independent super project agency or to consolidate two related departments into one. The donor and the host must have some image of how these institutional relationships will affect performance. This paper is addressed to improving these predictions.

There are several alternative models that come to mind. One is a *hierarchical command* type of organisation with clear lines of authority running to the top. The top authority has in mind the desired development recipe and issues the appropriate orders to people who are obliged to carry them out. Consolidation of related existing agencies under the direction of a single head is a popular approach to solving problems of failure to co-ordinate delivery of the various ingredients according to someone's view of the desired recipe.

For example, if the research and extension programmes are not mixed and timed correctly, it is conventional wisdom to advocate that both functions should be under the direction of the same person. An AID, Technical Assistance Project, in Guatemala noted that in the past there was one agency that was responsible for price and trade policy and another for market information and extension type programmes. The project was to provide assistance to a new combined agency responsible for both functions. The TVA in the USA is an example of a consolidated multi-functional super agency.

Another model is that of *bargained exchange* between agencies. Each agency has some set of responsibilities and resources. If it wants to combine a product or service from another agency with its own, it must negotiate with the other agency to secure its agreement. Where it is not possible to command, the desired action of others is achieved by making it worth their while. Something has to be traded. It can be in the present or a promise of future delivery. It can be money, client support, information, embarrassment, prestige, etc.

Most of what government does is co-ordinated by bargaining, although it is not usually seen that way. We have a habit of saying that if something is not internalised in one agency or executive, it is unco-ordinated. At the least, we apply the word 'co-ordinated' to actions of formal inter-agency bodies.

There are obviously many variations of hierarchical command and bargained systems. Not all agreement among parties is a matter of calculation or exchange. Some relationships are a matter of learned habit and recognition of status. There may be other types and the language used here may not capture the distinctions. That, in fact, is part of the research being proposed. What is the variety of organisational approaches for relating the many inputs and policies involved in development? It is useful simply to document that other approaches are possible so that further comparative research can be conceived.

The command system itself is never completely a command system. Some bargaining takes place within every organisation. Field offices bargain with the central office. The planning division bargains with the engineering division, etc. Each sub-group has some area of discretion and if a group wants the co-operation of another, it must bargain. The central authority cannot be everywhere at once. When two functions are consolidated in a single agency, they still bargain with each other.

What kind of conceptualisation can be used to document alternative inter-agency or inter-function relationships?

Perhaps the above abstract introduction can be made more concrete by reference to an example adapted from an actual case. The first element is the project *recipe*. Assume that there are three key material resources involved—a new imported hybrid seed (A); credit (B) and trucks to get the seed to the farms (C). These resources can be combined in different ways to secure different *outputs* such as agricultural yields and incomes and distributions thereof, as well as non-agricultural outputs. In this case the three ingredients can be combined to produce an increased output of wheat of 1 million bushels, largely going to small farms; or 1·5 million bushels, largely going to large farms, or some of these inputs (trucks in this case) can be used for non-agricultural outputs (road construction and repair). The next element in the model involves the *actor* or decision unit. Assume the Minister of Agriculture prefers the first recipe favouring small farms, the director of the agricultural credit agency (part of the Ministry of Agriculture) prefers the recipe favouring large farms and the Minister of Transportation wants to build roads.

The next question is: Who controls each of the three resource ingredients? In the broadest sense of the word this control feature will be referred to as a *property right*. Assume the Minister of Agriculture has a budget for seed and, in addition, is a friend of the President and has the right to fire the director of the credit agency. The credit agency director, however, has friends in the legislature who have appropriated funds for credit and are sympathetic to the director's views. The Minister of Transportation has a budget for trucks and road building. These are the materials that each actor can bring to a *transaction* with the other relevant parties. These trading materials can be exchanged as each actor tries to get the other parties to co-operate with his idea of the desired recipe and associated output. Perhaps the Minister of Agriculture will threaten the credit director with dismissal and offer the Minister of Transportation support for an expanded road budget year if he will loan the trucks to haul seed for a while. These conceptual dimensions are shown in Fig. 1.

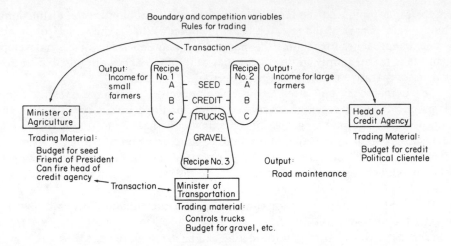

Fig. 1.   Model of inter-agency transactions.

The key question to be investigated here is how the structure of the inter-relationships between the actors affects whose idea of the desired recipe prevails. Reference has been made to the type of property rights of each party and this will be further elaborated below along with the rules for how these rights to resources can be used to obtain the agreement of other parties. Can an agency like AID predict what rules of the game are more likely to result in execution of a particular recipe and output favoured by AID? For example, will the small farmer wheat seed project gain if a separate new single project agency is created which controls all inputs, or can it be done by a new co-ordinating council made up of existing agencies, or still another set of features perhaps more palatable to the particular host government involved? It would be useful if we knew several alternative structures and substitutable features to accomplish a particular goal so that it can be fitted to different situations.

SHARED GOALS VERSUS CONFLICTS

It is important to distinguish between the task of problem-solving when there is agreement on goals and objectives (desired recipes and outputs) and a conflict over goals and objectives (Tuite et al.[10]). The above situation suggests a conflict of goals. The actors want inconsistent end results. This work will concentrate on these conflict situations. However, it is recognised that often the parties agree on broad end results (or could, after certain learning experiences), but, because of failure to communicate, etc., they do not act in a concerted fashion. This is the domain of much management and communications research and will not be further emphasised here.

Different actors often find themselves in a situation where concerted action creates mutual advantage. Each can gain by joint action. This still leaves the distribution of the gain among them to be bargained over.

PARTIES TO TRANSACTIONS

It is the intent here to provide a model that might apply to different kinds of levels of actors. These include someone who has responsibility for the whole of a complex project. This person must deal with many different people to obtain their services and goods. On the other hand, the same conceptualisation can apply to a lower level worker who, nevertheless, requires the complementary inputs of several other people. The decision-making unit to be observed, then, might be an entire agency, office, or down to an individual as these interact with other parties. This interaction will also be called a transaction. The essence of the transaction is to secure a desired action by some other party.

WHAT IS TRADED?

Goods

In the private market, when a consumer wants a producer to deliver a good, another good is offered in exchange (usually money). Is there an equivalent when one party with a certain project recipe in mind wants to get the agreement of another party to deliver a good under the latter's control? One possibility includes a *monetary payment*. The actor may be in a position to buy (contract for) the desired service or transfer part of his budget to another actor. It may involve a *trade in kind*. The Minister of Transportation agrees to loan the trucks in return for some surveyors from the Ministry of Agriculture, to be delivered later. Information and expertise can be shared. In sum, the flexibility of the actor's budget is a major resource at his disposal to get the agreement of others. This is related to the degree of agency functional specialisation (Simon et al.[8]).

Other types of goods can be much more subtle. If the one party has great *prestige and status*, he may secure the agreement of others by giving them approval and recognition and letting others know about it (Tannenbaum[9]). One party may be a friend of the President and able to put in a good word to help the budget of a co-operating party in the future. *Connections* to other sources of resources are then a bargaining asset. Time is the ultimate scarce commodity and prestige is useful in at least getting the attention of other busy decision-makers.

Research would aim at documenting both the amount and variety of goods available for trade.

Bads

Kenneth Boulding[2] has pointed out that bads and threats are exchanged, as well as goods. Students of international hot and cold wars are familiar with this situation. An actor may be able to get the agreement (desired performance) of another by threatening to deliver a harm or to reduce or stop a flow of goods which the other party previously enjoyed.

Just as prestige and connections with the President may be used to secure extra money for a co-operator, the same connection may be used to threaten a budget cut for a dissident.

A typical organisational reform for failure to achieve a given project recipe is to give someone additional authority. What does authority mean? In addition to budget allocation control, already discussed, it turns primarily on the right to hire and fire. In the case described above the Minister of Agriculture could fire the credit director but not the Minister of Transportation. An obvious reform is to reorganise the two Ministries with a single head who can threaten dismissal and pay reductions to all subordinates. This theme will be further explored below in a section on 'Internal versus External Bargaining.' However, the nominal right to dismiss and reward subordinates differs from its actual effectiveness. The factors affecting the ability of superiors to direct their subordinates have been detailed in the literature and need only brief mention here (Simon et al.[8]). This includes: the span of control, i.e. shape of the administrative hierarchy (Blau et al.[1]), spatial centralisation, mobility of administrators and their length of tenure (Pryor[6]), and degree to which behaviour is incorporated in standard operating procedures and a pervading professional or agency ethic. A prime factor appears to be things which affect the flow of information. An inventive cannot issue a command if he/she cannot tell what is going on or deliver the sanction to the right place.

Whatever the structure and degree of centralisation within the agency, this appears to be less associated with agency effectiveness in dealing with other agencies than the distribution of total rights and bargaining power between agencies (Tannenbaum[9]).

Information can sometimes be used to inflict harm on others. One party may be in a position to expose something causing pain for another. There are no doubt many other subtle ways in which to harm another party.

It is necessary to distinguish between agency resources and the resources of an agency's clients. There may be a gain from joint action, but the agency trying to get the co-operation of another agency may not be able to capture any of it to deliver either to the co-operating agency or to its clientele who might otherwise lose by the new action.

For example, if a new recipe can be delivered, Client A may greatly gain but unless the agency representing and serving them can trade some of this gain to clients of the potentially co-operating agency, the needed inputs will not be forthcoming. Sometimes this takes the form of log rolling where one agency agrees to support a future piece of legislation for another. This may, however, be insufficient if the desired co-operation inflicts a large damage to politically powerful clients of the other agency.

In summary, to answer the question: 'What is traded?', we have begun a list of items of the desired recipe that are subject to command by a given actor and items that can be traded to other parties who command other needed ingredients. Both of these involve 'ownership' of goods and bads which can be offered, withheld or threatened by a given actor.

BOUNDARIES AND COMPETITION

If a given recipe is to be implemented, one not only needs the material ingredients, but also the non-interference of other actors who also wish to duplicate the recipe and compete, or who wish the field left empty and the project never undertaken. In common parlance we talk about the mission or *functional boundaries* of a given actor or agency. Is it legitimate for the Ministry of Agriculture to do extension education or is education the exclusive domain of the Ministry of Education? Or can they both operate as competitors? There is a strong conventional wisdom that supports competition in private markets, but regards competition in public agencies as wasteful and duplicative. The performance consequences of exclusive versus overlapping functional and geographical operating rights need to be empirically determined.

Often it is not the use of a material resource that is needed from another agency, but rather its permission to operate. This may take the form of permits, licences, and veto powers. Somehow relevant third parties have given some agent the right to control entry to certain activities. (Economists familiar with market structure research will recognise this as the concept of barriers to entry.) Of course, the right to prevent entry into a certain line of activities and kinds of projects can be traded for other goods (or given up under threats of bads). Other material resources can be exchanged for permission to enter. So, in a sense, control over entry could be thought of as just another kind of trading material, although it is sufficiently different to warrant a separate category.

TRADING RULES

A given party may have certain trading resources but be constrained in their use. Again, a private market analogy may be useful. In markets there are contract rules. A seller may enjoy being in the position of being the sole supplier of a good currently in short supply. Potentially, the seller could use this power to secure the buyer's order for other goods as well. This is called a tie-in sale and is prohibited in the USA. Thus, the rules determine which of the potential resources the parties can actually use in getting the agreement of others.

An important factor affecting the ability to trade on one's resources has to do with the management of information. Do the parties have to 'show their hands?'. Public disclosure rules are equivalent to the rules that define fraud in private markets. Various procedural and notification rules for public hearings are other examples.

It is hypothesised that while private market rules are highly developed, the externally given rules governing bargaining among bureaucrats are few. This is so in part because of the conventional wisdom concerning how command systems work. We have often assumed there was no need or place for bargaining (people just issued orders and they were carried out), and therefore no attention was given to bargaining rules. You don't need a rule for something that is not supposed to exist!

It is further hypothesised that where few external bureaucratic bargaining rules are available, it will be very difficult to predict how the various development ingredients will be made available. In this case, the unique personal characteristics of the bureaucrats become all important. Their charisma and personal leadership qualities become the key to who can get the co-operation of whom.

INTERNAL VERSUS EXTERNAL BARGAINING

The model developed here focuses on negotiation between parties as each tries to secure the agreement of the other to a certain action. This may seem a strange concept for those who believe that there is a sharp discontinuity between structures made up of a number of semi-independent decision-makers (agencies) and those who market by hierarchical command. This discontinuity suggests a sharp difference between negotiation (bargaining) and an order or command. This leads to some simple-minded consolidation reforms when several agencies fail to implement a certain plan.

The beguiling simplicity of the hierarchical command model derives from the supposed ability of the commander to work his will without cost. He simply orders, and all the costs are on the other side. The view taken here is that this is a polar case seldom encountered in pure form. Returning to the earlier example, the Minister may not use his nominal power to fire the credit agency director without incurring some costs. The director doesn't hold his dissenting views in a vacuum, but because of some interest group, probably with some political power.

It is tempting to solve the problem of a recalcitrant, non-co-operating party who won't listen to 'reason' or won't trade by converting from an external to an internal transaction. This can make a difference, but it would be a mistake to believe that the internal transactions between nominally superior and inferior are costless to the superior. How many Ministers are able to work their will throughout their organisation? Part of the problem is one of information overload, but part is the fact that subordinates are not without rights of their own which causes accommodation (and negotiation) on the part of the nominal commander.

The hypothesis is offered that there are few command transactions based completely on the power of the boss to fire the subordinate without cost to the boss. Where this is the case, we expect to observe poor performance and execution of the command and also very expensive supervision costs. Some of this threat is probably involved in many bureaucratic transactions, but usually mixed with some 'carrots'. The reason is simply that unwilling (begrudged) participation is less productive (and socially unpleasant for all). A subordinate may have different objectives, but at some point there is enough 'carrot' involved that willing participation is possible. Most generals, and even dictators, have some understanding of this.

In summary, it is useful to enquire into whether the transactions are between external or internal parties. It should not, however, be assumed that internal transactions contain no elements of bargaining and that supervisors work their will without costs to themselves. A relevant research question is how often do we observe Party A getting Party B's productive assent when A's only resource is the right to fire B and when the only element of the transaction is communication of an order backed up by that threat of job or pay loss. In the present model, the threat of firing is regarded as just one among many resources that a party has which might get the desired action of another. The distinction between a request, an invitation, an offer to trade and a command or order is blurred. The receiver of all of these has a decision to make involving a calculation of benefits (including harm avoided) and costs (ends not served if the requests of others are heeded).

HOW ARE THE TRADING MATERIALS, BOUNDARIES AND TRADING RULES ESTABLISHED? AND HOW ARE THEY CHANGED?

Some of the resources a bureaucrat has are matters of personal characteristics. He/she may be a sharp debater, have a good memory, etc. Some resources involve acts of recognition and legitimation by outside groups. A property right is always a public or group phenomenon. An agency may have certain powers given by a constitution, by enabling legislation, or by habit and mutual assent. Its jurisdiction may also be a matter of assertion and, if others don't challenge it, power accrues by habit (Neustadt[5]). There may be additional rules which are given by outside decisions or are mutually developed by the participants themselves. There is also a certain dynamics involved. Initial power sources can be used to obtain more. Economic power is helpful in obtaining political power, and vice versa.

These questions obviously tie into some of the traditional concerns of political science with constitutional and political system issues. If an outside donor wants to suggest a certain administrative structure for project implementation in the host country as a condition for a grant or loan, it must certainly take into account the background politics of rule change. This is beyond this study which does not ask how a certain rule can be changed, but focuses on the probable consequences of a rule change which alters the bargaining material available to a given party.

SOME ADDITIONAL CONSIDERATIONS

The essence of the model has now been presented. Several additional questions need brief mention before we turn to relating the model to examples of different sets of the model's components.

Perception

Perception of the things being offered for trade is important. Ideally, it would be useful to check the perception on both sides. What resources does A think he has and what does B think A has, and which ones is B responsive to?

It should be sufficient to note general tendencies rather than to predict the outcome of each trade; *i.e.* when A has resources X_1, X_2, X_3 does he *generally* get assent of other parties more often than when he only has X_1?

In market trade, utilities for the same good differ among buyers and the smile of the seller may or may not be part of the exchange. Yet, we can observe some general tendencies without detailed knowledge of all the perceptions.

Bargaining implies that the objectives of each party are not identical at the outset. At that point we ask what resources A has to get B's assent. It is difficult to know just what resource of A is decisive for each B, but this knowledge is not necessary for our purposes. It should be useful to describe the nominal and apparent resources of successful A's. We can never be sure just which resources were the minimal necessary for a particular assent. But, if we can note that certain groups of resources are found to be available to successful A's more often than others, we can suggest packages that might be made available to any A that wants to increase the probability of its success. We may be able to suggest that when X_1, X_2, X_3 are not possible in a given programme that X_4, X_5, X_6 seem to be substitutes. This is a more modest objective than being able to say that in a particular negotiation with a particular party A could be successful with a minimum resource package of say X_2.

It should also be noted that misrepresentation of one's desired recipe may be part of a bargaining strategy. This makes research difficult since, if we compare two sets of rules where the actors try to achieve the same nominal recipe, the eventual performance may diverge because the original stated objective (recipe) of one of the actors was not his actual position.

Nominal versus actual rules

Research on this topic is also made difficult because recorded, nominal rules may not be the ones that the parties actually play by (Kornai[4]). There is also the situation where one has a nominal right, but its use can be made expensive by the other party. For example, there may be a rule that makes agency files available to another agency or to the public. But, if that agency doesn't co-operate, it may be very costly to get the information in a useable form. The agency may require the user to exhaust all procedural appeals before making the data available, etc.

Opportunities versus will to use them

The model developed here emphasises the structure of the opportunities (and exposure) of an actor. It is beyond the scope of the present study, but, nevertheless, the issue of the will and attitude of the actor should be noted. The actor may have opportunities, but no inclination to use them. Some bureaucrats have no vision of what they want to make of the world. They simply desire the perquisites of their offices and ride with the tide and adapt to any outside demands sufficiently to maintain their position and office.

In one of the case studies to follow, we observe an elite-trained high civil servant who has a passionate interest in small farmers and the poor, while his fellows do not. It is certainly relevant in a total model of development project success to explore how the attitudes of the actors are formed. For initial inquiry, however, research can focus on what factors shape the opportunities of an actor, rather than what attitudes. Nevertheless, we shall keep in mind that the two are often interrelated.

Learning and recipe development

The model so far has assumed that each actor enters the bargaining process with a clear and specific recipe and output in mind. This obviously is not always the case. The objective may be only broadly stated, such as improved marketing or income for small farmers, but neither actor is yet committed to any particular recipe. Thus, the interaction of the parties at the outset may be not where one is trying to get the agreement of the other to a preconceived plan, but where each is developing his idea of what should be done and how. Although the processes by which an actor develops his preferences for a particular recipe and output are very important, such processes, as well as organisational arrangements to facilitate learning and goal creation, are beyond the scope of this study.

It should also be noted that the very complexity of the development process can prevent anyone from having a complete picture of the necessary recipe for a large-scale project. One implication is that, as additional ingredients become clear, the rules of the game are critical in determining control over unplanned and un-expected events.

Relation of farmers to agency

The model has focused on inter- and intra-agency relationships. This is far from the whole story. There are many independent factors that affect the ultimate success of a project. A prime one is the behaviour of farmers. All of the physical inputs may be available, but the farmer may reject them. Planners may have even worried about tenure and price policies but farmers still will not shift to the new crop or whatever. We are reminded of the resettlement scheme where all inputs were made available, but the poor urban people would not leave the city for the rural area. Farmer perceptions are critical. Inputs may be available and embedded in appropriate policies (at least in the minds of the planner), but the farmer's per-ception may be something else.

The relationship of bureaucrat to bureaucrat is more likely to be face to face, and a bargaining and semi-contractual model seems plausible. The agency's relationship to farmers is, however, much more indirect. The agency cannot be sure for some time whether its offers of goods and services will be accepted and what behaviour ensues. We recognise that institutions are symbols and that the organisational format itself affects farmer perception and attitude towards the material services offered. We believe that these agency–farmer relationships are important, but research can be divided firstly into how inter- and intra-agency relationships affect what is made available to farmers and, secondly, on what they in turn do with these inputs.

SOME IDEAL TYPES

In order to visualise how the elements of the model presented above might be applied, it might be useful to formulate some combinations of the model's com-ponents that one might expect to find. These will be divided into primarily external and internal transactions. It should be kept in mind that over time the structure can change and that any given agency may be related to one party via one structure and to still another party via a different structure.

External

1. *Separate agencies for different inputs:* A commonly found situation is where different agencies have a piece of the action. Each has some trading resources, a mission and control over some of the ingredients to a large recipe. The number of ingredients controlled by any one actor and the kind and mix of trading materials

available (opportunities to offer goods or deliver threats and bads) are variables within this overall structural type. There is no one designated as a co-ordinator (except perhaps nominally a chief executive who always has limited time and other resources to utilise). No one of the agencies has any special mission to develop or secure an overall concerted action, but some may try to play such a role. The parties try to accomplish bilateral trades and agreements.

2. *A co-ordinating forum:* The above structure can be supplemented by some procedures whereby there is some occasion for formal meetings and communication among the parties. Agencies may be housed in such a way that informal communication is difficult. If there is some way to meet periodically the agencies can discover any mutual objectives and things that A could change to help B without much cost to A or even with mutual gain. No change is made in who controls what resources or recipe ingredients and consensus is required for action. The case of Comilla, to be described below, has this character.

3. *The planning agency:* The above structures can be further supplemented by a planning agency whose mission is to present plans of inter-related actions to the separate agencies. The planners have no authority to order execution of their plans. They usually have no project operating resources of their own or resources to trade to other agencies to get their agreement. Nevertheless, information and integrated plans are a motivating force in public debate. The planners may vary in terms of their attempts to play an organising role and this depends on the relationship of the planners to others in government who do have bargaining resources. In any case, the planners can act as brokers and facilitate trades among the separate operating agencies.

It is a small step from the planning agency to a formal mission to co-ordinate other agencies. This is a popular reform suggestion whose actual impact depends more on the range of resources the co-ordinator has than on his nominal mission.

Internal

The dividing line between internal and external transactions cannot be sharp. The above or below types could be placed on either side of the line.

1. *Contracting:* Some agencies do not control a certain function or have the necessary skills. They do have monetary resources which can be used to directly hire services from others. This is nominally an external transaction. It is, however, regarded here as internal since, if there are alternative supplies, the buyer may bargain over price, but little over content. In other words, the buyer gets what he wants or he searches for another supplier. This is a qualitative difference in the ability of others to influence the character of the project. How it works in practice is an empirical question, however. It is a way of organising the exact mix of inputs wanted when a party commands the necessary budget, but where there may be internal constraints to the use of new employees. A common problem is the civil service rules which prevent certain practices. The ability to contract out can get

around these and also constitute a bargaining resource when an agency head is trying to get agreement from his subordinates.

Contracting can also secure an appearance of separation of responsibility. The person hired serves to isolate the buyer from the client group served and absorb some of the possible criticism of performance.

2. *Centralised:* The centralised agency has all of the recipe ingredients in one organisation with all parts linked in a hierarchical chain of command. Superiors at least have the nominal power to fire and affect the salaries of employees, among their other bargaining resources. An example would be combined research and extension functions under a single dean of a college of agriculture. This functional centralisation can be with reference to a single project or involve many activities.

(a) Special Project Agency

Some international grant and loan agencies who are involved in major projects such as irrigation or land settlement schemes prefer to have new, independent agencies who can control all of the necessary ingredients for the particular piece of geography involved. Of course, the words 'all ingredients' are still relative, because eventually everything is tied to everything else. An agency may have control over seeds, fertiliser, water and extension for a project area, but at some point the production enters a distribution system and is subject to world markets and policies. The special project agency may have exclusive rights to work in an area and exclude competitors. The Puebla–Rockefeller project is of this general type.

(b) Super Agency

If there are problems in fitting together ingredients in a particular project area from two departments, they can be consolidated into a new super agency with a single head. This differs from (a) above since more than one project and programme may also be involved in the super agency. This expands the trading materials available to the top decision-makers since material from project A can be used to secure the assent of others for project B. This is fine for supporters of B, but not for A who is exposed to this predatory action (and vice versa).

It should be kept in mind that large-scale organisations are usually formed of functional or geographical (or both) divisions. One might expect bargaining and negotiations among them and the power of the top executive is limited by the bargaining resources of subordinates.

WHO GETS TO DECIDE WHAT THE PROBLEM IS?

Most approaches to administrative and institutional structure assume some development plan or recipe and ask how can it be implemented. This is not an unreasonable question, but its answer depends on insight into how alternative institutional structures affect what recipe of development is chosen. One of the reasons it is difficult to achieve a given variety of co-operation among bureaucrats is that they represent different views of what the problem is. For example, each bureaucrat has certain habits, relationships with third party agencies and with clientele. If he/she changes activity there are costs which must be borne. Unless these costs can be offset, change will not be forthcoming. Different clientele have different problems. Any particular development scheme seldom helps all equally and may harm some. Few are interested in growth of GNP, but rather in their own individual net product.

Thus, all groups are seldom agreed on the optimum recipe for development. Different bureaucrats reflect the real conflicts among the public. When a bureaucrat does not co-operate with a certain development plan, it may be because the interest group he/she represents does not find it in their best interest. The research question then becomes one of predicting how institutional alternatives affect whose interests will dominate development activity. For example, what organisational structures give the most (or least) access to the money lenders, construction firms, large farmers, feed grain farmers, etc. By 'access' we mean, who has a good bargaining position.

The users of any information produced by this research may be varied. It might be used by someone who wishes to implement a particular plan. It might be used by someone who wishes to defeat or modify the same plan. Institutions are both means to an end and themselves are part of the system that chooses ends. We shall not talk of institutional or project failure in the abstract, but rather seek positive knowledge of the relationships between the rules and whose recipe prevails.

GENERALITIES VERSUS CONCEPTUAL HANDLES

Much of the work in development institutions has tried to identify the successful (by someone's definition) pattern and then to recommend its duplication in other countries. Much effort must have been expended around the world trying to create the same combination of agricultural research and extension as is found in the USA which is based on some kind of general prediction that similar results can be obtained. There is much discussion, for example, on whether the Comilla, Bangladesh, approach can be duplicated elsewhere.

We are open minded on this, but not hopeful of finding these types of general-isable propositions. A more modest objective is to try to develop a set of questions and concepts which can be used to get a handle on a variety of situations. Economists do not carry around in their heads a set of input mixes for each unique commodity and production situation. They do have a set of concepts which can organise inputs and outputs into useful relationships. Perhaps something similar is possible in the study of institutions.

The hypothesis is that there is something useful to be learned, for example, by studying the structure of inter-agency co-ordinating councils, whether they be in

Costa Rica or the USA. If nothing more, it will show that there is more than one way to skin a cat. Perhaps we can identify certain functional attributes which are related to performance, but for which there are a number of specific substitutes.

The utility of the above model can be suggested by application to an actual case. The first step in applying such an institutional model is to search for attempts by a development agency to implement its preferred recipe or plan. The next step is to discover the conflicts between the various agents that control different inputs to the plan. What costs are created for whom if the particular recipe is implemented? Another step is to inquire what resources were available to the initiating party which could be used to get the appropriate participation of others. Finally, what institutional rules affect the supply of resources available to the initiating party? Some indications of this can be suggested by an individual case but the ultimate test is to compare alternative institutions to see which ones most enhance the ability of a given actor to implement a plan or to indicate substitutes when a particular institutional form is unobtainable.

THE MODEL APPLIED

The following single case is only meant to be suggestive and provide illustration of model components such as type of trading material, mission boundaries, competition, and trading rules.

The Comilla project in what was formerly East Pakistan has three components: (1) the organisation of credit co-operatives; (2) organisation of local government and encouraging co-operation between local level representatives of the major national government departments; (3) training of personnel involved in the programmes mentioned above. These programmes require different degrees of co-ordination. The training function is relatively self-contained, requiring little input from other agencies (except to send the trainees). On the other hand, substantive development efforts require the integration of the services provided by different national agencies such as education, health, co-operatives, animal husbandry, fishery, and agricultural technical assistance. The timing and mix of these inputs from different sources has an impact on the speed and kind of development. For purposes of this inquiry programme item (2) above would be of most interest. However, the inquiry was not able to focus on this exclusively.

Interviews with the project director, Akhter Hameed Khan (personal interview, 29 January, 1974), were an open-ended exploration of how he was able to survive; *i.e.* what factors helped him when he had to bargain with others and persuade them to co-operate, but primarily to keep others off his back? He listed five major factors, as follows.

1. *Support of the President.* The President has indicated publicly that he supported the project and this was widely known. This meant that enemies of the project could not destroy it for fear of incurring the displeasure of the President.

This support was not sufficient to obtain specific action by other agencies since there is a limit to Presidential attention, but it did prevent interference by others. In sum, it appears that the degree of publicly voiced support for a project by top political figures is a relevant variable in the bargaining resources of a project manager.

2. *Prestige of support from outside authority figures.* Such groups as the Harvard Advisory team let it be known that they believed in the project. The team director visited the project quarterly. This support gave the project extra credibility and brought it to the notice of high level administration in the Capitol. This meant the attention of top administration could be had without going through lower levels. This does not necessarily mean they did what Khan wanted, but he could be assured of their attention.

3. *Financial resources.* Foreign aid was available for capital outlay (Academy buildings) and staff. This meant that new functions could be added without major re-allocation of existing budgets. It is hypothesised that the availability of financial resources from outside so that change does not threaten old budgets is an important bargaining factor for a new project.

4. *Power vacuum.* Khan purposely chose to work at the local level. At the district level many ambitious people were already competing and interest groups were focused there. This left an opening where a new programme could be quietly initiated. It also allowed a longer period of trial-and-error without the glare of publicity and the need for showing immediate results.

Also the role of the education institution was an advantage. It initially at least was seen as neutral and non-competitive with other established interests.

5. *Prestige of the director.* Khan was the status equal of all the civil service people he had to work with. He had their respect and attention. He was not regarded as a rival.

Khan cannot return to the new state of Bangladesh. He is going to work with a sister Academy in Pakistan. He was asked how the above factors will differ in the new situation and what can be substituted for them if any are absent.

1. He will not have the support of the President.

2–3. Foreign aid and prestige is no longer politically palatable in the same degree, so it is not a major bargaining asset.

4. There is less of a power vacuum at the local level, but there is the advantage of an ongoing organisation (of the Academy). It has some inertia and has established a claim to operate in the area.

5. The Pakistan civil service is young and not known to Khan. He will not be regarded as a harmless dreamer, but as a competitor.

6. Depth of conflict. The money lenders and large farmers are much more entrenched at the expense of small farmers.

7. Creation of new pressure groups. Khan says, 'the under-privileged must have their own separate organisation.' He implies a labour model and says management and labour cannot be put in a single organisation. This aspect needs further

probing. In Comilla, Khan played a role in creating a new political force. He did not take the prevailing power groups as given, but nurtured them. In effect he may have created his own political capital. He created experience in organisation and small farmer co-operation via co-ops. Once this experience is gained, however, it can be used for more political purposes.

Analysis of the above new situation does not give one confidence that Khan's new assignment will succeed in bringing major change to small farmers. The first six factors generally give him less bargaining power in getting the assent of others than he had in Comilla. Whether creation of new pressure groups or other trading material can substitute remains to be seen.

MODELS OF INTER-AGENCY AND AGENCY–CLIENT BARGAINING

The Comilla Academy itself was not primarily a provider of direct goods and services. It has a role in creating new institutional relationships between the agencies that did provide the substantive inputs. The prior situation provided for national government departments, each with its own line of authority to field officers. These field people had little contact with each other and were physically separated in their offices. The local people and their leaders related to each officer individually and came as petitioners and pleaders for service. The officers complained that they could get no co-operation from the local people—for example, bringing all cattle together at a central location to be immunised. The people complained that service was poor and not related to their priority needs.

This system changed with the institution of the Academy and the Basic Democracies programme. In the new system, the local officers had to make a formal report of activities to a local government council. The Academy was instrumental in getting all of the officers physically located together. Regular meetings of all officers were called and chaired by the Circle Officer (CO), a national government person responsible for local government operation. The CO had no direct jurisdiction over the other officers who reported to their own departments and had their own funds and promotion processes. He did have some funds to use in his own programme and, because of his general responsibilities, was in a position to try to exercise some overall leadership.

The major change, then, was that the various officers began to talk to each other and to local government leaders. No dramatic change in authority or jurisdictional boundaries was involved. However, new lines of communication did reveal new possibilities for mutually advantageous action; e.g. the animal husbandry officer could make it clear that he could not give innoculations unless the cows were assembled. The local government leaders knew, then, that if they helped with the assembly the job would get done. This made the officer look good in his report to his superior when more cows are vaccinated/month. In this case we are not talking about any major conflicts of interest. The officers want to vaccinate, the farmers want the vaccination and local leaders are able to organise farmers on a given day and place. Each has something to offer and all can gain by mutual accommodation if they just know of the opportunity.

The above example is representative of tremendous opportunities. There are many common interests and new organisational formats can discover them. However, alas, the world is not always without conflict. Some officers were pushing programmes that some in local government or other offices did not want. Here a particular officer did not want to get feedback from others. At times officers refused to attend the common meetings. Since the CO had no direct authority (and neither did local government), attendance could not be ordered. Other bargaining resources to encourage attendance and co-operation are not evident (at this point in the inquiry). Evidently, at the time of the revolution and creation of Bangladesh, the CO was evolving into a stronger figure. The role of the Academy in creating a public demand and support for this needs investigation.

The possibilities of discovering mutual beneficial trades and actions should not be underestimated. But, we should not expect new debating forums (co-ordinating councils, etc.) to overcome deep-seated conflicts and cause much change in existing power distributions. Important background information here is that the case study area is *relatively* homogeneous in terms of farm size. Also, the traditional money-lender class had departed earlier when the Hindus left when the predominantly Moslem state was partitioned from India. In essence, the conflicts here were not as deep-seated as in many areas. Where conflicts are large, it can be hypothesised that new programmes of development to help small farmers will not make much progress just by instituting new opportunities for communication. Change would require major new rights and bargaining resources for the small farmer interests.

Some agency officers felt threatened by the forum and would not attend the meetings called by the circle officer. No one could force them to attend or force agreement on action, even if they did attend. This leads some observers to suggest that a locally based co-ordinator be given authority over the other agencies, replacing their line ties to their parent agency in the Capitol (Hunter[3]). In terms of our model this changes the institutional *structure* from one of bargaining between equal, independent agencies to one of bargaining (and command) between a superior and a subordinate. But how does it change the actual *resources* available to the would-be co-ordinator? The organisation chart structure is a factor, but it does not tell us enough about what the co-ordinator's resources are that can be used to get assent of others. Just because the legislature or executive says that so and so can co-ordinate others does not automatically bring it about. Can the co-ordinator fire and control the salary of a recalcitrant animal husbandry or health officer? Will the President really ask the officer's department head to fire the officer or affect his promotion? What are the civil service personnel rules? Does the co-ordinator actually control a discretionary budget which can be allocated among the officers? Will the powerful local farmers opposed to new programmes be able to get the co-ordinator removed if he goes too far?

These same bargaining resource questions could have been asked within the old institutional structure. There are many would-be co-ordinators in spirit, if not in name. Several of the specific officers may have a developmental recipe of how the various officers should work together. What affects whether any one of them will be successful in achieving his recipe? What does any particular officer have at his disposal to get the assent of others?

There are *some* necessary links between structure and resources. With independent agencies there is no possibility of command (and firing) which may be a feature of a new co-ordinator office or integrated super-agency. But, even in the latter, this resource may be limited and insufficient if not combined with other kinds of resources of a 'carrot' nature. In many instances knowledge of *structure* alone will not reveal very much about effective bargaining *resources*.

It is important to search for substitutes in both structure and resources. Often it may be politically impossible to make a frontal attack on established agencies and create a new super-agency or formal co-ordinator that can survive. It may be possible, however, to more subtly add to the bargaining resources of one of the agencies whose concept of a recipe you agree with so that it can get more agreements from others.

In summary, a model has been presented which suggests how institutional factors affect the resources available to a given actor to implement a complex development plan or project. Where an actor lacks bargaining resources, he will have to modify the original recipe to accommodate the interest of others. If this is severe, the original performance objectives may not be met at all.

ACKNOWLEDGEMENTS

This paper is a portion of Midwestern Universities Consortium for International Activities subgrant, AID/csd-2958-8. The authors appreciate the helpful assistance of Richard Blue, Gary Wynia, Brian Coyer, Robert A. Solo, Warren Samuels and Robert Stevens.

REFERENCES

1. BLAU, P. M., *et al.* (1966). The structure of small bureaucracies, *American Sociological Review*, **31**, 179–92.
2. BOULDING, K. (1973). *The economy of love and fear*, Wadsworth, Belmont, California.
3. HUNTER, G. (1973). Agricultural Administration and Institutions. *Food Research Institute Studies in Agricultural Economics, Trade and Development*, 13, 233–51.
4. KORNAI, J. (1959). *Over-centralization in economic administration*, Oxford University Press, London.
5. NEUSTADT, R. E. (1960). *Presidential power*, John Wiley and Sons, New York.

6. PRYOR, F. L. (1973). *Property and industrial organization in communist and capitalist nations*, Indiana University Press, Bloomington and London.
7. RAPER, A. (1970). *Rural development in action*, Cornell University Press, Ithaca, New York.
8. SIMON, H., *et al.* (1956). *Public administration*, Knopf, New York.
9. TANNENBAUM, A. S. (ed.) (1968). *Control in organization*, McGraw-Hill, New York.
10. TUITE, M. *et al.* (1972). *Inter-organizational decision making*, Aldine, Chicago.

7
CITIZEN PARTICIPATION IN MICHIGAN
DISTRICT COURTS
Josef M. Broder

Introduction

For more than a decade, Michigan's local courts have been a subject of much public and legislative concern. As part of a nation-wide reorganization trend, Michigan's efforts to reorganize its local courts began with a 1963 constitutional convention which replaced the decentralized justice of the peace system with a centralized, consolidated and professionalized system of district courts, staffed by locally elected judges and financed primarily by local monies. Local court centralization legislation now pending would prohibit payments of local judicial supplemental salaries and transfer the functions of court financing from the local to the state level under a system of state-wide financing. A move toward abolition of competitive judicial elections in favor of judicial appointment has also been the subject of considerable public debate in Michigan and other states. This chapter summarizes the findings of a recent study[1] in which social indicators on court performance were constructed to measure how Michigan District Courts are performing under current methods of court financing and judicial compensation and selection, and what citizens can expect from a change to state-wide district court financing and district court judicial appointment. An attempt is made to examine implications these findings have for local participation in court policy formulation.

The relationship between local court reforms and citizen participation is not well documented. In adopting the centralized, consolidated and professionalized district courts, legislators relied primarily on court reform theory and reform models drafted by legal professionals and adopted in other states. Court reform in the face of conflicting interests as to "what courts should be doing" and "how much should the community pay for local courts" usually leaves some citizens worse off. The unforeseen consequences of previous local court refort in Michigan are instructive of the distributional consequences of governmental reorganization and our current state of ignorance on the impact of reforms on citizen participation.

166

This chapter summarizes the result of the study which first described how Michigan district courts were operating under current methods of judge election and court financing. This is accomplished by the formulation of court performance indicators describing the court's policy in cases involving driving under the influence of liquor (DUIL) and other traffic offenses, disorderly persons, simple larceny, shoplifting and marijuana possession also, an attempt was made to inform local residents of how much it was costing them to operate their courts as well as how much revenue was being generated.

The second objective of the study is to suggest the effect on court performance from changes in the method of judge selection and compensation and to explore the extent to which the mode of public participation changed through these reforms.

The allocation of court services was described within a marketing context as an administrative system of resource allocation. Not unlike decision makers in the private sector, it was hypothesized that judges respond to the preferences of citizens who create or have the potential for creating costs and benefits for them and their courts. Similar to producers behaving in response to the cost and benefit creating effects of price changes, the judge is thought to respond to the preferences of groups who can create costs and benefits to him by being instrumental in judge selection and court financing. Using this administrative behavioral model an attempt was made to resolve the following issues: (1) Are there differences among courts? (2) Do judges make a difference in affecting the content of the outputs produced by the court? (3) Whose preferences are being reflected in the services produced by the court? (4) Does the particular structural organization of the court have an impact on the content of the services produced by the court and on the ability for local groups to maintain access to court policy formulation.

Social Indicators of Court Performance

Early in the research, it was discovered that the types of trial court activities which were being monitored left much to be desired by decision-makers, contemplating alternative judicial candidates, court budgets or methods of judge selection and court financing. The initial conceptual problem in designing performance indicators address the question of "what do courts produce?" When viewed from the citizen/taxpayer perspective, courts produce a service which is not so much consumed as it is enjoyed or realized. As consumers of court services, citizens have an interest in the content or substance of court decisions (i.e., how the court is disposing of drunk drivers, shoplifters, etc.) and in the administrative costs of court operations (i.e., how much is it costing taxpayers to operate their trial courts). Not unlike other public agencies, trial courts must compete for alternative sources of financing which include revenue generating penalities and state and local contributions. In making allocative decisions, state and local funding units must weigh the cost and content of court services against the budgetary demands made by other public service agencies. To facilitate a better understanding of the cost and content of court activities, a distinction was made between **substantive court decisions** made from the bench (arraignments and dispositions) and **administrative court decisions** made by the judge as chief administrator of the court (expenditures, revenues and scheduling). In this research the concept used to describe administrative and substantive dimension of trial court activities is known as court **performance.**

Are There Differences Among Courts?

Availability of performance information is a prerequisite to citizen participation in public decisions. Selected court performance data indicate that courts differ with respect to the costs and benefits they create to defendants and local residents. The differences in the distribution of costs and benefits go beyond operating expenditures and revenues to include associated costs of using the court and perhaps most importantly, the substantive performance of the court or the manner in which the courts affect the distribution of opportunities among local residents. More specifically, this research found substantial differences in: fines and costs assessed to traffic offenders, average court operating expenditures-per-case, average net revenues-per-case generated by the court, and costs associated with using the courts. The performance indicators are as follows.

The **Ten Minor Moving Traffic Offense Average** represents the mean fine and cost assessed to first offenders charged with the ten most frequently committed minor moving traffic violations under the states uniform traffic code. These data were compiled from minor traffic fine and cost schedules used by limited jurisdiction trial courts for the acceptance of first-offender guilty pleas. The average fine level ranged from a high of $36 in one county to a low of $12 for another.

Average expenditures-per-case give one indication of how much it is costing to operate the court. These data were computed by dividing the total number of cases heard by the court (civil and criminal, traffic and non-traffic) into the totally locally funded court budget including amounts spent for magistrates and probation departments. When compared with total expenditures, average expenditures-per-case give a better indication of expenditures performance because of caseload differences across counties. Not included in these data are the costs of appeals from limited jurisdiction courts. Expenditures ranged from $6 per case to $137.

Average net revenues-per-case generated by the trial courts gives decision makers a measure of net revenue performance across courts as well as an indication of the size of the public subsidy required in the processing of cases. Net revenues-per-case were computed by subtracting average locally funded expenditures-per-case from average locally retained gross revenues-per-case. The inclusion of non-revenues-generating cases into the computation of this performance indicator results in some negative values. The implicit or explicit policy conclusion to be drawn from the level of net revenues-per-case is that courts differ in their attitudes as to how the cost of court operations should be shared. Negative values imply that the general taxpayer will contribute to court operating costs while positive values suggest that litigants bear these costs. Net revenues ranged from $27 to a minus $50.

Citizens in rural and sparsely settled areas of Michigan expressed dissatisfaction with the amount of costs associated with utilizing these centralized and consolidated trial courts.[2] The costs of locational and temporal accessibility were measured in the form of police waiting time in and travel time to and from court. Because of caseload differences and differences in the amount of police business brought before trial courts, police waiting time was expressed as a ratio of productive (time spent in trial, giving testimony signing complaints) to unproductive court time (time spent waiting for commencement of court trial). Similarly, police travel time was expressed as a ratio of time spent traveling to and from court to time spent in productive court activities.

This study did not ascertain the extent to which the mean and variances of these data differed from some desired level, rather these data are presented to give substance to citizen debates on court performance in traffic cases and to give decision-makers a point of reference from which to measure the impact of court reforms aimed at reducing sentencing disparities across courts.

Court performance in selected misdemeanors was also measured in this study. In disposing of DUIL, disorderly persons, simple larceny and possession of marijuana cases, courts differed with respect to their first offender policies, their repeat offender policies, the frequency and extent to which jail and probation were used, the average fine and costs assessed to select offenders, the uniformity or variance with which fines and costs were assessed and the extent to which plea bargaining took place.

If court performance data were available to citizens they could better ask themselves if their local court meets their own preferences. Citizen participation would be enhanced through public dialogue inquiring why one court performs differently from its neighbor. The policy philosophy of legislators, governors and mayors emerges from press accounts. Candidates for such offices run on their records and challengers indicate how their policies would differ. However, in the case of the judiciary there is no readily available record and in fact, judicial candidates are prohibited from advertising how they would dispose of certain types of cases (for example, whether they would use maximum fines for speeders and drunks). If data such as those reported here were readily available, voters could better match their preference to those of judicial candidates.

Differences among courts can be interpreted in two ways. From the **point of view of the offender,** there may be a preference to receive the same punishment for the same offense regardless of geographical location. From this view, the data in this study show that offenders receive different punishment in different courts and gives support to policies to consolidate administration to achieve great geographic uniformity. From the **view point of a local community,** the difference among courts may be interpreted as an expression of differences in majority preferences among communities. Just as some local governments prefer to spend more on roads and less on libraries than their neighbors, some prefer to try to reduce speeding by higher fines while other communities prefer a different environment and use their judicial resources in other ways.

The data on difference among courts is useful for choice of judicial candiates by voters and also to inform debate on whose preferences and point of view should count. But, these differences say little about the probable effect of court reform. Court reform might be expected to change the mode of citizen participation in judicial selection and the personalities who occupy judgeships. Observed differences among courts could be due to difference in cases presented for disposal rather than who is the judge. Thus, the next step in understanding the probable effects of judicial reform is to inquire whether judges make a difference in court performance when other variables are held constant.

Do Judges Make a Difference?

The outputs of the local legal system reflect decisions made by several participants ranging from the citizen who files a complaint to the corrections administrator who is engaged in rehabilitation. In addition to the lack of knowledge as to the differences in court performance, there seems to be a similar lack of knowledge as to which participants in the local legal system account for various performance differences. The judge, as a participant in the local legal system, was found to make a unique contribution to the outputs of the courts.

Since judges are thought to respond to a variety of behavioral incentives, demonstrating that the judge is in effect using his discretion required more than restating the existing statutes on the discretionary power of the judges. In other words, a distinction was made between capacity and desire to have a unique input into court policy. A re-examination was made of the often heard argument that cases in a particular jurisdiction would be diposed of in a similar fashion regardless of the judge, since the judge is merely applying the law in an objective fashion.

To test the extent to which judges had a unique input into the court's output, two alternative methodologies were used. One approach employed analysis of variance to test for fine and costs mean and variance differences across judges in multiple judge courts where other factors affecting court performance were held constant. A second approach involved regression discontinuity time series analysis which examined what happens to some court performance measure over time as the judgeship changes personnel. This approach is similar to binary variable techniques used by a price analyst to test for seasonal shifts in prices or quantity relationships.

By examining the behavior of judges in multi-judge courts where cases are randomly assigned to judges, it was found that judges exposed to similar community, administrative, economic and legal influences differed significantly in some of their substantive decisions, both in the level of fines and costs assessed to persons originally charged with drunk driving, disorderly persons, simple larceny and possession of marijuana and in the variation with which these fines and costs were assessed.

Some weak evidence of the judge making a unique contribution to the performance of the court was found by examining policy changes associated with the arrival of a new judge with regression discontinuity time series analysis. The study found that incoming judges may have, in the past, changed the court's policy toward specific types of offenses and that such substantive policy changes tended to take place in single judge courts. Such policy changes were confirmed in conversations with judges and court personnel. Since the majority of the courts in rural Michigan are of the single judge type, the propensity of rural judges to alter court performance upon entering office has important policy implications for rural residents' ability to influence court policy. As a mode for public participation, voting in the non-partisan judicial election in rural areas becomes more than just staffing the court with a passive functionary.

Despite the active role which rural judges may have taken in altering the court's policies upon taking office, the electorate is left uninformed of the alternative policies available to them at judicial elections.

The above evidence suggests that who occupies the judgeship does make a difference for court performance. If judges make a difference, then the institutional rules for judge selection and court finance may affect court performance and the ability of various groups to hold courts accountable for their performance.

Court Performance Model

In addition to describing the state of the judiciary and documenting a point of reference from which the effects of future reforms can be measured, these administrative and substantive court performance data were compiled for purposes of predicting the impact of reforms altering the manner in which judges are selected and courts financed on the ability for citizens to maintain local inputs into court policies. Under current arrangements, Michigan's limited jurisdiction trial court judges are elected locally, except in instances of interim vacancies, at which time the governor appoints a judge who must subsequently stand for re-election. A distinction was made between judges who initially entered office through election and judges who initially entered office through appointment. This distinction between initially appointed and elected judges was incorporated as an institutional factor into a model designed to explain differences in administrative performance and to predict probable consequences from a system of appointed judges. The locally funded salary paid to the judge as a supplement to the fixed, uniform state funded salary was included as a second institutional factor in the model to test the relationship between local funding and administrative performance and to predict some probable consequences of state-wide financing.

In order to test for the effect of institutional alternatives, the effects of non-institutional variables which might affect performance must be controlled. These include community sociological, criminal population, and economic variables.

Institutional: Methods of judge selection and court financing serve as an expression of the relationship between the judge and groups associated with the court or the mode of public participation available to citizens. It was hypothesized that altering the methods of judge selection and court financing, in effect alters the mode of public participation through changes in the size and content of the political boundaires of individuals who have an input into judge selection and court financing. To the extent that preferences across groups are heterogeneous, differences in court performance are related to differences in preferences of groups with access to the court policy making process. Groups who form a state-wide majority to influence gubernatorial appointments may differ from the majority of the local electorate.

Community Sociological: Court policies are made in the context of values associated with the larger community. The sociological nature of the community, as measured by political party affiliation, religious preference, wealth and rurality is thought to have conscious effects on the judge's habits, attitudes and beliefs to the extent that he was socialized in the community or to the extent that the judge feels a sense of obligation to majority preferences in the community.

Criminal Population: Since communities differ in criminal populations, court performance is thought to be affected by the court's efforts to deal with different crime rates, crimes, and consequences of criminal activities. Included in this set of variables are defendant attitudes and behavior in contesting charges brought against them in addition to the mix of cases brought to court (civil and criminal; traffice and non-traffic).

Economic: the court's administrative performance is thought to be affected by various economic and management factors associated with the court. Included in these sets of factors are court size, court location; the extent to which the court utilizes the services of specialized functionaires (court administrators, magistrates, and traffic bureaus) and measures of court congestion as reflected by police waiting time.

Substantive Performance: The courts ability to offset all or part of their operating costs by revenue generating penalties creates an interdependence between decisions of legal substance and administrative performance. Included in these substantive performance variables are the level and mix of revenue generating penalties (fines and costs) and non-revenue generating penalties (jail and probation).

Multiple regression was used to measure the extent to which differences in performance across courts were explained by combinations of the above explanatory variables. Within the context of the general model, the search for the "best" set of explanatory variables was faciliated with automatic search procedures generally using the conventional 90% level of significance as the criteria for eliminating non related explanatory variables. In addition to estimating the degree of association between a dependent administrative performance variable and some combination of independent or explanatory variables, multiple regression analysis was employed to make statements (test hypotheses) about the significance, direction and

magnitude of the relationship between the dependent performance variable
and specific explanatory variables when the remaining explanatory variables are held constant. The results are not conclusive but rather they are
intended to be first approximations and to raise questions for further
research. Some specific questions addressed in the multiple regression
analysis were:

1. What can local residents expect from a system of judges appointed
    by the Governor?
2. Does the local judicial supplemental salary serve as a mechanism for
    local input into the courts' substantive and administrative policies?

In the process of resolving what local residents can expect from proposed
reforms which would alter the manner in which judges are selected and
courts financed, some additional questions were raised and entertained by
this research.

3. To what extent are economies of scale present in Michigan's district
    court system?
4. What is the relationship between administrative considerations
    associated with court operating expenditures and substantive per-
    formance with respect to the court's fine and cost policies?
5. Do local crime rates have any bearing on the types of penalities
    handed down by the court?
6. What factors account for differences in the uniformity which exists
    within courts?
7. To what extent can the court's fine and cost policy be manipulated
    to alter the court's revenue performance?
8. To what extent do associated costs of going to court affect the court's
    expenditure and revenue performance?

Probable Effects of Court Reform

Several findings of particular relevance to local residents were inferred
from relationships within these equations. In terms of court substantive
decisions, courts with appointed judges were found to be more lenient in
assessing fines and costs to offenders of minor moving traffice violations
and appointed judges per se were found to be more lenient in possession of
marijuana cases. Courts with appointed judges required fewer expenditures-per-case, although when considering both expenditures and gross
revenues, these courts generated lower average net revenues-per-case than
courts with elected judges. If the relationships which existed in 1975

remain in the future, the policy implication of these findings is that under a system of appointed judges, courts will tend to be operated with lower average expenditures-per-case, offenders of traffic and marijuana violations can expect lower fines and costs and the taxpayer may have to share a larger burden of the costs of operating the courts.

No difference with respect to fine and costs variation was found between judges who entered office initially through election and judges who entered office initially through appointment. For those groups desiring greater uniformity within courts, it appears doubtful that a move toward state-wide appointment of judges will accomplish these desires.

Evidence was found that the local judicial supplemental salary tends to be related to average court operating expenditures-per-case, average net revenues-per-case generated by the court and the extent to which judges vary fines and costs in selected misdemeanor cases. Courts with larger local judicial supplements required fewer average expenditures-per-case and created less of a burden on taxpayers through the amount of average net revenues-per-case generated to the local funding unit. The positive relationship between the amount of the local supplement and fine costs variation suggests that the local supplement may have served as an incentive for the judge to use more discrimination in disposing of selected misdemeanors or that the local supplements served to attract judges which used greater discrimination in disposing of these cases.

To the extent that the local judicial supplement and local court financing facilitate interaction between the judge and members of the local funding unit, it is believed that the relationships between local funding and court performance gives evidence of the local units' ability to have an input into the operations of the court in their area. For whatever narrowly defined cost redistributions which will be forthcoming from a system of the statewide court financing, the relationships between the source of the funding and court performance suggests that local influence into the operations of the court will be decreased by measures which would remove the court financing function from the local government.

In much of the court reorganization literature there is a general belief that expanding the size of the court through centralization and consolidation, saves the taxpayers money because of economies of scale believed to be associated with local courts. Some evidence suggesting that diseconomies rather than economies of scale exist in Michigan's district court system was found by testing the direction of the relationship between average locally funded expenditures-per-case and caseload. In light of nationwide trends to centralize and consolidate local courts, doubts are raised whether such reforms can be justified on the basis of reducing average operating expenditures-per-case.

Any discussion relating court size with average expenditures-per-unit of output begs the question of how are court outputs to be defined. Size and expenditures-per-unit of output comparisons are valid only to the extent that the content of the output in question remains constant throughout production levels. Evidence found by this research suggests that the content of court outputs changes with court size. More specifically, the size of court as expressed in the number of judges on the court and the number of cases heard by each judge was related to the variation in fines and costs assessed in selected misdemeanor cases. It was hypothesized that court size and the number of cases heard per judge affected the court's ability or willingness to use unique judgements in assessing fines and costs in each case. In large multiple judge courts, with fewer percentages of cases going to trial and large numbers of cases per judge, there was a tendency to assess more uniform fines and costs.

The relationship between the court's fine and costs policies and average court operating expenditure levels suggests that courts are not immune to the economic forces which confront decision makers in the private sector. Courts requiring high average expenditures-per-case tend to assess higher levels of fines and costs, suggesting that fine and costs the defendant received were among other considerations, related to the average amount of resources required to dispose of a case. To the extent that courts take expenditure requirements into consideration in their fine and costs policies, court reform measures designed to achieve greater uniformity in fines and costs across courts must deal with differences in court expenditure performance. Greater fine and costs uniformity across courts in the face of differences in expenditures-per-case requirements would alter incidence of burden as to who pays for the operations of the court. Greater uniformity in fines and costs paid by defendants would result in less uniformity in the jurisdiction's policies as to the ratio of the taxpayers to the defendant's contribution to court operating expenditures. Freedom on the part of the defendants to receive the same fine and costs regardless of where the crime is committed means a loss of freedom on the part of the local community in deciding how the court operating expenditure burden will be shared.

Courts are often criticized for being too lenient on criminals relative to other participants in the local legal system. While the assessment of each participant's contribution to the local legal system was beyond the scope of this research, a general statement can be made regarding the court's awareness and responsiveness to local crime rates. Courts were found to be responsive to local crime rates as evidenced by courts in jurisdictions with higher crime rates having assessed higher fines and costs.

There is evidence that increasing costs to stricter law enforcement may have taken place in courts which assessed high fine costs. The negative relationship found to exist between average net revenues-per-case, and the average fine and costs assessed in moving traffic cases, suggests that higher fines and costs may be more costly to assess because of the greater incidence of defendants' contesting their cases at higher fine and costs levels. To the extent that this relationship is an accurate description of what is taking place in the courts, the taxpayer is faced with the tradeoff between bearing some of the costs of operating the court and having laws strictly enforced.

Median family income of the jurisdiction was also found to be related to average fines and costs assessed in moving traffic cases such that courts in poor communities tended to assess higher fines and costs. While this does not preclude the possibility that judges take "ability to pay" into account when assessing fines and costs on an individual case basis, the traffic fine and costs schedules across courts in general did not appear to be established with the community's "ability to pay" in mind.

From a court financing standpoint, the negative relationship between traffic fines and costs and average net revenues-per-case raises the question of to what extent will an increase in fine and costs levels increase court revenues. Evidence suggests that increases in fine and costs were associated with reductions in average net revenues-per-case. It appears to be costing the court proportionately more to assess and collect higher fines and costs. Attempts by courts to alter net revenue performance through changes in fine and costs levels must take into account the consequences which these changes have on defendent pleading behavior and the crime rate.

Related to evidence of diseconomies of scale in Michigan's local court system is the impact which police waiting time has on the court's revenue performance. It was found that courts with large relative amounts of Michigan State Police waiting time also generated poor net revenue performance records. While the reasons for police waiting time were not fully explored in this research, informal observation suggests that police waiting time is an indication of court congestion due to inadequate court staffing and court facilities. From the standpoint of the entire local legal system, decision makers should weigh losses in revenues attributable to court congestion resulting from police waiting cost and other associated costs of utilizing the court against the costs of adding court personnel, expanding of physical court facilities or other measures designed to reduce congestion.

Conclusion

This research has been an attempt to raise the level of understanding about the operations of local courts. Not only do courts differ with respect to their substantive and administrative decisions, but judges make significant contributions to differences between courts. For local and non-local residents, this means that the kind of justice delivered by the local court depends to a certain extent upon the judge. While there is much about the judge's behavior which is not known, evidence suggests that the institutions which surround the judge's office affect the type of judge which gets into office the decisions made by the judge while in office and the mode of citizen participation in court policies. Court reforms which would alter the manner in which judges are selected and courts financed should take into consideration the effects which the interaction between the judge, local residents and local governing units have on whose preferences are taken into account in the court's production function.

While in several categories of offenses, the property rights inherent in the method of judge selection and finance make a difference for performance and who counts, other categories show no such effects. This is not surprising since the rules may represent more of a potential capacity for preference articulation than is actually being utilized. This is because of the fact of high information costs to citizens in comparing actual or future court performance to their preferences. Where performance indicators are not readily available to the public, which is the case with the judiciary, citizens are choosing in the dark. At the current time, data on administrative performance is more readily available than the outcome of cases. This perhaps explains why there is a stronger relationship between institutional alternatives and administrative performance than for the substantive outcome of judicial decisions.

Footnotes

[1]Josef M. Broder, *The Provision of Court Services - An Inquiry Into the Allocation of Opportunities to Rural Communities.* East Lansing: Department of Agricultural Economics, Michigan State University, Unpublished Ph.D. Dissertation, 1977. This reference contains all of the statistical detail summarized in this chapter.

[2]Josef M. Broder, *Selected Impacts of Michigan's 1969 Lower Court Reorganization on Rural Citizens,* Unpublished Masters Thesis, 1973, Department of Agricultural Economics, Michigan State University, East Lansing, Michigan.

8
MEDICAL COST CONTAINMENT: AN EMPIRICAL APPLICATION OF NEO-INSTITUTIONAL ECONOMIC THEORY

A. Allan Schmid and Ronald C. Faas

One of the governmental responses to the rapid rise in health care costs was a 1970 amendment to the Public Health Services Act (P.L. 91-515). It was observed that part of the cost increase was associated with some degree of over-investment in medical facilities and equipment. For some given geographical region there was an excess of beds per population unit, and expensive equipment was duplicated, leading to higher than necessary per user cost.

The usual policy suggestion from neo-classical economics for over-investment is to induce competition in the market for medical services. But this prescription is blocked by a feature of medical service which violates one of the preconditions for the usual claimed benefits of the competitive market. Product information costs to the consumer are high. It is hard for the patient to determine need. This means that the consumer does not fully determine the quantity and quality to be purchased, but instead relies on health professionals to make the decision. It has long been observed that doctors are both suppliers and demanders. This applies not only to their labor services but also to decisions on facilities and equipment made by hospitals which are heavily influenced by doctors. Doctors and other health care providers had the opportunity to influence the demand for their services and create a supply whose costs could be passed on to users who had little power to reject it.

Earlier legislation had required regional (multi-county) agencies to review all proposals for health capital investments. When this did little to slow cost increases and

Michigan Agricultural Experiment Station Journal Article # 9330.

179

facility expansion, it was hypothesized that investment planning was controlled by providers, so it was formally mandated in 1970 that a majority of the governing boards of these Comprehensive Health Planning agencies (CHP) must be consumers. It was predicted that if consumers made the decisions, over-investment would be reduced.

It is the function of theory to suggest instrumental policy variables and predict how they might affect performance. Two main sets of variables are identified by neo-classical theory. One has to do with variables related to the degree of competition and the other with factor ownership. Where market competition is inapplicable that leaves the alteration of factor ownership to try to affect performance. Usually this takes the form of changing the distribution of land or stock ownership. In the case of public or not-for-profit firms, it takes the form of how boards of directors are determined. The attempt to prevent rising medical costs via mandatory consumer dominance of planning agencies is in the neo-classical tradition of focusing on factor ownership.

The purpose of this paper is to supplement neo-classical theory with that of institutional economics and to test hypotheses derived from that theory using public health planning as an illustration. The data are obtained from the records of Comprehensive Health Planning agencies in Michigan in 1974 and 1975. For details, see Faas (1977).

Institutional Economic Theory

The Congress seemed to assume that nominal ownership is the same as control and participation in decision making. But a classical theme in institutional economic theory, since the path-breaking work of Veblen and later Berle and Means (1968), is that control may be separated from ownership. Applying this insight to health planning suggests that specifying nominal membership (ownership) is not enough. Complex organizations provide an opportunity for actions to be taken which are not consistent with the preferences of the nominal owners or those at the top of the hierarchy.

One of the reasons for this divergence is information and contractual cost. The central board can't make all decisions and process all information. When some of its decision power is delegated, it can lose some control. This is why institutional scholars give attention to the internal organization of firms and their operating procedures. Thus, internal procedures constitute property rights affecting the opportunity sets of the participants just as much as nominal membership (ownership). Yet, the procedures are not mandated by law.

It is expected that the governing board will assign some information processing to committees who will make project approval recommendations to the board. It might be further hypothesized that if the project review committee has the same consumer dominance as the board, it would make decisions consistent with consumer interests.

All of the Michigan CHPs followed the law's mandate and a majority of the members of the governing board were consumers. These boards all established project review committees who made recommendations to the board. The law is silent on membership and procedures for the review committee. In fact, 12 of the 17 review committees had a provider membership majority.

Neo-Institutional Theory

Why do consumer-dominated boards appoint provider-dominated review committees? To explore this behavior requires an examination of modern institutional economics. An important component of neo-institutional theories is a focus on various product characteristics which create human interdependence and the opportunity for one person's actions to affect another. Institutional policy alternatives then shape and direct this interdependence by giving opportunities to some parties and denying them to others. One of the important product features is related to transaction costs, especially those related to access to information. Another is the cost of excluding anyone from product benefits. For a detailed exposition of this theory, see Schmid (1978).

What incentives does a consumer member of a CHP board have for vigorously pursuing cost containment efforts? To be well informed on technically complex health investments requires much effort. The board members wholly bear these costs but receive only a minute fraction of any cost-saving benefits if and when they become patients. The general public is a free rider on any cost reduction benefits and pays none of the high transaction costs borne by board members. On the other hand, the provider members have a great deal to gain individually if large facility investments are made. The provider members are paid to represent provider interests. Going to meetings and reading supporting material is part of their everyday job, while it is not for consumer members.

This difference in incentives could cause consumer-dominated boards to let providers have more members on project review committees. This hypothesis is not directly tested here, but is consistent with the observation that providers have a majority of review committee membership.

Further attention to the project review committee seems warranted by the fact that their recommendations are seldom overturned by the board (less than 3 percent).

Institutional theory with its interest in transaction costs does lead to other testable hypotheses. Something as ordinary as travel costs to attend meetings takes on great significance. Again, membership is one thing, actual participation is another. If provider members are more likely to attend than consumer members, the influence of consumers is potentially further eroded. As already noted, the provider members are likely to have travel and attendance costs covered as part of their job. It is hypothesized that provider members will have a higher attendance than consumers and that provider share of attendance will increase with distance traveled to meetings. In fact, actual attendance as a percentage of membership was less for consumers than provider regardless of location. It is expected that members from core counties where the meeting is held will have higher attendance than those from counties adjacent to the county where the meeting is held and from still more distant non-adjacent counties. The overall result in Michigan was that the provider share of total committee attendance increased from 56 percent in core counties to 64 percent in adjacent and 72 percent in non-adjacent counties.

The data suggest that there are some nitty-gritty standard operating procedures which become important property rights affecting the opportunities of conflicting parties. The size of the region affects travel costs as does the location of the meetings. If the meeting place were rotated, it would remove the systematic advantage of providers located in the most populous urban centers. While a great deal of political debate has focused on mandating consumer membership on the board, it turns out that what might appear as minor details of committee membership, region size and meeting location can affect actual participation in decisions.

Is there any way to structure opportunities and incentives via property rights to offset the high transaction costs faced by consumer representatives relative to the benefits they can capture? One can imagine the consumer member who is heroic and is committed to the cause regardless of individual cost-benefit relationships. Reinforcement from the general public will be slight since they are not likely to notice the heroic effort. To the contrary, those consumers who follow the providers' suggestions are likely to be applauded along the way by people who have prestige because of their professional positions. This suggests that consumer members will tend to be captured by the providers.

One institutional response to the above dilemma of cost-benefit disparity is the professional political entrepreneur. The politician can afford to invest in information and other transaction costs to obtain political office rather than merely a share of the lower health care costs. This suggests that if a limit to health investments is to be imposed, it must be done by the regular political system and not by volunteer citizens. The politician can afford to make an issue of health care cost and support state agencies in setting some overall budget constraints. This can take the form of setting a limit on the number of hospital beds that can be built in a region.

The health planning laws provide for such a procedure. The State of Michigan sets a limit on the number of hospital and nursing home beds for each health planning region. The impact of this "budget constraint" can be determined from the data. The bane of empirical institutional research is the passage of uniform laws which allow for no institutional variation to be observed. Fortunately, the "budget constraint" applies to investments in bed capacity, but not to other equipment purchases. It is hypothesized that projects subject to a state-mandated budget constraint will be subject to more rigorous review by the regional CHPs than non-constrained projects. Review committees recommended approval of 44 percent of the 113 projects subject to budget constraint, but 89 percent of projects not so subject. If consumer dominance of board membership is the key instrumental variable in expanding consumer control of health costs, then this difference in performance should not occur. But, the fact is that simply mandating consumer membership (factor ownership) is not enough.

Some further insight with the above results is afforded by institutional theory. Randall Bartlett (1973) argues that decision making is surrounded by different degrees of uncertainty and information cost. Decision makers must balance the costs of making an incorrect decision by not being informed and the costs of acquiring information. This means less than complete information is often the rational level to secure. Thus interest groups can influence public decision makers by subsidizing information favorable to that group's interest. This changes the relative prices of different types of information faced by decision makers (p. 27).

In the project review process, the provider applicant has an interest in subsidizing information favorable to the applicant's project. Damaging information must be supplied by someone else. If projects are reviewed serially one by one, each applicant puts forward the best picture possible and other providers remain silent. It is up to the board to obtain other information. If consumers knew what questions to ask, they might get their professional staff to supply this information. Even so it would be costly. An alternative source of information on applicant A's project is applicant B. But B has no incentive to question A's data if the projects are not competing. This competition can be created if the board collects a number of applications and considers them together. If there is a budget (bed) constraint, the board is more likely to consider projects in batches. This, in fact, is confirmed by the data. It is hypothesized that information will be provided to a greater degree by applicants as a group when projects are considered together. This hypothesis could not be tested directly. But its effect on project action can be partially tested. Projects subject to a budget constraint and considered with reference to a similar project received the lowest percentage of endorsement and the greatest reduction in dollars approved relative to dollars requested (cost containment coefficient). Projects subject to budget constraint but not considered in a group were subject to less rigorous review. But both of these categories were more rigorously reviewed than projects subject to no constraint. Competition among suppliers is an important institutional variable as it influences the availability of information to public decision makers (buyers).

An ideal empirical test would be provided if the performance of alternative institutions (property rights and rules) could be compared in terms of actual medical costs to users. It is difficult to utilize time series data when other cost-affecting variables are present and can't be experimentally or statistically controlled. This leaves us with having to utilize proxies which seem plausibly to move in the same direction as actual costs. In this study we used measures of interest group participation in decisions. We are aware that just being present when a decision is made does not assure control, but it does seem like a useful starting place. Likewise, the measure of percentage of projects approved and the ratio of dollars approved to dollars requested is not ideal. Over time applicants may learn to play the "ask for more than you need" game commonly played by public agencies in budget requests, though this may be less prevalent in newly instituted investment control bodies.

Conclusions

Institutional theory has come a long way even if actual policy has not yet caught up. Policy in the health planning field (and many others) is still mired in the simplistic belief that nominal ownership (in this case membership on decision bodies) is the instrument of power allocation among conflicting groups. But institutional theory suggests that we look elsewhere to find the property rights which effectively control the many sources of human interdependence among which transaction costs (particularly information costs) are particularly important in this case. While it is considerably less amenable to simplistic slogans, the empirical evidence points to a number of internal procedure rules which affect the incentives of the various actors and the costs of participation that they face.

References

Bartlett, Randall. 1973. Economic Foundations of Political Power. New York: The Free Press.

Berle, Adolf A., Jr. and Gardiner C. Means. 1968. The Modern Corporation and Private Property.

Faas, Ronald C. 1977. Decision Making in Project Review: Processes, Participation and Performance in Michigan Multi-County Comprehensive Health Planning. East Lansing: Michigan State University, Agricultural Economics Report No. 328.

Schmid, A. Allan. 1978. Property, Power and Public Choice. New York: Praeger.

9

COMMENTARY: AN ECONOMIC PERSPECTIVE ON THE COMPENSATION PROBLEM
Warren J. Samuels

The legal profession customarily approaches the problem of determining whether to compensate private persons for loss or injury sustained through change from a perspective which is essentially normative. The relevant literature is directed largely toward the quest for principles, rules, or tests,[1] and within each proffered solution is a set of judgments as to the propriety of compensation.[2] The purpose of this Article is not normative, although it may suggest a different view of compensation policies. Rather, this Article is intended to be a theoretical exploration into the nature and scope of the compensation problem. It is premised on the belief that a full understanding of the problem requires a return to the fundamentals of law and economics. The compensation problem arises from nonlegal, or market, changes as well as from legal changes.[3] Because it involves redistribution of wealth and economic opportunity, it is an important part of the management of social change and has inherent potential for influencing the course of future social change. Conceptually, however,

The author is indebted to Allan Schmid, Victor Goldberg, Warren Gramm, Richard LaBarge, A. Wayne Lacy, Todd Lowry, Mark Perlman, Alan Randall, Paul Craig Roberts, Howard Sherman and Robert Solo for comments in various forms on an earlier draft of this paper; to Victor Goldberg's manuscript, "The Peculiar Normative Economics of a Public Choice-Property Rights Intersection" and Alan Randall's manuscript, "Information, Power and Academic Responsibility"; and to the members of my seminars on Political Economy: Institutions and Theory (Winter, 1973) and Law and Economics (Summer, 1974).

1. Most recent discussion has centered on Michelman, *Property, Utility, and Fairness: Comments on the Ethical Foundations of "Just Compensation Law,"* 80 HARV. L. REV. 1165 (1967); Sax, *Takings, Private Property and Public Rights,* 81 YALE L.J. 149 (1971); Sax, *Takings and the Police Power,* 74 YALE L.J. 36 (1964).

2. The task is, indeed, invaluable. That this article adopts a different perspective should not be taken as disparagement of the normative approach.

3. Legal change is defined here as change in common, statutory, administrative, or constitutional law. Nonlegal change is defined as change in market conditions, *e.g.,* changes in technology or in the price structure, and includes changes in the behavior of economic actors.

the compensation problem involves much more than intentional redistribution. The argument of this Article is: (1) That the compensation problem is ubiquitous; (2) that uncompensated takings are inevitable; (3) that, for purposes of compensation, there is no analytically significant distinction between legally and nonlegally imposed changes; and (4) that analytically equivalent situations inevitably require different normative treatment.

The value system primarily responsible for definition of the compensation problem was John Locke's ideal of government and law as protectors of property rights. In the Lockean context, the purpose of compensation is to protect the ownership, enjoyment, and status quo economic value of those property rights. The Lockean view is attractive, but also problematical because it biases legal rights to compensation in favor of past uses and users.[4] A more important problem is that the Lockean approach is not and cannot be descriptive of reality, even in a society founded in the Lockean tradition, and therefore realization of the Lockean ideal is impossible. Reality dictates a high degree of selectivity in the application of Lockean principles. That is to say, although the payment of compensation for loss or injury due to change is highly sanctioned in both law and economics, the pervasiveness of legal and nonlegal change presents an inevitable necessity of choice: many "takings" must remain uncompensated. Perhaps it will come as no surprise that full compensation is impossible, but it may be surprising to see how selective the process actually is. Of primary importance, then, are the factors governing when compensation will be required, but discussion of them is beyond the scope of this article. The purpose here is to identify the character of the compensation problem.

Part I presents a descriptive survey of the scope of the compensation problem. Part II examines an economic theory of the compensation problem: the theory of rights and opportunity sets. Part III discusses the legal resolution of the compensation problem. An attempt is made throughout to generalize and broaden the conceptual perspective and to break away from the closely analyzed lines of specific problem-oriented case law.

---

4. *See* Michelman, *supra* note 1, at 1203-05.

I. Scope of the Compensation Problem

In 1919, at the annual meeting of the American Economic Association, Thomas Nixon Carver, an eminent Harvard economist of deeply conservative persuasion, engaged in a discussion with Harry Gunnison Brown, a lifelong exponent of Henry George's single tax. The discussion concerned a paper by Carver which proposed striving for a "balanced industrial system" through effective education—what today probably would be called manpower retraining or general manpower policies. In Carver's view, such an educational system would provide for sounder economic growth and wider diffusion of wealth and economic or industrial power.[5] Brown argued that Carver's scheme was vulnerable to the same criticism conservatives had levied against the concept of a tax on unearned increments in land value, namely, that it would confiscate vested rights, destroy existing values, and change the rules of the game while the game was in progress.[6] Under Carver's plan, the income of individuals who had entered high-income occupations because of the prospect of continued superior incomes would decrease because of the increased supply of workers generated by manpower retraining. Carver's manpower policies would visit economic injury or loss upon certain groups as an effect of deliberate government action no less than George's single tax. "If vested rights is a good enough argument in the latter case—and it is the argument which usually counts most, whatever else may be said against the proposal—it should be a good enough argument in the former case," wrote Brown, "and it should be a good enough argument for conservative economists to use against any proposed reform which seems likely to cause loss or decreased income to any group of persons."[7]

Manpower retraining and a tax on unrealized unearned increments in land value are, in other words, analytically equivalent

---

5. Carver, *Some Probable Results of a Balanced Industrial System*, in Papers & Proceedings of the 32d Annual Meeting of the Am. Econ. Ass'n 69 (Am. Econ. Rev. Supp. March, 1920).

6. Brown, *A Balanced Industrial System—Discussion*, in Papers & Proceedings of the 32d Annual Meeting of the Am. Econ. Ass'n 81 (Am. Econ. Rev. Supp. March, 1920).

7. *Id.* 84. For a similar and extended critique see Hale, *Coercion and Distribution in a Supposedly Non-Coercive State*, 38 Pol. Sci. Q. 470 (1923), discussing T.N. Carver, Principles of National Economy (1921).

in their effects. The two may be treated differently only by selective adherence to the Lockean principle.

Consider, also, the following examples of unquestionable economic loss sustained as a direct or proximate consequence of legal action: the imposition of a tariff, which effectively transfers real income from consumers to producers (or, conversely, the lowering of a tariff, which effectively transfers real income from producers to consumers); labor relations legislation and protective labor legislation, which change the relative market power of employees and employers and of union and nonunion employees; urban renewal projects, which may cause wholesale reshuffling of social and economic opportunities and values; anti-inflation policies, which may produce unemployment; anti-unemployment policies, which may produce adverse inflationary effects on the recipients of fixed incomes; changes in Federal Reserve monetary policies, which rearrange opportunities of borrowers and lenders; the legal recognition of amenity rights, which constrain the rights of factory owners, managers, and employees; legislation restricting highway advertising, which reduces or alters the economic opportunities of certain landowners, the billboard industry, and certain workers; consumer protection statutes; changes in the legal standards governing class action suits; changes in product liability law; statutes and ordinances changing landlord-tenant relations; changes in common law remedies for nuisance, trespass, and so on; rezoning from high density to low density, or *vice versa*; changes in the law of copyright, *e.g.*, governing royalties payable for large-scale photocopying or faculty-university rights to instructional materials at state universities; failure to recognize, in appropriate proceedings, condemnation blight, injurious affection, interim depreciation, highway noise damage, access loss, and lost economic rent; changes in the rights to use public resources such as parks; regulations banning fishing privileges with gill nets; and forced destruction of pesticide-contaminated chickens.

In some instances, compensation is paid, while in others, compensation is not even seriously considered. All of these cases, however, have analytically equivalent effects: economic damage, loss, or injury. It is only because the losses are selectively perceived or evaluated that they are treated differently. It may be objected that in some instances the losers do not have compensable rights. But this objection is self-serving: as will be seen below, part of the compensation problem is that some losers are not treated as having rights. Whatever one thinks of the normative rules used to justify differences in treatment, the fact remains that analytically equivalent cases are treated differently.

Consider, too, that compensation would sometimes work against the objectives which compel the government to cause the loss. For example: (1) If eminent domain principles were consistently applied to regulation, such as public utility regulation, so as not to adversely affect preexisting economic value, regulation would perpetually protect the very monopoly returns it was designed to reduce; (2) "expropriation" through eminent domain in the United States has in fact been "purposefully used to allocate resources, to influence entrepreneurial opportunities, and even to provide effective subsidies for favored types of business enterprise, often at high cost to 'vested rights' in property";[8] (3) absorption of the Law Merchant by the common law was designed to reformulate the normative input and output of the legal system and to encourage the development of new interests, new values, and a new class, altering the economic position of all those doing business with business;[9] and (4) some common law changes were intended to facilitate the growth of various markets at the expense of preexisting rights of long standing.[10]

In short, legal change is pervasive and, consequently, potentially compensable losses are virtually infinite.

II.   AN ECONOMIC THEORY OF THE COMPENSATION PROBLEM

This part will examine the economic significance of rights, the dual nature of rights in terms of the welfare economics theory of opportunity sets, and the functional equivalence of legal and non-legal change. The goal is to identify the fundamentals of the compensation problem.

---

8. Scheiber, *Property Law, Expropriation, and Resource Allocation by Government: the United States, 1789-1910*, 33 J. ECON. HISTORY 232, 234 (1973).

9. Lowry, *Lord Mansfield and the Law Merchant: Law and Economics in the Eighteenth Century*, 7 J. ECON. ISSUES 605 (1973).

10. *See* Holdsworth, *A Neglected Aspect of the Relations Between Economic and Legal History*, 1 ECON. HISTORY REV. 114 (1927-1928).

A. The Economic Significance of Rights

Legal rights permit economic actors to participate in economic decision-making as buyers and sellers; they represent the abstract acknowledgement of the legitimacy of claims to income and to participation in resource allocation. The economic value of rights depends upon a wide range of legal and market variables. The economic value of Alpha's[11] rights is a function of the legal identification and assignment of rights to Alpha; of Alpha's own past and current decisions to exercise his rights; of Alpha's relationship to Beta's exercise of rights; and of changing market conditions, including technological, resource base, population, demand-supply, and other changes. Alpha's rights are, then, relative to at least three other factors: the legal limitations inherent in their identification and interpretation, the exercise by others of their rights, and legal and nonlegal change. The present market value of a right involves the capitalization of all of these variables. The economic significance and value of rights is thus a function of both law and market.

The Lockean protection-of-rights approach and an egalitarian resolution of the compensation problem require the clear identification and definition of rights. Yet rights are relative to the rights of others, and, furthermore, it is not always possible fully to specify a right in terms of other rights, because there are many other rights to which any one right is or may become relative. Moreover, in a dynamic economy, relationships between rights are constantly changing in a Schumpeterian process of creation and destruction of opportunities.[12]

Selective perception operates to obscure the ephemeral nature of rights. Each present right is only one successful claim or expectation among others which did not materialize, yet this realized right is believed to have been pre-existing. This belief is reinforced by the legal pretense that rights have an abstract antecedent existence that government is obligated to protect. The economic reality is that rights which are protected are rights only

---

11. "Alpha" represents one individual in society. "Beta" represents one individual or, alternatively, all other individuals in society.

12. Schumpeter argued that capitalism is a system of innovation which both creates and destroys opportunities, typically for different people. *See* SCHUMPETER, CAPITALISM, SOCIALISM AND DEMOCRACY (1950).

because they are protected; they are not protected because they were preexisting. Rights are made and remade, through both the law and the market; they are not found. Actually, however, common law rights and changes in common law rights are almost always ex post facto, *i.e.*, determined, rather than enforced, by judicial action. The beliefs described above serve a socially useful purpose by legitimizing conflict resolution through the legal process. But they should not obscure the ambiguity of rights and the impossibility of their unambiguous definition.

Each right, then, is a "package of possibilities"[13] within a structure and process of dynamic interplay. As one commentator has said:

> The essence of property, as we actually use the term, is not fixity at all, but fluidity. Property is the end result of a process of competition among inconsistent and contending economic values. Instead of some static and definable quantity, property really is a multitude of existing interests which are constantly interrelating with each other, sometimes in ways that are mutually exclusive. We can talk about a landowner having a property interest in "full enjoyment" of his land, but in reality many of the potential uses (full enjoyment) of one tract are incompatible with full enjoyment of the adjacent tract. It is more accurate to describe property as the value which each owners has left after the inconsistencies between the two competing owners have been resolved. And, of course, even then the situation is not static, because new conflicts are always arising as a result of a change in the neighborhood's character, or in technology, or in public values. These changes will revise once again the permitted and permissible uses which we call property. Property is thus the result of the process of competition.[14]

In sum, the economic significance of rights, and of the power and freedom they imply, is "in significant part determined by existing conditions of economic resource employment"[15] in the total social, legal, and moral universe.[16] Rights of one period govern the

---

13. Michelman, *supra* note 1, at 1234.

14. Sax, *Takings and the Police Power, supra* note 1, at 61 (footnotes omitted).

15. Michelman, *supra* note 1, at 1167.

16. Thus if rights are allowed to be changed only through the market, the existing distribution of rights, and, thereby, of income, wealth and power, will be protected. It is also true that changes in market prices alter and redistribute rights, and, thereby, income, wealth and power, by inflicting different injuries and benefits. The reason is that the

interaction of that period, which in turn governs rights for the next period, and so on.

B. Rights and Opportunity Sets

The decision-making process inherent in the preceding analysis may be articulated in terms of the following general model.[17] Each individual—each legal person of economic significance —has at any point in time an "opportunity set" from which he may make choices. An opportunity set consists of the available alternatives for action or choice, each with a relative opportunity cost, which are open to the individual. The choices each individual makes determine the character of his future opportunity set. An opportunity set is also a function of two factors: power and mutual coercion. "Power" is the capacity to assert choices or to participate in decision-making. It is a function, among other things, of one's position in formal and informal organizations and, especially important here, of one's rights. "Coercion" (the word is not used pejoratively) refers to choices by Beta which have an impact upon Alpha's opportunity set without Alpha's consent. In a system of general interdependence, the impact is mutual. The substance of the impact, furthermore, includes benefits as well as injuries. The substance—benefits and injuries—of mutual coercion may be defined as "externalities"—positive and negative.[18]

---

economic significance of rights is a function of both law and market, with market forces themselves partly a function of legal rights. See text at notes 17-21 *infra*. When rights are allowed to change only through the market, *i.e.*, when legal change is proscribed, the status quo rights structure is given effect and protected. Expressed differently, the economic value of rights is partly a function of marginal productivity forces *and* marginal productivity forces are partly a function of rights.

17. The model is elaborated and applied in Samuels, *The Coase Theorem and the Study of Law and Economics*, 14 NAT. RESOURCES J. 1 (1974); Samuels, *Public Utilities and the Theory of Power*, in PERSPECTIVES IN PUBLIC REGULATION 1 (M. Russell ed. 1973); Samuels, *Welfare Economics, Power and Property*, in PA. STATE UNIV. INST. FOR RESEARCH ON LAND & WATER RESOURCES, PERSPECTIVES OF PROPERTY 61 (G. Wunderlich & W.L. Gibson, Jr. eds. 1972).

18. Sax emphasizes

a view founded on a recognition of the inter-connectedness between various uses of seemingly unrelated pieces of property. Once property is seen as an interdependent network of competing uses, rather than as a number of independent and isolated entities, property rights and the law of takings are open for modification.

Sax, *Takings, Private Property and Public Rights, supra* note 1, at 150. Sax also noted:

Property does not exist in isolation. Particular parcels are tied to one another in complex ways, and property is more accurately described as being inextricably

To summarize the foregoing decision-making model, Alpha and Beta make choices from their respective opportunity sets. Those sets are a function of their power—position, rights—and of the impact of their choices on each other. For example, Alpha and Beta each have finite amounts of wealth, and each will use that wealth in one way or another. The uses which are actually chosen will affect the alternatives, and their respective opportunity costs, open to the other and the relative power position of the two individuals, in part, through the acquisition and valuation of economic assets, including property and position.

The *interdependence* of their relationship is critical. While it is true that both may gain from a mutually desired exchange,[19] the nature and terms of the exchange and its significance to each of them will all depend upon their respective opportunity sets. Whatever affects the power or coercive status of the one will tend to have an opposite effect upon the other. In other words, loss is built into the process.

Alpha's relative capacity to participate in mutual coercion is a function of his power, and his power is determined in part by his rights, specifically, by his legal rights of economic significance and by anything functionally equivalent to the coercive impact of rights. Whatever affects Alpha's rights, especially vis-á-vis Beta's rights, will *pro tanto* affect Alpha's opportunity set and his economic well-being. The economic value of Alpha's property is protected by law from robbery, but not from erosion by market forces—*e.g.*, by a change in Beta's spending patterns.

---

part of a network of relationships that is neither limited to, nor usefully defined by, the property boundaries with which the legal system is accustomed to dealing. Frequently, use of any given parcel of property is at the same time effectively a use of, or a demand upon, property beyond the border of the user.
Id. 152.

19. The presumption is very great that an exchange between a willing buyer and a willing seller is a positive sum transaction, *i.e.*, that both parties gain. However, it cannot be emphasized too strongly that all transactions have both positive and negative sum aspects. Exchange, of course, can take place within a great variety of market and institutional contexts, and no exchange between a willing buyer and willing seller exists independently of those conditions. In particular, changes in legal rights affect the equilibrium of exchange. Nonetheless, the positive sum aspect of transactions is important. This Article, however, focuses on the negative sum aspects—specifically, on the negative externalities generated by the assignment and exercise of rights in Alpha-Beta rights conflicts.

Alpha and Beta thus exist in an economic relationship to each other in which each may act within his legal rights in a way which, intentionally or unintentionally, reduces the economic value of the other's rights. Legal rights, then, do not exist in isolation, but always relative to other persons who may bear the negative externalities of the rightholder's choices or actions.[20] For Alpha to have a right is for Beta to have an exposure, and vice versa; for Alpha to have a new right is for Beta to have an additional exposure to Alpha's decision-making, and vice versa. Thus a change in legal rights creates a pair of externalities: a benefit for Alpha and an added exposure—a constricted opportunity set or increased opportunity cost—for Beta. Governmental regulation of Alpha through the exercise of the police power is the functional equivalent of assigning Beta a right. Indeed, what is taken for granted as rights is often largely a product of past regulation.[21]

Rights therefore have a *dual* nature: the opportunity-set enhancement of those who have rights and the opportunity-set restriction of those who are exposed to them. Creation of a right means creation of both the enhancement and the restriction; legal change of rights means alteration in the pattern of enhancement and restriction. To grant or change a right is ipso facto to generate losses in opportunity sets and in the economic value of pre-existing rights.

The legal significance of these economic realities is that every change of the law enhances some and restricts other opportunity sets and therefore both benefits and injures the economic value of pre-existing rights. Furthermore, the very existence of every right creates a compensation problem because of the inherently

---

20. As Hohfeld stressed, rights must be understood within the larger matrix of jural correlatives and jural opposites. What is designated here as *rights* comprises, in Hohfeldian terms, the sum of right, privilege, power and immunity, which are *correlative*, respectively, to duty, no-right, liability, and disability; and which are *opposite*, respectively, to no-right, duty, disability and liability. One may have the legal ability to alter legal relations (power) or one may not (disability); one may have affirmative claims upon another, including control over another's conduct (right) or one may have no such claim or control (no-right); and one may be exposed to having one's legal relation altered by another (liability) or one may be exempt from such exposure (immunity). W. HOHFELD, FUNDAMENTAL LEGAL CONCEPTIONS (W. Cook ed. 1964). On the Hohfeldian analysis vis-á-vis the model of mutual coercion, see Samuels, *The Economy as a System of Power and its Legal Bases: The Legal Economics of Robert Lee Hale,* 27 U. MIAMI L. REV. 261 (1973).

21. Samuels, *The Coase Theorem and the Study of Law and Economics, supra* note 17, at 12.

dual nature of rights. Legal change only alters the patterns of exposure and loss and of interests which the law protects; it should not be overlooked that the prior identification, assignment, and exercise of rights also created injury.

Because of the relative and dual character of rights, they may be viewed from numerous perspectives. What is perceived as freedom by one person may seem tyrannous to another. At work is a subtle process of selective perception of rights and injuries. For instance, governmental action may be sought to defend Alpha's right from Beta *because* Alpha's right is more easily seen or understood. There is a failure to perceive or identify with Beta's right, and this failure accounts in part for the failure to perceive Beta's loss. Consequently, there are windfall gains and windfall losses.

Rights are thus truly problematical. First, each "package of possibilities" is subject to all the variables of the social system, including changes in technology, market conditions, political conditions, and natural phenomena. Second, the action, nonaction, and forbearance of parties, including the government, all produce rights and generate losses to opportunity sets through the abortion or foreclosure of other potentialities—*i.e.,* of what otherwise would have been effective rights in a different structure of relative rights. Third, an economic actor does not always know that he needs or has a right until he knows what other actors can do to him. Finally, economic change often arbitrarily permits some but not others to take advantage of new opportunities and thereby to realize more of their rights potential. Generally, the effects of change are favorable to owners. However, a favorable result is only partly a function of ownership; it is equally true that effective ownership is a function of favorable results. In other words, rights are both independent and dependent variables in an interdependent decision-making system.

C. The Compensation Problem

The compensation problem involves determining which interest to protect, in each Alpha-Beta conflict, or, in other words, to which potential losses existing values may be exposed.[22] The

---

22. *See* Sax, *Takings and the Police Power, supra* note 1, at 61.

selective perception of injuries and of potentially compensable losses influences the process of choice. If Beta's injury is not perceived, the compensation problem is not fully perceived—although it may be normatively resolved through legal change.

The selectivity of perceived loss is caused largely by the traditional distinction between legal and nonlegal change. The compensation problem does not arise solely from legal change. Governmental action is inextricably involved in every private action; for purposes of compensation, nonlegal and legal change are functional equivalents.[23] The perception of loss should therefore encompass all gains and losses which result from the coercive economic behavior of others. Many nonlegal sources of change—changes in technology, resource availability, population, taste, market structure, demand-supply relations, and so on—are only nominally "market" phenomena. They are in many respects more significant than legal sources of change, yet they are also less conspicuous and are perceived selectively.

The fundamental complication inherent in the compensation problem is that Beta's loss is theoretically compensable only by imposing an opposite set of adverse effects upon Alpha. Nonlegal change can occur only because legal support is given to one relative right vis-á-vis another. Usually, if not always, nonlegal change involves at least Alpha's exercise of legal rights and governmental failure to protect those of Beta's rights which are injured by Alpha. In short, freedom to exercise private choice is grounded in a legal foundation; economic actors can produce

---

23. That nonlegal change is functionally equivalent to legal change does *not* mean that they necessarily have the same normative status. This Article does not normatively equate coercion through price changes with coercion by the state or with coercion by an armed robber; it does not normatively equate power through work with power through seizure. Rather, this analysis emphasizes the importance of a normative basis for distinguishing between actions pejoratively deemed coercive and those not so deemed. In a very profound sense, the need to differentiate between acceptable and unacceptable coercion is the premier valuational task of man. But opportunity-set analysis of rights indicates that all types of coercion function equivalently in their effects on opportunity sets—even when the changes are normatively differentiated.

Also, while this Article argues that there is no objective justification for the existing distribution of rights, that does not mean that all claims are equally arbitrary. The absence of an objective or independently determined basis for rights (one preexistent and preeminent to man or to human choice) dictates the necessity for a normative basis for differentiation. That is the role of principles and tests of compensability.

coercive impact on others because the law permits their choices to overcome the choices of others. The interests which the law protects may change through nonlegal means, but the adverse effects on Beta are the same as if the law itself has changed. Indeed, Beta may seek countervailing legal change.[24]

Legal and nonlegal change can also be functionally equivalent as economic alternatives. Private power-holders can use one or the other to achieve their goals: a private cartel or captured administrative regulation;[25] market dickering or influencing the exercise of the power of eminent domain;[26] a market skewed in favor of a ruling class or out-right governmental paternalism.[27] In every case, the law is used to reach economic objectives by enhancing certain right potentials and inhibiting others.

Although it is customary to conceptualize the compensation problem as an eminent domain matter, government also compensates for *nonlegal* change, through legislative and other judicial channels. Farm subsidies, tariffs, and designation of disaster areas for special federal assistance are all examples of such governmental aid for nonlegal change. Legal change may be produced by, or may be used to ratify, nonlegal change. Furthermore, public "takings" may be used to prevent or compensate for private "takings": Alpha's power may be restricted to prevent Alpha from visiting opportunity-set injury on Beta, or courts or legislatures may selectively perceive the "victim" of private or public takings. In both cases, someone loses and is not compensated for the loss. In general, government determines which interests to protect as rights. In every case, government takes a position on compensation through its action or inaction in the face of Alpha's or Beta's exercise of opportunity-set choices. One ox will always be gored.

In short, compensation is a reciprocal problem. "The real question that has to be decided is: should A be allowed to harm B or should B be allowed to harm A?"[28] Further, if Alpha is

---

24. *See* Samuels, *Interrelations Between Legal and Economic Processes*, 14 J. LAW & ECON. 435 (1971).

25. Samuels, *Public Utilities and the Theory of Power, supra* note 17.

26. *See* Scheiber, *supra* note 8.

27. Seidman, *Contract Law, the Free Market, and State Intervention: A Jurisprudential Perspective*, 7 J. ECON. ISSUES 553 (1973).

28. Coase, *The Problem of Social Cost*, 3 J.L. & ECON. 1, 2 (1960).

compelled to compensate Beta, should Alpha be compensated because his rights potential or opportunity set had included the possibility of his action without compensation to Beta?[29]

The concept of compensation should also allow for injury to the security of expectations. Because rights are relative to other rights, each economic actor's opportunity set is in part a function of the expectation of security—security *from* the adverse consequences (negative externalities) of others' choices and security *to* make choices that produce consequences adverse to others. Security in both respects is a volatile phenomenon, and conflicts of expectations are inevitable. The point here is that a decision to protect one will tend to deny the other, typically without compensation. The same analysis is applicable to demoralization costs.[30] Common law legal change may minimize demoralization costs and maintain the illusion of overall equity, but it too must decide whose demoralization costs deserve compensation, and the loser will tend not to be compensated.[31]

D. Other Considerations

At least three other considerations deserve mention: the relative nature of rights, once again; the significance of asymmetrical or unequal positions between economic actors; and the relationship of rights to costs.

1. *The Relative Nature of Rights*. According to the approach taken in this Article, rights are protected not because they are

---

29.

> During the debates in the British Parliament in the early nineteenth century on abolition of slavery, the early adherents of the Compensation Principle were maintaining that the masters must be compensated for the loss of their investment in slaves. At that point, Benjamin Pearson, a member of the Manchester School, declared that "he had thought it was the slaves who should have been compensated." Here is a stark example of the need, in advocating public policy, of an ethical system, of a concept of justice. Those of us who hold that slavery is unjust would always oppose the idea of compensating the masters, and indeed would think rather in terms of reparations: of the masters compensating the slaves for their years of oppression.

Rothbard, *Value Implications of Economic Theory*, 17 AM. ECONOMIST 35, 37 (No. 1, 1973).

30. *See generally*, Michelman, *supra* note 1, at 1214 *et seq*.

31. The same conclusion results from consideration of the problem in terms of externalities. Rights are rights to create externalities. The problem is not whether or not there are to be externalities, but, rather, *which* externalities. See Samuels, *Ecosystem Policy and the Problem of Power*, 2 ENVIRON. AFFAIRS 580 (1972); note 17 *supra*.

rights, but they are rights because they are protected. Rights are whatever interests government protects vis-à-vis other interests when there is a conflict. Thus, rights can be viewed as absolute, to the extent that they are independent of legal change; they can also be viewed as relative, *i.e.*, as including provision for legal change and as always subject to it within established procedural and other constraints. In the absolutist's view, rights are preexistent and preeminent to law; in the relativist's view, rights are subject to law and to change through law. Rights therefore may be defined in such a way that every act, private and public, modifies a right; or in such a way that no act, private or public, modifies a right. The difference is that the latter definition builds in the concept of modifications, *i.e.*, of externalities. In the former view, the revolutionary coerces changes in rights, while in the latter view the revolutionary is only exercising his right to engage in revolution.[32]

The absolutist view is functionally useful as a conceptual device for limiting or channelling change. However, the economic reality is that the absolutist view is wrong: the rights that count are the rights recognized and enforced by law. There is no right beyond the controlling law; there is only a change of the interests which the law protects, albeit with a loss, which may or may not be compensated because of the relative and dual nature of rights. The relativist view does correctly reflect reality, but it requires a determination of which relative right to protect or compensate. This raises the question of why certain interests are designated as legal rights and the further question of why certain of these rights attain the stature of "property rights" while others do not. By both absolutist and relativist theories, however, there is potentially compensable injury; only the status of the injury differs.

2. *Asymmetry.* The relative positions of economic actors are not always symmetrical or equal. In fact, there is considerable inequality, and this inequality is both a cause and a consequence of asymmetrical legal rights. Asymmetrical access to government—to lawyers and lobbyists and therefore to courts, legislatures and executives—tends to produce asymmetrical definitions

---

32. Stubblebine, *On Property Rights and Institutions*, in CENTER FOR THE STUDY OF PUBLIC CHOICE, EXPLORATIONS IN THE THEORY OF ANARCHY 43 (G. Tullock ed. 1972). *Cf.* Michelman, *supra* note 1, at 1240.

and distributions of rights, of economic security, and of opportunity sets. In short, asymmetrical access to the law leads to unequal economic performance. Conversely, unequal economic performance leads to asymmetrical access to the law. Asymmetry in the power structure of the market and in society generally tends to lead to, reinforce, or duplicate asymmetry in legal rights.[33]

This asymmetry is relevant here because it affects the perception of compensation claims. Asymmetrical recognition of relative rights may skew the process of mutual coercion and therefore the distribution of income and wealth. One of the purposes of legal maneuvering is to accomplish precisely this result. For the present analysis, it suffices to note that asymmetrical recognition of rights inevitably also means asymmetrical legal solutions to the compensation problem. The compensation problem would of course exist without such asymmetry or inequality; the asymmetry is an additional and important complication.

3. *Rights and Costs.* There are two different perspectives on the relationship of rights to costs, each applicable to different situations. First, it is clear that rights are partly a function of costs. The value to Alpha of his rights depends on the opportunity costs of each alternative, including consideration of the negative externalities of Beta's choices. If money costs rise and prices do not, net income falls and with it the capitalized economic value of the enterprise or property. Second, the reverse is also true: costs are a function of rights. Legal determination of rights governs whose interests are to become costs to others. From Alpha's point of view, the economic value of his rights is a function of his costs; but his costs are a function of Beta's rights.[34]

---

33. Rights are only partly a function of social and material power; other factors, *e.g.*, the market, are also operative, especially in a society of substantially diffused power. Power therefore is not absolutely self-reinforcing.

Nevertheless, although the asymmetry described in the text is only a tendency, it is important. Note, for example, that although landlords have a right to be compensated for urban renewal takings, tenants do not have a comparable right. Michleman, *supra* note 1, at 1254-56. It is also important to note that in the complex political battle for urban renewal benefits, lobbyists for the poor had to use a substantial amount of their political resources to gain a rough equivalent of compensation in the form of relocation payments. Consequently, the poor fared worse than they would have had their right to compensation been recognized. That is, if the law views Alpha's claim as uncompensable, Alpha will have to use up political resources, to protect himself. Alpha's loss may be termed a political opportunity cost. I am indebted to Victor Goldberg for urging this point.

34. See notes 17, 31 *supra*; *cf.* Schmid, *Nonmarket Values and Efficiency of Public Investments in Water Resources*, 57 AMER. ECON. REV. 157, 162 (Supp. 1967).

This dual perspective is easily misconstrued or misapplied. It cannot properly be argued that because rights are partly a function of costs, they should be determined on the basis of efficiency. Efficiency is a function of rights rather than the other way around.[35] The lawmaker considers the costs to *both* Alpha and Beta in defining and assigning rights, and thereby determines whose interests are to become costs for the other. Lawmaking thus requires either official value judgments about whose costs should "count" or official legitimization of the status quo distribution of income and wealth.[36]

Indeed, rights are themselves important tools for protecting and compensating interests, since the designation of some interests as rights elevates those interests above others by according them legal status. However, to change rights means to change costs without compensation. To make Alpha's interest a cost to Beta is to refuse to allow Beta's interest to become a cost to Alpha. It is impossible to compensate all losers. What is important are the factors governing which injuries will be identified and compensated.

III.   LEGAL RESOLUTION OF THE COMPENSATION PROBLEM

A.   Modes of Legal Resolution

Analysis must differentiate the outcome of legally resolved conflict from the principles developed to resolve that conflict—the modes of legal resolution of conflict between rights. Since rights are substantive, as well as relative, the principles developed to affirm or deny them are readily reified. However, the seeming certainty of legal principles tends to obscure the fundamental element of choice which is still involved in applying the principles.

The most important mode for the legal resolution of compensation claims takes the form of distinguishing between application of the power of eminent domain and regulation through the police power.[37] In this process, the contract, due process, and

---

35. Schmid, *supra* note 34, at 164. "Efficiency depends on the relevant input-output categories, and it is collective judgment expressed in property rights which determines relevancy." *Id*. 163.

36. See note 16 *supra*.

37. Theories and principles developed to deal with compensation problems are: inva-

equal protection clauses are balanced against the public interests protected through exercise of the police power. The cases and commentators incorporate a wide range of rational and folk-wisdom considerations, but these considerations are *plural* and choice is required. Other constitutional modes of legal resolution are the balancing of the commerce clause against the fifth and tenth amendments and of the tenth amendment against the supremacy clause. A variety of subsidiary constitutional doctrines are also relevant, *e.g.*, fair return on fair value and state action. Also relevant are the public purpose clauses in state constitutions. Tort law has developed a wide range of theories for compensating loss, including negligence, proximate cause, assumption of risk, contributory negligence, strict liability, and nuisance—all used to adjudicate relative rights. The law of negotiable instruments, business associations, and contracts have a comparable variety of theories to deal with compensation. Procedurally, the concept of standing to sue for compensable injury is important. Finally, the very designation of certain claims as "property rights" is itself a mode of resolving compensation problems, especially when the competing interest is not recognized as a property right or is a nonproperty right considered inferior to the property right.

In all of the foregoing modes of legal resolution, law governs the distribution of sacrifice in society by balancing a variety of considerations, tests, principles, and interests. It does this through the selective perception of injury and interpretation of the law, subjective balancing of relative hardships, and a subjective sense of justice. Within each selective exercise there is an essential normative element. For example, much American law is designed to promote technological innovation and material growth, yet another even more fundamental premise of the legal system is that many longstanding expectations deserve legal protection. Almost all American law places a high value on consumer tastes and changes in consumer tastes, and therefore permits consumer sovereignty without requiring consumers to bear the

---

sion, noxious use, diminution of value, conflict mediation versus governmental enterprise, balancing social gains against private losses, maximum total net benefit, private fault and public benefit, and considerations of efficiency and fairness. *See* Michelman, *supra* note 1, at 1184-1213, 1226-45; Sax, *Takings and the Police Power, supra* note 1, at 36.

primary costs. The choice between *caveat emptor* and *caveat venditor* as alternative approaches to risk and loss distribution exemplifies what is here called selective perception: selective emphasis upon one side or the other in an Alpha-Beta rights conflict. An additional complicating problem concerns which branch of government is the appropriate one to make these choices.

Yet much legal resolution of the compensation problem is never considered and never challenged. Rights are determined, often only implicitly, in a process which amounts to fitting each case into one of two empty boxes: one which requires compensation for injury and one which does not. The legal process yields determinate solutions, and in this respect does not differ substantially from welfare economics. Welfare economics classifies externalities as pecuniary or technological and as Pareto-relevant or Pareto-irrelevant; it has both narrow and broad definitions of injury and of evidence of injury. All the economic principles function with great flexibility to differentiate between compensable and uncompensable loss.

It is not possible to formulate a consistent and definitive rule (for example, no compensation for losses of less than 250 dollars) which will avoid forcing one party to bear opportunity-set loss.[38] No test will completely eliminate uncompensated loss, because no test can solve the fundamental compensation problems which arise when a right is created for Alpha, with a resultant opportunity-set injury to Beta, or when a rule is changed to benefit Beta, thereby imposing an opportunity-set loss upon Alpha. The tests and theories, considered separately and together, represent analytical frameworks still requiring choice and still necessarily inflicting uncompensated losses on opportunity sets.

Indeed, the tests and theories obscure the loss to the "other" party. They legitimize results and set minds at rest that there is long-term equity. But all tests require the valuation of interests in relative-rights determinations. They lack substantive specificity until it is provided by the decision-maker—and then it is the substantive relative-rights determination that counts. Most im-

---

38. *Cf.* Goldblatt v. Town of Hempstead, 369 U.S. 590, 594 (1962) ("There is no set formula to determine where regulation ends and taking begins"); *see* Michelman, *supra* note 1, at 1171.

portant, for present purposes, is the fact that each test or theory functions to deny the value of one opportunity-set loss. It is this loss which is obscured. The fact that one is convinced that a particular case involves the police power rather than eminent domain does not necessarily preclude compensation for the losing party. The issue may be said to turn on what is or is not "legitimately" within opportunity sets; but that determination, like all the others, will incur opportunity-set losses.

B.   The Joint Rights-Loss-Compensation Determination Process

In *Pennsylvania Coal Company v. Mahon*,[39] Justice Holmes, speaking for the majority, wrote:

> Government hardly could go on if to some extent values incident to property could not be diminished without paying for every such change in the general law. As long recognized, some values are enjoyed under an implied limitation and must yield to the police power. But obviously the implied limitation must have its limits, or the contract and due process clauses are gone. . . .
>
>   . . . .
>
> The general rule at least is, that while property may be regulated to a certain extent, if regulation goes too far it will be recognized as a taking.[40]

Mr. Justice Brandeis, dissenting, stated:

> Every restriction upon the use of property imposed in the exercise of the police power deprives the owner of some right theretofore enjoyed, and is, in that sense, an abridgment by the State of rights in property without making compensation. But restriction imposed to protect the public health, safety or morals from dangers threatened is not a taking. . . . The State merely prevents the owner from making a use which interferes with paramount rights of the public.[41]

Although each leads to a different result, the two views about the nature of property rights are substantially the same: rights are relative to legal limits and to legal change as well as to the rights of others, and there may be what substantively amounts to tak-

---

39. 260 U.S. 393 (1922).

40. *Id*. 413, 415.

41. *Id*. 417.

ings under the police power. The two justices differed in their weighing of the interests: Holmes emphasized the magnitude of the taking, the "extent of the diminution,"[42] or the degree of economic harm,[43] while Brandeis was concerned primarily with protecting the public from noxious uses. More important than the analytical differences is the fact that each reached a different conclusion about which box the case belonged in. It should be noted, also, that while the language of the case is cast in terms of affirmation of rights and powers, the decision actually determined rights, loss, and compensation.

The significance of the analysis of opportunity sets and of the dual character of rights is that the determination of whether to compensate for legal change is part of the process in which rights themselves are determined. The decision to compensate is simultaneously a decision, or the functional equivalent of a decision, to grant a right. The joint nature of the process is even more evident in a statutory award of compensation. Any legal recognition and protection of a right enables the flow of payment to one party and not to the other. The same joint rights-loss-compensation process determines the compensation and the loss, and the loss is usually uncompensated.

The joint rights-loss-compensation determination process affects the composition and structure of opportunity sets (the distribution of economic opportunity), the distribution of income and wealth, and the direction and rate of social change, including technological and economic development, and the choice of technological alternatives. The compensation problem is thus part of the problem of determining which factors and forces will govern technological, legal, and social change.

IV. Conclusion

This study has been an effort to identify the scope of the compensation problem. That problem has been seen to be larger, more complex, and more subtle than the eminent domain concept of "takings." The economic significance of rights is a function of the opportunity sets which rights help determine and of the pres-

---

42. *Id.* 413.
43. Sax, *Takings and the Police Power, supra* note 1, at 41-46.

ent economic value of the future income stream generated by choices made from opportunity sets within a system of mutual coercion. This necessarily means that there are ubiquitous uncompensated opportunity-set losses. These losses may be perceived only selectively; and they are selectively, if not deliberately, imposed. The problem of determining when compensation should be made is a matter of public choice. Normally, this determination is made selectively and imperceptibly—one reason the system works as peacefully as it does.

The joint rights-loss-compensation determination process has a significant influence on the distribution of economic wealth and therefore should be of profound interest to both lawyers and economists. Resolution of the compensation problem is a highly selective process, which in a broad sense represents the ubiquity of choice and the elements of arbitrariness and sacrifice which are necessarily involved in the reconciliation of competing interests. The agnostic approach taken in this paper will not be congenial to some; certainly, it is abrasive to the legitimization of rules and to the legal and economic pretense of consistency. Human nature seems to call for a sense of orderliness, coherence, and propriety, and legal and economic orthodoxy tends to fulfill that need. The joint rights-loss-compensation determination process, however, has an emergent and indeterminate character. The approach taken here may be helpful in understanding the dynamics of an important social problem.

10
THE ROLE OF THE COMPENSATION PRINCIPLE IN SOCIETY
Warren J. Samuels and Nicholas Mercuro

The compensation problem is explored in light of radical indeterminacy, selective perception, and the nature and operation of the legal system. The compensation principle is shown to be functional as psychic balm and legitimation of the institution of property and the basic organization of society, and not the protection of particular property rights, except selectively. Conventional legal and economic treatment of compensation issues—for example, the conflicting, conclusionary and tautological taking issue—thus is shown not to reach the fundamentals of the system of property, the legal system, and the roles thereof in society.

210

Private Property: ... which consists in the free use, enjoyment, and disposal of all his acquisitions, without any control or diminution, save only by the laws of the land. ... that sole and despotic dominion which one man claims and exercises over the external things of the world, in total exclusion of the right of any other individual in the universe. [W. Blackstone, in Ehrlich (29), pp. 51, 113.]

The real question that has to be decided is: should A be allowed to harm B or should B be allowed to harm A? [Coase (18), p. 2.]

When reason argues about particular cases, it needs not only universal but also particular principles. [St. Thomas Aquinas, in Viner (107), p. 47.]

General propositions do not decide concrete cases. [Oliver Wendell Holmes, *Lochner v. New York*, 198 U.S. 45, 74 (1905).]

One generation's misfortune is a later generation's cause of action. ... [R. Smith (95), p. 122.]

Any radical change in the structure or content of law expropriates former holders of power. [Friedman (41), p. 47.]

In the past it was the railroad's responsibility for protection of the public at grade crossings. This responsibility has now shifted. Now it is the highway, and not the railroad, and the motor vehicle, not the train which creates the hazard and must be primarily responsible for its removal. [Interstate Commerce Commission, quoted in Van Alstyne (106), p. 50n. 232.]

All we can seek is consistency, coherence, order. The question for the scientist is what thought-scheme will best provide him with a sense of that order and coherence, a sense of some permanence, repetitiveness and universality in the structure or texture of the scheme of things, a sense even of that one-ness and simplicity which, if he can assure himself of its presence, will carry consistency and order to their highest expression. Religion, science and art have all of them this aim in common. The difference between them lies in the different emphases in their modes of search. [Shackle (92), p. 286.]

The purpose of this article is to explore the role of the compensation principle in the legal and property systems of society. The discussion is analytical and nonnormative; there is no effort to establish or assess any particular test of "taking" or compensability. The analysis is developed primarily with regard to the taking clause of the Fifth Amendment[1] but has wider applicability. The materials covered include both case and statute law but also "nondecisions"—areas and issues wherein the compensation problem either does not explicitly arise or does not receive formal, written, legal disposition. The problem of prediction—that no singular or simple explanation suffices for the imposition or nonimposition of the compensation requirement—arises in a manner which reaches to the fundamentals of the system of property, the legal system, and the roles thereof in society.

Section I summarizes various aspects of the problem of compensation. Sections II and III explore radical indeterminacy and selective perception, respectively, as fundamental explanatory principles. Section IV presents a general theory of the relevant nature and operation of the legal system, in part with regard to property rights and regulation, in respect to the role of the compensation requirement. Section V explores the several specific roles of the compensation principle in society.

I THE PROBLEM

It is possible to secure a number of different handles on the compensation problem.[2] In each respect, the problem is seen as intractable.

From an analytical perspective, the compensation problem is ubiquitous; uncompensated takings are inevitable; there is no analytically significant distinction between legally and nonlegally imposed changes; and analytically equivalent situations inevitably receive different normative treatment. These conclusions are predicated upon the dual nature of rights and the reciprocal character of externalities.[3]

From a practical perspective, widely stated findings show that no clear rule exists to rationalize the taking-compensation, or eminent domain-police power, cases[4] and that the decisions are conflicting, essentially tautological, and frequently transparently conclusionary.[5] Indeed, the reality is that almost every decision has an opposite number.[6] There are different holdings in almost every taking area, including inverse condemnation, even in the same state, with regard to similar fact situations.[7] Several different possible perceptions of loss or "takings" are possible [Kramon (57), pp. 149, 158, 160, 161]: The polluter's actions[8] [Michelman (65), p. 1236], the inaction or lack of government control [Large (61), pp. 1062, 1069–1070, 1077, 1083; Kramon (57)]; and the legal control of the polluter.[9] Each may be perceived as constituting a taking. It *is* impossible to formulate a rule which will compensate for all losses in a world of reciprocal externalities and dual rights. The legal system can appear to do so only by not recognizing certain losses as losses. Yet even without this understanding, and offering no other rationale, both the courts and commentators stress the helter-skelter situation in the cases.

The predicament extends further than the absence of any clear, dispositive or explanatory rule and reliance upon conclusionary and tautological language. Compensation is a universally recognized principle; its universal recognition is stressed in the literature: Cormack (21), p. 221; Costonis (22), pp. 1026, 1032; and ample literature emphasizes the propriety of compensation: Furubotn and Pejovich (44), p. 1142; Stoebuck (100), pp. 606–608; Buchanan and Tullock (16); Michelman (65). Yet the literature also contains admonitions that it is impractical and undesirable to compensate for all losses;[10] that there is in fact not only a ubiquitous compensation problem—(Olson (72), p. 447—but a wide array of inevitable uncompensated losses: Sax (88), p. 53; Michelman (65), p. 1258; Downs (27), pp. 71–90; Costonis (22), p. 1075; and Note (115); that "it is universally agreed that not every harm caused by governmental activity should be compensated for" [L. Berger (8), p. 169]; and, *inter alia*, that the always-compensate rule is one "which, manifestly, society has rejected" [Williamson (110), p. 124]. Moreover, there is an asymmetry between payment for losses (itself capricious) and recovery of windfall benefits and gains. Persons equally injured in some sense are not equally compensated. "In many situations, the injury or loss to the individual is exactly the same, and whether he recovers or not depends wholly on how the court characterizes the exercise of governmental power involved" [Elias (31), p. 31]. Locally concentrated losers are not compensated, for example, out of funds raised by special taxes upon locally concentrated gainers. "The absence of both of these devices can be considered indirect evidence that the public affected prefers to risk suffering uncompensated losses in order to have a chance to benefit from unrecaptured gains" [Downs (27), p. 92]. Given the widely perceived capriciousness in the area of compensation, the lottery interpretation is not inapposite.

The compensation principle thus seems both visionary and capricious. The Lockean desideratum of protecting property through the compensation requirement seems vacuous and impossible. In what context does the compensation principle have meaning and to what is that meaning restricted?

II RADICAL INDETERMINACY IN SOCIETY

The compensation predicament is one manifestation of a deeper and enveloping existential problem. Society is neither given nor fixed but open, with its future created through human action, choice, and interaction, specifically with regard to the details of individual and organized life. For reasons of personal psychology and social control, pretense often is maintained concerning the absoluteness, finality, pre-existence, and pre-eminence to man of social arrangements; see Levi (63), p. 1. Human society and organization, including law, does exist. *Ex post*, social arrangements are determinate. *Ex ante*, however, society is radically indeterminate and open. Making and remaking social arrangements, including law, is the existential burden of man. In so doing, man neccessarily confronts certain fundamental problems. One of them, the "problem of order," is discussed below. In general it can be said that there are "eternal issues or problems . . . in the sense [of] . . . formulations of human dilemmas on so high a level of abstraction that they cannot ever really be resolved"; see Friedman (40), p. 828. In attempting partial, halting, and limited resolutions of these issues, problems, and dilemmas man makes and remakes society.

In every society, throughout time, a sense of order and coherence is imposed upon both the physical and social worlds by man, a major function of ideologies, religious, economic, social, and political. Individuals are thus provided comfort in an otherwise ambiguous and changing world. "Institutions are now experienced as possessing a reality of their own, a reality that confronts the individual as an external and coercive fact"; see P. L. Berger and Luckmann (10), p. 58. Such social definitions are opaque in places, but they nonetheless are transmitted through socialization processes. Each system is defined on its own (current) terms. It is accordingly difficult to differentiate between the objectivity of natural phenomena and the objectivity of social formations, including the concepts through which they are reified (p. 59).

However, social arrangements are in fact artifactual, made and remade by man. "Social order is a human product, or, more precisely, an ongoing human production. . . . Social order exists *only* as a product of human activity" (p. 52). "Neither God nor a mystical 'Natural Force' created society; it was created by mankind"; see Mises (67), p. 515. "Culture exists or operates in human beings, who, by their patterned conduct and way of life, create whatever order there is. . . . Social order arises, therefore, not from some mysterious cosmic mechanism but from the patterning of human behavior into the conduct approved by the group traditions"; see L. K. Frank (37), pp. 550, 551. The order which man perceives as given and even externally generated is thus a creation of man himself. That creation is a product of both deliberative and nondeliberative decision-making. The institutional order is the result of slow accretion. Normally changes occur gradually and incrementally, in part through direct confrontation with issues resulting in change but also in part through halting and tortuous adjustments which combine to effectuate changes of substance and/or direction. (This is particularly true of the common law system.) Moreover, as studied in the social sciences and in jurisprudence, all such decision-making, that is, change, occurs within the constraints and regularities of behavior and interaction. It is from these changes that determinate solutions and thereby social reality exists, that is, the changing status quo point through time. All this is true of both the economy and the legal system. Over time, both are made, not found, so far as humanity as a whole is concerned. The social reality which is thereby constructed is heterogeneous, ambiguous, and marked by unresolvable dilemmas and conflicting subordinate principles and tendencies.

The existential burden of man is the process of choice, including the choice of constraints upon choice. Indeed, there is an infinite regression of choice encountered in analyzing human arrangements and institutions. "Facts" on one level tend to be grounded on choices at some deeper level.

Given the radical indeterminacy-choice nature of society, the most relevant social process is the identification, confrontation, clarification, and selection of values. Choices must be made, and the valuation process operates, among other things, to treat what may be analytically equivalent as normatively unequal. Externalities may be reciprocal but the valuation process adjudges one visitation of harm to be superior, or of greater propriety, than the other. Compensation rules function as part of the valuation process to differentiate normatively between applications both among the compensation rules themselves and among other rules which compete with them. Out of these processes and applications, society is made and remade. *Ex post* determinateness is achieved through coming to grips with *ex ante* radical indeterminacy, openness, and the necessity of choice.

Part of the processes outlined above is the rationalization, legitimation, and sanctioning of the choices made, including, and for present purposes especially, the choices of rights and exposures to rights. Legitimation will be further discussed below.

The legal system, then, participates in the overall valuation process with regard to norms, rules, and choices. There is, in fact, necessary incremental legal choice making and remaking the structure of socioeconomic-legal relations so typically articulated in terms of rights. Both social control and our own psyches induce us to believe in final, definitive rights but such is impossible. Among other things, change produces new Alpha-Beta conflicts and the problematical legal and economic significance of rights. Legal terminology, the necessity of decisions, and deterministic economic theory together operate to create the appearance of precision and certainty; moreover, the legal and economic systems do provide determinate results *ex post*. Conflicts between rule and discretion approaches are complicated by the plurality of rules. There is a high demand for a sense of operational certitude, which would psychologically compensate for, yet conflicts with, the imprecise nature and nonmechanical application of rules and the inevitable roles of discretion and uncertainty as between rules; see Friedman (40), pp. 789–794, 829–837. On the level of jurisprudential philosophy, analytical jurisprudence conflicts with legal realism.[11]

As a consequence of the operation of the legal system, there is a normative structure—a chosen structure—of society organized in part through legal rights. This normative structure governs the distribution of power, the disaggregation of scarcity and, *inter alia*, the distribution of the burdens of uncertainty and sacrifice. There is differential capacity among people to insulate themselves from adverse changes and to capture the benefits of change. This differential capacity is a partial function of the randomness or capriciousness of results, radical indeterminacy, and the chosen normative structure.

In short, radical indeterminacy signifies both a necessity of choice marked by inconsistency, as the unresolvable must somehow be given more or less temporary and partial solutions, and an arbitrariness, as those solutions, as functional as they may be, have no ultimate rationale or foundations but instead depend upon and reflect human choice.

III SELECTIVE PERCEPTION

The fundamental force at work in the resolution of the compensation problem is *selective perception*. Beyond the complex process of choice itself, the general phenomenon pervading the entire compensation problem is the differential perception of analytically equivalent situations capable of different and contradictory identifications depending upon perspective. The valuational element contained in underlying selective perceptions enables decision-makers to go from ostensible *is* propositions to *ought* conclusions. One cannot derive an *ought* from an *is* alone; the way in which it is often done is through selective, and therefore valuational, perceptions and identifications contained in the *is* part of the analysis. This process is present in all takings cases and reasonably clearly evident in at least some. Selective perception is functional for normative differentiation, and the normative conclusion drawn is likely to be tautological with an antecedent premise involving selective perception.

Each society has a socially constructed, subjective definition of reality which each member of society internalizes as part of his/her mental equipment. Sociologically, we share a subjective consciousness acquired through societization and inculcated and reinforced through ideology, material interests, and social sanctions. Psychologically, this subjective consciousness involves personal identity definitions, motivational orientations, and specific attachments of individual psychic meaning which help define the self and one's place and role in the social system, in which societization is both internalized and individualized. Actual objective social reality develops and changes as individuals and groups act on their particular subjective view of social reality, both giving effect to and altering its subjective construction; see P. L. Berger (9), P. L. Berger and Luckmann (10). Each individual has a complex and changing personal attitudinal structure from which arises selective perception of relevant events. Social and legal development is at least in part a process of restructuring perceptions as well as giving effect to them. This process is multifaceted and involves the evolution of norms and conceptions of entitlement and propriety; see Tapp and Kohlberg (103), pp. 85–86 and *passim*.

In partial analytical amplification, the following may be noted. First, a large number of losses are not perceived as such by decision-makers (or by the losers themselves). Typically, one person in an Alpha-Beta conflict is perceived not to have a loss vis-à-vis the other's deemed entitlement; similarly, this is true with respect to parties in reciprocal externality conflicts. Second, it is difficult to differentiate between active perceptions and the arguments manipulated by skilled advocates. Third, it is difficult to differentiate selective perception as such from the form which it takes—private versus public, harm-benefit tests, or benefit-cost calculations. Fourth, selective perception may inform the analyst as much about the person undertaking the perception as the object or event identified. Finally, in part because individuals have differential "sensitivity" and values [Laitos (59), pp. 448, 449 and *passim*], the goal of "greater sensitivity"[12] may not yield the same lessons or perceptions to all parties.

There are a multiplicity of instances[13] in which courts, legislatures, and commentators make conclusionary and tautological assertions. In each case, the words give effect to an underlying selective perception. Some interests are recognized as rights and others not, although both may have had previous putative legal status and protection. Some losses are perceived as such and others not. Decisions are rendered in each conflict, often by divided courts or narrow legislative majorities. Selective and conflicting perceptions are inevitable, ubiquitous, and reflected in the incoherence and inconsistency of decisions, statutes, and tests of "taking."

Perhaps the most important respect in which selective perception and identification is exercised is in regard to "injury," "damage," and "loss." The definition of injury, evidence of injury, and the criteria of compensability for injury—that is, the fact, nature, and degree of harm [C. J. Berger (7), p. 823; Levi (64), pp. 404–405; Funston (43), p. 277]—are all subject to selective perception.[14] The widely cited common-law maxim *sic utere tuo ut alienum non laedas*—use your property as not to injure the property of others—requires an additional, or independent, determination of injury, and, indeed, there has been changing perceptions of injury in relation thereto; see J. Smith (94), pp. 389–390; Carmichael (17), p. 759. Similarly, the *de minimis* rule is subject to selective interpretation and application, as is the *damnum absque injuria* (damage without legal injury) rule.[15] What Holmes called the "petty larceny" of the police power is not petty to all participants and observers in particular cases; see Van Alstyne (106), p. 4.

Perception of injury may correlate with selective perception of rights. Judgment as to the reasonable use of property may be seen as justification for damages to a neighbor, but "harmful" or "noxious" use may permit control without compensation; Kratovil and Harrison (58), p. 627. Injury may be perceived of as a *de facto* vis-à-vis the *de jure* taking date; Sackman (79) pp. 163, 169, 170; Arnebergh (3), p. 324. Different attitudes may be held with regard to injury consequent to breach of contract; Birmingham (11), pp. 283ff. Injury may be seen as incidental or material enough to destroy the essential elements of ownership, or as necessarily incident to the ownership of property [Sackman (79), pp. 163–173, 179–181], or as already capitalized in the market. Injury may be seen as capricious, disproportionate, and unprincipled exploitation; Michelman (65), pp. 1217, 1230. Unemployment or inflation may be seen as injury and either or both may be seen as a function of policy decisions, as systemic, or as aberrational; Ackerman (1a), pp. 146ff; Cohan (19); Spengler (98), p. 538. The sense of entitlement, vis-à-vis which injury tends to have meaning, likely will differ between wetlands and marshes [Ackerman (1a)], nonreturnable bottle production and use, billboards, breweries, and massage parlors or pornographic book businesses. Amortization for the recapture of investment may be seen as inadequate vis-à-vis loss of use and business opportunity; Holme (51), p. 284; Van Alstyne (106), pp. 44ff. Damage may be perceived as substantial or incidental, permanent or temporary; Ruegsegger (77), pp. 336, 340, 341. Rendering of property totally useless for economic purposes may or may not be perceived as a legal injury requiring compensation.[16] Access loss may be perceived as substantial or incidental; Sackman (80). "Deprivation" may be seen as lawful and thus not legally injurious; Sackman (79), p. 182. Transfer of development rights (TDR's) may or may not be seen as constituting uncompensated loss to development zone landowners; Barrows and Prenguber (6), pp. 549ff. Damages may be seen as consequential (meaning incidental to government action and compensable) or as inconsequential (remote and noncompensable).[17] In all these and many other respects, selective perception is exercised in Fifth Amendment taking cases (and other areas of the law of damages) and in the relevant interpretive literature. [In general, see Lesser (62), p. 144; Ditwiler (26), pp. 669, 671; Large (61).] In each instance, more than one party can complain of injury, and choice has to be made and usually is made with selective perception.

The role of selective perception and identification also applies to the frequent dictum that cases are, and should be, decided on the basis of the "facts." In numerous cases, the validity of regulation is said to depend "upon the facts in each particular case," that is, "each case must be decided on its own facts" [see cases quoted in Lesser (62), pp. 136, 137, and Van Alstyne (106), p. 45]. On the other hand, commentators have remarked that factual assessments are "subjective" [Harris (50), p. 667], and that "facts" are real and certain only to the extent that they go unchallenged; Friedman (40), p. 805. There are numerous cases wherein two fact situations (that of the instant case and that of a possible precedent) are interpreted differently by majority and minority, with no appreciable difference in their respective treatment of the governing law but with opposite holdings as to takings and therefore compensation.[18] *Res ipsa loquitur*,[19] but differently to different persons.

IV THE NATURE AND OPERATION OF THE LEGAL SYSTEM

Within the context of radical indeterminacy and the principle of selective perception, we present here an analysis of the nature and operation of the legal system as the necessary context of meaning of the compensation principle and the roles which it performs. Some of the statements made herein are dependent on chains of reasoning, some are statements of observable fact, and others are essentially interpretive. In every regard the intent is positive description and interpretation; in no respect are specific normative implications intended.

The role of the legal system, including both common and constitutional law, is to provide a framework or process for conflict resolution and the development of legal rights; see Tribe (104), p. 556. This is the primary mode through which Alpha-Beta rights conflicts are formed and resolved. There is a fundamental and ineluctable necessity of choice with regard to inconsistent or competing interests, in part, with allocative and distributive consequences [Keeton (55), p. 1333; Sax (89), p. 174; Samuels (82, 83, 84)]. It is not surprising, then, that different and conflicting views of law develop. Law is in fact both a mechanism for sanctifying what is perceived or advocated as tradition and a resource for facilitating what is perceived or advocated as desirable change; see Tapp and Kohlberg (103), p. 89. Given the dual nature of rights and ubiquitous reciprocal externalities, there will be legal change, and change of the interests to which government gives its protection regardless of which perspective one adheres to. That there are different attitudes toward government (state, law) is understandable: Law is a source and/or enforcer and protector of rights and it is also an infringer on rights. It is a universal father-figure with both negative and affirmative images [Freud (38); Laitos (59), p. 430]. There is desire both to use and to limit use of the state. There has been a greater policy consciousness [Friedman (41), pp. 37–38] during recent centuries, although this must be juxtaposed to the continued pretense of, and apparent desire for, finality which is at least in part a function of a desire to promote continuity and to legitimize decisions. But policy consciousness cuts two ways: Along with clearer appreciation of the artifactual and therefore normative and contingent character of arrangements has come a sharper sense of loss (which no longer is attributed to nature and perceived as inevitable) and thereby resort to government for redress of felt loss and iniquity.

Change and Conflict

Two characteristics of legal history have been *change* and *conflict*. Apropos of the former, there has been continuous change, typically of an incremental or gradual character. There have been ubiquitous changes of rights (among other things) by common, statute, and constitutional law. The legal system has initiated, reacted to, and ratified change originating within other sub-processes of society. Rights and principles of law have undergone historical evolution. New technology has elicited new bodies of law, new rights, and changes in the consequences of old rights and principles; see Friedman (41), p. 26. Law has been made through judicial decisions (although the Fifth Amendment just compensation provision has not been applied to common-law legal change); Sax (88), p. 51; (89), p. 180 and n. 64; Kratovil and Harrison (58), pp. 614, 632, 645; Michelman (65), p. 1181. However, most legal change has not been perceived as change.[20]

Although the process of legal change has been gradual, it has been continuous and accordingly has led to major transformations of the legal system and of the patterns of rights and, thereby, of the systems of economic organization and control. Large-scale systemic evolution has resulted in every field of law and of the economic system; Laitos (59), p. 426, n. 9; Horwitz (53); Commons (20). The real world of law and economics has been transformed from an agrarian to an industrial capitalist, nonlanded property system with an emphasis on capital accumulation. Present concepts and doctrines have been adapted from a simpler, agrarian society [Costonis (22), p. 1038]; but changing society always has meant changing rights; Dales (23), p. 503. Consequently, the process of change has involved a continuous interaction between legal and economic systems (Laitos (59), pp. 424, 429; Samuels (82), with the economic role of government having changed significantly in the process; Laitos (59), pp. 423ff; Auerbach (5); Solo (96).

Change has meant, perhaps inevitably, conflict over costs and benefits. American legal history is also characterized by conflict between gainers and losers, or over escaping costs and capturing gains; Friedman (42); Horwitz (53); Commons (20); Schumpeter (91). There has been conflict both about and through the legal system, conflict over legal change and the broken eggs of economic development;[21] Fusfeld (45), p. 905. Some, but by no means all, conflict has arisen over the fact and consequences of inequality of income and wealth. Attention to conflict should not obscure the fact that relative harmony or social peace has prevailed and endured in American society. But it should be noted that these conditions are sustained only through the successful resolution of conflict. The realities and pretenses of harmony should not obviate the realities of conflict, which is what controversy over the compensation principle is largely about. Scarcity has meant conflict which has contributed to the inability of rights to be absolute or fully protected, especially in a changing world. The legal system has been unable to avoid controversy, in part because of its deep involvement in the distribution of sacrifice—Michelman (65), p. 1258—and advantage[22] in society, whether through legal or market change (the latter involving differential legal protection).

The Problem of Order

In every society there is a fundamental "problem of order"—Spengler (97), the necessity for a continuing reconciliation of freedom with control, change with continuity, and hierarchy with equality. "Order" can be defined under any of these six terms; which definition is adopted and followed influences one's conception of law; Friedman (41), p. 15 and *passim*. There is great tension between the principles representing each of the terms comprising the three conflicts. At the most abstract, and most open, level, the problem of order involves all three conflicts. For a full appreciation of what order involves, including the sacrifices, a totalist view is necessary; that is, every system of freedom must be seen as operating within the system of control, including legal controls, necessary for it, and that both maintenance and change of the status quo require legal controls. Any change, including any legal change, may be evaluated on its own terms or under the criteria of the status quo which it proposes to change. Inasmuch as every system involves both change and continuity, it may be observed that the market economy involves not only "secure" rights but also the opportunity to create change thereby (more or less fortuitously) both destroying and creating others' rights; see Schumpeter (91).

The legal system is a mode of creating both a sense and the reality of order. The politico-legal system is part of the process for working out piecemeal solutions of the conflicts which comprise the problem of order as well as incremental results of the social valuation process; Jerome Frank (35) pp. xix-xx; J. P. Frank (36), p. 409. Thus, a major function of law is social control; Friedman (40), p. 796. For example, the courts perform the role of moral leader; Levi (64), pp. 417, 422. The question, however, which must be worked out is: Law and order on whose terms? With respect to the economy, the legal system is intimately involved with its organization and control, and with its power structure, in part through the property system; Parsons (73), Commons (20), Friedman (40), pp. 788, 796. A key question is: To whose interests does "order" give effect through law? The problem does *not* involve more versus less government but the interests to which the law is to give effect and the changes which are to be made therein. It is through the continuing (re)determination of the interests to which government will help give effect that the problem of order, the normative structure of society, and a sense of coherence, security, and orderliness are worked out. Throughout all this, too, is the problem of "who decides"; Friedman (40), p. 788. It is true both that rules of law function in part to distribute power *and* that the rules are a function of power: The law allocates power *and* is an instrument of power. "The law itself is an instrument of power, and the person who knows it, or controls it, or both, has a weapon of many megatons of force. ... Legal systems ... are clearly used as weapons in struggles for political power" [Friedman (41), pp. 47, 48]. Thus there is conflict both over use of the legal system and between the legal system and the market (between those who predominate in each). The law is an object and means of economic control and the market is an object of legal control. Out of this, order is produced—and inevitable noncompensated losses.

Politics and Self-Government: Legislature and Judiciary

Governance connotes decision-making or choice and involves having to differentiate between analytically equivalent cases on normative grounds (Alpha can do this to Beta but not that). The problem of order is complicated in systems of self-government or politics. The nature and structure of these systems governs the form in which freedom versus control and continuity versus change conflicts arise. Belief in and practice of self-government, or democratic politics, is functionally equivalent to the mutability of rules, that is, legal change through politics. In nondemocratic systems, it is the total legal-political process which makes policy and alters rules. Further, inasmuch as democracy tends to imply "equality" of some sort, for example, of rights, democratic politics is necessarily (and perhaps paradoxically) involved in treating Alpha and Beta unequally due to the dual nature of rights, quite aside from distributive inequalities.

In a system of self-government or politics, law is not the command of a sovereign above the population but is (re-)created in part through more or less majoritarian election of representatives. Consequent to legal change, the compensation requirement becomes instrumented primarily through litigation involving the taking clause of the Fifth Amendment. Such litigation, and the policy process which it engenders, involves the juxtaposition of, and conflict between, legislature and judiciary.

It should be clear that both legislature and judiciary are exercising the power of governance. The differentiation of governance into the two branches[23] is a function of the disaggregation of the power of government through the system of checks and balances. It represents a pluralist politico-legal system. Such a division of power within government implies limits, review (accountability), and ambiguity of authority; see Friedman (40), p. 796. It also implies eternal conflict over jurisdiction, exercise of discretion, and substantive policy. Both branches are sources of substantive rights and legal change of rights. Each has its own evolving institutional ideology.

The institution of judicial review, especially with regard to the "constitutionality" of legislation, is a function of this division of power, at least as it has worked out in this country from the jurisprudential architectonics of John Marshall.

Constitutional law provisions and doctrines (many if not most of which are not explicit in the document, being a result of judicial introspection) acquire an aura of objective reality. Content is ascribed to them as part of the evolution of society and the interaction of the several branches of the politico-legal system (including power struggle, however moderated and channeled by the supplemental institution of political parties). Insofar as they are functional, the provisions and doctrines operate as part of social reality as both determined and determining variables and are meaningful only (for present purposes) in their functioning with regard to the organization and control of the politico-economic system.

Judicial attitudes with regard to reviewing constitutionality are necessarily ambivalent. Their application generally is within the extremes of abrogating any such role, leaving policy fully up to the legislature, and always substituting (or being willing to substitute) its own wisdom for that of the legislature [Ackerman (1a); Large (61), pp. 1062, 1076, 1077]. In taking cases, the issue arises in the form of conflict between narrow and broad conceptions of the police power as the latter is juxtaposed to private (property) rights.[24] There is no ultimately given role for the courts and the legislature vis-à-vis each other; they must and do work out continuing accommodations to each other. Their relationship is necessarily something that is worked out and subject to continuing mutual adjustment; Friedman (40), pp. 797–798, 822. The judiciary's conception of its role—for example, rules of reception vis-à-vis refusal of cases, or, following Ackerman (1a), judicial activism, reformism, or deference—enables and alters the realization of the effective demand for courts which is derived from the demand for rights; Friedman (40), pp. 810, 815. Such roles have complex behavioral consequences. For example, pressure for legislatively adopted systems of compensation increases in response to greater willingness of the courts to permit restrictions on land use; Bosselman (12), pp. 684, 685. In any event, the Fifth Amendment taking clause is, *inter alia*, a mode of grounding legal decisions (choices).

As implied above, the legislature may adopt compensation as a matter of policy.[25] Even without judicially determined (or anticipated) constitutional "necessity" for compensation, the legislature can award compensation (and in magnitudes independent of the scope of actual loss) at its discretion.[26]

Finally, while it is more or less obvious that deep judicial decision-making is obscured by invocation of constitutional (or common law) doctrines, it must be recognized that the hard (controversial) decisions often are left to the courts, both intentionally and otherwise, by the legislature; Ditwiler (26), pp. 672, 675. At the same time, there are serious limits to judicial policy determination as a mode of governance. [The limits imposed by the narrow confines of cases and case law have been discussed by Pound (74); Large (61), p. 1062; and Laitos (59), pp. 429 n. 10, 437, 444, 448.]

The Matrix of Legal Principles

Each principle of common and constitutional law exists within a matrix of correlative and opposing principles. Each principle has at least several significantly rival meanings or interpretations. Each principle has its highest level of meaning within the context of the matrix, or network, formed by all principles with which it interacts. The conflict of the Fifth Amendment just compensation clause with the state police power (through the Fourteenth Amendment due process of law clause) and with federal powers, of eminent domain with police power principles, or of the police power with property rights, however expressed, has meaning ultimately only within the larger matrix formed by their juxtaposition, as well as the juxtaposition of such other constitutional provisions as the commerce power with the Tenth Amendment, the supremacy clause with the Tenth Amendment, and, *inter alia*, the state police power with other provisions of the Fourteenth Amendment. The same is true on the state constitution and common law levels. Economic and general policy conflicts in American society tend to become ultimately expressed in constitutional terms, in part as each side attempts to pre-empt the high ground of argument and rhetoric and in part because it is in constitutional terms that conflict resolution takes place.

Each principle is seemingly total, broad and absolute, yet each requires a definition of terms and confrontation with conflicting principle(s). The matrix of principles forms a conceptual system which helps define and structure problems but which does not automatically solve them. It functions to abet social peace by enabling the articulation in its terms of both sides of particular issues, perhaps especially the assertion of new claims of right. It provides a semantic and conceptual system with which issues are articulated and decisions are phrased. Interests and aims can be expressed in terms of common and constitutional law, in each case often heightening the sense of conflicting "guarantees"; Abraham (1), p. 291. Continuity and change, freedom and control, hierarchy and equality, and Alpha-Beta rights conflicts are resolved and "balanced" within the matrix, each solution being expressed in terms of the superiority of this or that principle.

In all this, the court system, as a norm and decision-producing process, interacts (reinforces and conflicts) with the political system. Common, statute, and constitutional law form a process; a set not of absolute principles or rights but of relative principles or rights each perceived as absolute.

Constitutional law, for example, is "not a fixed body of truth but a mode of social adjustment"; Waterman (109), pp. 933–934. "General legal rules and principles are working hypotheses, needing to be constantly tested by the way in which they work out in application to concrete situations ..."; Dewey (25), p. 26. Claims (and findings) of principle and right may function to support certain interests or their rivals. The precise meaning of conservative or liberal with regard to the status quo depends on empirical content; thus "the slogans of the liberalism of one period often become the bulwarks of reaction in a subsequent era"; (ibid.). The pattern of meaning formed by the matrix changes. As a mode of the resolution of the problem of order, however, the matrix necessarily incorporates principles supportive of freedom, control, change, continuity, hierarchy, and equality as these come to be constituted in a world of radical indeterminacy, selective perception, and the dual nature of rights. Perhaps needless to say, there is much sophisticated and subtle power play exercised over the principles, the matrix, and the conceptions of society and interests for which, at any point in time, they are symbolic and functional. The myth of absolute and/or fixed legal principles is overwhelmed by the realities of the matrix of which each is a part and by the change which each, and the pattern of the total matrix, undergoes.

The Matrix of Legal Rights

Similarly, each right has meaning as part of a network of rights and interdependencies. Each right has problematical meaning only within the total matrix of rights and their interaction through time. Each right has economic and practical significance only with regard to the rights of others with which it is interdependent.

Persons and groups can form either absolutist or relativist metaphysical views of rights. The approach of absolute rights is generally the analytical or normative equivalent of a continuity-oriented definition of the problem of order. Yet not only are rights in reality relative (as described above) but each absolutist identification of rights tends to specify them differently, thereby requiring choice, which the very notion of absolutism was intended to avoid. Arguments over rights are essentially arguments over continuity versus change (always selectively) or over inconsistent uses. Appeals to rights are claims to certain conduct by others; Tribe et al. (105), p. 108.[27] Each argument presumes the object for which it attempts to adduce support. As one unusually perceptive and candid court said, "We cannot start the process of decision by calling such a claim as we have here a 'property right'; whether it is a property right is really the question to be answered."[28]

Among other things, rights protect interests, channel behavior, and enable participation in social decision-making. But each right is relative to other rights (that is, in part, their correlative obligations or duties) and the exercise of other rights as well as to the exercise of governmental conflict resolution. The protection accorded to each is necessarily limited by the protection accorded to conflicting rights and expectations.

Property rights, and indeed all rights, are simultaneously both private and public in nature. They are manifestly private in their assertion or ascription of entitlement and ownership; they are clearly public, first, in their legal generation (definition and assignment) and, second, in their dual and externality-producing nature. Notice how readily the very idea of private property gives rise to conflicting themes: Property may be seen as the right to injure others [J. Smith (94), p. 383], as not the right to injure others,[29] and as the right to be free of injury caused by others; Carmichael (17), p. 749, cf. p. 755. That is, the matrix of rights is highly kaleidoscopic. It is in continual flux due to changes in economic conditions, technology, values, attitudes, problems, and law. Because of such change and also because of the complexities of the problem of order, interdependence in the forms of the dual nature of rights and the reciprocal character of externalities, and radical indeterminacy, rights are contextual, contingent, and problematic in nature.[30] Rights are limited, altered, destroyed, and enhanced in their socioeconomic and legal significance through both the market and the legal system. The creation of a new right for Alpha necessarily constitutes alterations of the circumstances and reach of some Beta's rights. Rights are inevitably ambiguous due to change and the multiplicity of other rights with which they may come in conflict.

There is, then, an ultimate necessity of choice as to who will have what rights and who will be exposed to the exercise of the rights of others and in what way or within what limits, that is, who will have what capacity to act and to inflict gains and losses on others. The cloud of ambiguity is partially lifted in each court case as conflicting claims are weighed and one interest is made to yield to the other. The process of determining compensability is one such mode of creating and destroying rights.[31]

For instance, every person takes his/her "rights" as given, real, substantial and known—until the person confronts a problem. At that time the person learns that there is a difference, and perhaps a significant difference, between what he/she took for granted as his/her "rights" and the complexity of human arrangements arising from the confrontation of right and right or legal principles. The person has discovered radical indeterminacy. What had been taken as objective reality is now seen as "but" a sign of subjective meaning and revealed to have illusory or at best problematic substance; P. I. Berger and Luckmann (10), pp. 2, 35, cf. pp. 22, 24. Granted that all rights are not equally problematical, it is *not* true that "At any moment of time there is a legally sanctioned structure of property rights in existence" [Furubotn and Pejovich (44), p. 1142], if these rights be seen as fully, clearly, and permanently defined.

The matrix of private property is part of the larger matrix of rights which, as has been argued above, must be seen in conjunction with the matrix of legal principles. Contrary to our tendency to reify property rights as absolutes, which *is* part of our reality, is the further reality of the dynamic matrix of property:

> The essence of property, as we actually use the term, is not fixity at all, but fluidity. Property is the end result of a process of competition among inconsistent and contending economic values. Instead of some static and definable quantity, property really is a multitude of existing interests which are constantly interrelating with each other, sometimes in ways that are mutually exclusive. We can talk about a landowner having a property interest in "full enjoyment" of his land, but in reality many of the potential uses (full enjoyment) of one tract are incompatible with full enjoyment of the adjacent tract. It is more accurate to describe property as the value which each owner has left after the inconsistencies between the two competing owners have been resolved. And, of course, even then the situation is not static, because new conflicts are always arising as a result of a change in the neighborhood's character, or in technology, or in public values. These changes will revise once again the permitted and permissible uses which we call property. Property is thus the result of the process of competition.
>
> Once reoriented to this more fluid concept of property as economic value defined by a process of competition, the question of when to compensate a diminution in the value of property resulting from government activity becomes a much less difficult one to formulate. The question now is: to what kind of competition ought existing values be exposed; and, from what kind of competition ought existing values be protected.[32]

Ambiguity of the property right status quo is a function of radical indeterminacy, the dual nature of rights, the reciprocal character of externalities, and legal-economic (including technological and knowledge) change. Further, the ambiguity underscores the role of compensation determination in the process of selectively redetermining rather than merely protecting pre-existing rights.[33]

Property Rights, Regulation, and Taking

From the perspective of normative decision-making, the taking issue is the differentiation of taking from regulation. The treatment accorded the problem is often conclusionary and tautological, as in the proposition that a valid exercise of the police power does not require compensation: Olson (72), pp. 445, 446, 450, 451, 458; Roby (76), pp. 508, 513.[34] The distinction is increasingly seen as illusory; Waite (108), pp. 292, 293. Whether seen as a taking (requiring compensation) or regulation (not requiring compensation), the governmental action at issue operates to diminish rights, opportunities, freedom, and value for one party (parties) and to enhance same for another('s). Thus we read that:

> In a sense, all governmental restrictions on property use deprive the owner of valuable opportunities to profit from property to which he has formal title. As restrictions grow, it quickly becomes difficult, if not impossible from a purely economic standpoint, to distinguish a formal condemnation and seizure of property from the regulatory destruction of valuable use rights; ... Note (115), p. 1018.

> The sharp dichotomy that exists in the law between inverse condemnation, calling for full compensation, and a police power exercise, with no compensation, has always been rather questionable. In many situations, the injury or loss to the individual is exactly the same, and whether he recovers or not depends wholly on how the court characterizes the exercise of governmental power involved; Elias (31), p. 31.

In each case, the distinction seems to be dependent upon the identification of the interest to be protected as a right, although this premise is not understood or at least not often clearly stated. Is regulation a taking or is it a prevention of a private taking? Whether regulation is a prevention of Alpha from harming Beta, or having Alpha return to Beta what Alpha improperly acquired from Beta, or a "sense of fair play translated into adequate law" or the use of government to correct abuses arising from the hitherto otherwise unregulated private economy [Eisenhower (30), pp. 811, 812], or a taking from some Alpha, will depend upon the legal choice of property definitions and assignments. Upholding government action as permissible regulation means that the claimed property right is nonexistent or inconsequential and that some other claimed private or public interest is protected; asserting that the governmental action is a taking requiring compensation means that the claimed right is affirmed—and that some other claimed private or public interest is negated. To say that a compensation award implies that a property right has been abridged is misleading [Kratovil and Harrison (58), p. 612]; the award itself constitutes or connotes abridgment. Both regulation-holdings and takings-holdings may be said to stabilize values in the market, but different values are stabilized depending upon the holding; Lesser (62), pp. 135, 138.

The fact of the matter is that statutory regulation is a mode of protecting interests such that regulation is the analytical equivalent of (common law or court-determined) rights. In this respect, regulation functions in the same manner as holding a governmental action subject to compensation: Each affirms, and negates, claims of interests. Most, if not all, regulation creates rights; Dales (23), p. 492; Samuels and Schmid (87), pp. 102, 103, 105. Regulation is a mode of changing and adjusting rights; Waite (108), p. 284. Although the myth is predominant that newly articulated rights have an antecedent existence, and although there is widespread failure to recognize regulation as a mode of creation and protection of rights— Netherton (70), p. 51—all new protections of interests and solutions to new Alpha-Beta conflicts, whether identified as regulation or rights, involves the more or less creeping abrogation of existing rights. Courts may invent certain easements to extend protection to the "reasonable" interests of property owners [Kratovil and Harrison (58), p. 613]; in such and many other cases, the courts are—and necessarily so—creating rights [Waterman (109), pp. 928, 933; Kratovil and Harrison (58), p. 630] in a manner analytically equivalent to the legislature when the latter is said to "regulate." The irony is that if *regulation* may be said to be a taking requiring compensation, so too may *deregulation*: In each case there are losers. Deregulation is not typically associated with an affirmation of compensation, in part because of selective identification or specification of the status quo. The interests of those protected by regulation are not given the status of rights. That ubiquitous compensation is neither theoretically nor practically possible, as above, is another matter. Regulation as opposed to rights cannot dispose of the compensation question.[35]

The point is, of course, that the matter cannot be fully and conclusively dispositive of the regulation versus taking issue. We desire to infuse human dignity with rights, the idea that individuals have rights not only vis-à-vis each other but also against the state—Murphy (69), p. 303; Buchanan (15). The problem lies in the conflict of the democratic "right" to self-government with the democratic "right" to be protected from a majoritarian will—all quite aside from the ostensibly nondemocratic nature of judicial decision-making. Again, the matter involves inexorable choice, the division of the power of governance, and radical indeterminacy.

The decisions and the commentaries in this field, understandably, are somewhat schizophrenic. [The most recent major work, that of Ackerman (1a) posits two essentially mutually exclusive but coexisting legal analytics.] They posit an absolute takings limitation or an absolute police power, or emphasize that private property rights and public interests (the police power) must somehow be "balanced." They have promulgated a number of tests, criteria, principles, and requirements with which to distinguish compensable takings from noncompensable exercises of the police power.

The tests include: physical invasion, noxious use, diminution of value, conflict mediation versus governmental enterprise, balancing social gains against private losses, maximum total net benefit, private fault vis-a-vis public benefit, and considerations of efficiency and fairness.[36] The use of these tests is essentially selective and arbitrary. Their use in any particular case is a matter of decision, of ultimate pure choice. They are not deducible by deductive logic or by inference from the facts. There is no automatic litmus test by which the tests themselves can be selected for applicability. They are categories (empty boxes) with variable selective contents whose adoption is almost if not wholly subjective. They neither individually nor collectively provide a formula or calculus by which Fifth Amendment takings can be distinguished from unprotected police power actions.[37] Each test represents a relevant, however imprecise, consideration or basis for differentiation but collectively they both permit and require the exercise of choice in their selection and application. The very use of these tests functions to legitimize takings which escape their use while also functioning to obscure the inevitable choice and specificity of application involved. Such is the inexorable existential burden of radical indeterminacy.

There is concern both that overemphasis upon the just compensation requirement may severely limit public action and that a broad and permissive interpretation of the police power may emasculate the protection provided by the compensation requirement.[38] It is no wonder that both courts and commentators find confusion, diversity, and contradictions in the relevant decisions. This situation is due, as argued above, to the necessity of choice which is mandated by the reciprocal character of externalities and the dual nature of rights. Given this necessity of choice, the irony of the matter lies in the impossibility of a complete Lockean policy. Although the compensation requirement is predicated upon conservative values, such a requirement cannot be uniformly conservative due to the inevitability of ubiquitous uncompensated losses arising from the reciprocal character of externalities and the dual nature of rights. Constitutional rhetoric about the integrity of the just compensation requirement and of the police power (and other similar powers) will not obviate this situation. The problem, in fact, is not the protection of property against governmental takings but which mode of change and of sacrifice, and which distribution thereof, is to be given legal sanction.

V THE ROLE OF THE COMPENSATION PRINCIPLE

It will be seen that although the protection of particular property rights is not the function of the compensation principle (except selectively), the requirement does function to protect the *institution* of private property and therefore the basic organization of society.

Service in the Framework of Legal Policy-making

The compensation principle must be seen as one principle within the matrix of principles with which the politico-legal system articulates and seeks solutions to problem-of-order and value-clarification-process conflict.[39] It is one rule in competition with other rules (and its subsidiary rules — the "tests" of taking — are each one rule vis-à-vis other rules). The compensation principle is a vehicle for the introduction into policy analysis and decision-making of certain interest claims. It is one mode of giving effect, however selectively (because of the dual nature of rights and the reciprocal character of externalities), to continuity-oriented considerations. In this regard, it must be clear that the "legalism" of the compensation requirement does not necessarily operate to support the status quo; rather, it is part of the process of restructuring the status quo: Sax (88), pp. 54–58; Friedman (39), p. 168. The use of the compensation principle is one example of the use of legal fictions and principles to permit change without open admission thereof; Friedman (41), pp. 35, 37; (40), pp. 839–840. As will be further seen below, the role of the just compensation requirement, paradoxically, is to tend to legitimize all legal change, compensated or not. In a narrow sense, the compensation requirement is often invoked as a strategic limitation to prevent change. More broadly, however, the requirement is part of the mode of judicial and societal determination of the maximization of net benefits, as it were, not only within extant rights but through changing rights; Sax (88), pp. 48, 61–62. As such it is only one facet of a larger matrix of principles. It is, as Sax (88), pp. 53, 55, 56, cf. Michelman (65), p. 1179, has insisted, a myth to believe that the function of the taking provision of the Fifth Amendment is to maintain and protect existing values; as, he has also argued, its chief role is in problem-solving [Sax (89), pp. 185–186], and it so functions as part of the total matrix of legal principles only in the terms of which the principle has meaning.

Service as a Check on Arbitrary and Tyrannical Power

The availability of the compensation requirement serves to institutionalize the sense and values of procedural fairness; Sax (88), pp. 40–41, 54–57, 58–60, 64; Stoebuck (100), pp. 596 ff, cf. 586–587. It does this by enabling the effectuation of the division of power within government,[40] especially through judicial review. It permits the disgruntled to have their day in court without the necessity of more elaborate rules provided in advance; Friedman (40), pp. 835–836. It provides a sense of participation in the legal order. It also reinforces the "independent" role of lawyers' law vis-à-vis statutory and administrative law.

This service of the compensation requirement, however, must not be understood in exaggerated or idealized form. The Fifth Amendment taking provision does in one respect limit governmental authority and power. It limits or checks the unilateral exercise of the powers of governance by the legislature. The courts also unilaterally exercise their powers of governance in these matters. However, the compensation requirement has not been imposed (even selectively) upon their decision-making. Insofar as the compensation requirement serves as a check on arbitrary and tyrannical power, it does so only through the use of governmental power to check other governmental power the exercise of which in its totality remains arbitrary. In so functioning it operates to channel the exercise of arbitrary government power in one direction rather than another, to protect one set of private interests rather than another. While the compensation requirement serves as a check on arbitrary power it is the remaining functions of the compensation requirement which are paramount.

Psychic Balm

Scarcity, as manifest in the dual nature of rights and the reciprocal character of externalities in a radically indeterministic world, implies the reality of conflict and therefore the necessity of choice among inconsistent or disharmonious interests. Decisions must be reached as to which interests, claims, and expectations are to survive and which are to perish. Sacrifice, and redistribution of income and wealth, are inevitable; Michelman (65), pp. 1166, 1208, 1258. Considerations of policy, that is, of expediency modified by public sentiments—J. Smith (94), p. 384—necessarily control; Cormack (21), p. 259. In this process the state is not merely an umpire but a critical factor in the continuing process of reformulating the matrix of rights. The burden of this process is not solely the ubiquitous inevitable noncompensated losses which occur but also the anxiety consequent to the realization of policy consciousness. The pretense of a law which is found and applied is preferred; attitudes of law obeying and law maintaining are elevated over the attitude of law making; Tapp and Kohlberg (103). Yet the reality of legal choice forces its way upon consciousness. Grandiose ideological systems, among other things, function to produce and rationalize systems of sacrifice so to minimize the perceived costs and antagonism thereto; P. L. Berger (9).

All politics, in the broad sense inclusive of common and constitutional law, is at least in part a matter of hurt feelings [Goedecke (46), pp. 10–11]; in such a context, justice is the relating of feelings of injustice to reality (*ibid*), p. 11. The compensation principle serves by its very existence (and our belief in its objective reality) to overcome anxiety over change (and especially what is perceived as legal change) in social affairs.

The primary role of the compensation principle lies not in its use as such but in its very presence. The role of the compensation principle is to serve as a psychic balm in the face of radical indeterminacy. It functions to obscure the necessity of choice, to absorb the reality of loss through reference to high principle, and to soothe the realization of instrumentalism and rationality; Friedman (41), p. 39. Belief in the compensation principle sets minds at rest—Shackle (92), pp. 288, 288–289—creates and reinforces a sense of fairness, and beautifies "what is disagreeable to the sufferers."[41] Even infrequently awarded compensation aborts conflict and anxiety and reinforces the sense of security and legitimacy; Friedman (41), pp. 39, 63. Thus the psychic balm function of the principle in general is infinitely more important than the existence of a coherent and consistent compensation policy. The fact of definite decisions, and the omnipresent availability of the principle, is more important than the content of the decisions, at least within ambiguous limits. It is an open question as to how well the system would work if the truth be known: "The thoroughly liberal society, in short, cannot know what makes it work."[42]

Legitimation

In performing the above functions, especially the psychic balm role, the compensation principle also serves a legitimation function. The compensation principle is part of the process of legal change and its legitimation, in which man seeks congruence between his behavior and his beliefs and attitudes; Holsti (52), p. 15. Decisions are justified by linking them with some rule or law of unquestioned legitimacy: Friedman (39), p. 161; R. Smith (95); legal principles and constitutional clauses are rules by which other rules and decisions are made and legitimized; Friedman (40), p. 795. What is legitimized includes specific substantive legal changes (for example, changes in the differential legal protection accorded to interests or rights), the existing decisional system and structure, and the mode of thought (the legal style of thinking, definition of reality, and normative structure of social reality). Successful legitimation keeps the peace, avoids dissatisfaction, complaint, criticism, and especially insurrection and attack.[43] Conclusionary and tautological declarations and absolutist principles serve the legitimation function, as well as the psychic balm role, often admirably well.[44]

The Fifth Amendment just compensation provision, quite paradoxically, tends to legitimize all legal change (in the sense used here) whether or not compensated.[45] The legal system compensates in some or many cases but in having the compensation provision available it induces the acceptance of legal change without compensation. The loser in a litigated (or lobbied) Alpha-Beta conflict has been given a hearing, has learned that another principle—often one which carries its own readily comprehensible rationale—is superior, and, having lost, can now retire to lick his wounds. However the matrix of rights and of exposures to rights has been changed, the system of law and the property system remain unassailable. The loser has given his cause a good try, within the system, and the system and the substantive decision are legitimized. The ultimate irony is that the compensation principle, ostensibly a check on legal social control, is itself a mode thereof. It is one means through which "most victims are prepared to bear such losses or can be educated to be willing to accept them"; Keeton (55), p. 1347.

Such are the paradoxes of legal social control.

FOOTNOTES

The authors are: Professor of economics, Michigan State University, and assistant professor of economics, University of New Orleans, respectively. The authors are indebted to Jurgen Backhaus, Daniel Bronstein, James Buchanan, Daniel Chappelle, Philip Favero, Leighton Leighty, H. H. Liebhafsky, Daniel Saks, Allan Schmid, Robert Solo, George Stigler, Richard Zerbe, and an anonymous referee for discussions in various forms bearing on this article; to numerous persons in state and federal governments for discussions relating to particular problem areas in their experience; to Jon Wesa, Thomas Kennedy, and Mary Jo Tormey for uncommonly helpful research assistance; and to the members of Professor Samuels's seminars on Political Economy: Institutions and Theory (Winter 1973) and Law and Economics (Summer 1974).

1. "... nor shall private property be taken for public use without just compensation," U.S. Constitution, Fifth Amendment. All states except North Carolina have a similar clause, some of which read "taken or damaged." (In North Carolina the just compensation requirement has been reached through judicial interpretation of the due process clause of the state constitution.) Compensation is neither inherent nor originally included in the power of eminent domain (the right to take) but has been added as a limitation; see Netherton (70), p. 39, and Stoebuck (100), p. 575. Land was early appropriated for roads without compensation; Sax (88), p. 53.

2. Injunctive relief is an alternative course of action which, if successful, voids the offending action thereby obviating the need for compensation. In recent years, "inverse condemnation" cases have proliferated in which private plaintiffs assert compensable takings by government action typically otherwise unobjectionable.

3. *Dual nature of rights*: For Alpha to have a right is for some Beta to have an exposure to Alpha's right (and the actions and choices enabled thereby) and vice versa. Thus, Alpha-Beta conflicts.

Reciprocal character of externalities: The injury (cost, damage) which the polluter visits upon others has as its reciprocal the injury which pollution control visits upon the former polluter and others. Neither party is the "cause" alone and either party can be exposed to the burden. A policy to promote or require "internalization," say, upon the polluter, actually may mean a change in the patterns of rights, exposures, and adjustments. Compensation is a problem of which interest, among inconsistent interests, to protect and which to inhibit and is part of the process through which rights, loss, and compensation are *jointly* determined; see Samuels (85).

4. The courts on several occasions have been quite candid: "There is no set formula to determine where regulation ends and taking begins"; *Goldblatt v. Town of Hempstead*, 369 U.S. 590, 594 (1962). "No rigid rules can be laid down to distinguish compensable losses from noncompensable losses"; *United States v. Caltex, Inc.*, 344 U.S. 149, 156 (1952). "The amendment does not contain any definite standards of fairness by which the measure of 'just compensation' is to be determined"; *United States v. Cors*, 337 U.S.

325, 332 (1949). "A compensable taking under the federal constitution ... is not capable of precise definition"; *Harris v. United States*, 205 F. 2d 765, 767 (10th Cir. 1953). It is a matter of no surprise, then, that commentators have said such things as the following: "The predominant characteristic of this area of law is a welter of confusing and apparently incompatible results" Sax (88), p. 37 ... the impression that the Court has settled upon no satisfactory rationale for the cases and operates somewhat haphazardly, using any or all of the available, often conflicting theories without developing any clear approach to the constitutional problem" (*ibid.*), p. 46. The court decisions are "often vague, conflicting, and without pattern" Harris (50), p. 636. There is "a crazy-quilt pattern of Supreme Court doctrine," "a haphazard accumulation of rules," "no 'specific constitutional limitations,'" and "floundering and differences among judges and among generations of judges" Dunham (28) pp. 63, 64, 68, 105. There is "judicial schizophrenia" Large (61), p. 1055, n. 60; "lack of uniformity" Sackman (80), pp. 335, 336; "no definite rules or standards" Kratovil and Harrison (58), p. 597; "confusion, uncertainty and diversity of rules and results" Note (110a) p. 162; "highly ambiguous and irreconcilable decisions" Broeder (14), p. 228; decisional results "liberally salted with paradox" Michelman (65), p. 1170; "artificial distinctions without basis other than in semantics" Aloi and Goldberg (2) p. 647; "a judicial maze of inconsistent and arbitrary opinions" Note (112), p. 693; and, *inter alia*, "conceptual confusion, inconsistency, and utter absence of logic ... are part and parcel of eminent domain law" Kanner (54) p. 58.

5. In the absence of rules uniquely dispositive of litigation and with strong elements of pure normative choice in a world of reciprocal externalities and dual rights, it is not surprising, further, that decisions are "often explained in conclusionary terminology, circular reasoning, and empty rhetoric." Decisional results are stated. "Why this result necessarily follows from the legal premise, however, is seldom explained. Often, on the apparent assumption that the connective reasoning is self-evident, the result is merely announced in conclusionary form." On important points, "typical judicial decisions are generally uninformative"; Van Alstyne (106), pp. 2, 29. Courts reach *ex post* determinate results by placing each case in this or that empty box, the decisional language being conclusionary and tautological with regard to either or both the choice and application of rules. Decisions never systematically identify or classify the conflicting interests; rather, they tend to be replete with "hyperbolic images" [Funston (43), p. 281 n. 110; cf. Van Alstyne (106), p. 35]. Principles and tests are often stated in "seemingly inflexible terms"; Van Alstyne (106) p. 34. It has been said that the distinction between compensable and noncompensable government activity "is not altogether precise, and can readily be manipulated to reach divergent results"; (*ibid.*), p. 26. The nature of the phenomenon has been aptly characterized by a perceptive court: "It is possible to manipulate concepts by the selection of a different level of verbalization, that is, a different level of generalization. An entirely different result can be 'logically' forced. ... That kind of analysis is fruitless because the conclusion is dictated by the way one starts the train of reasoning"; *Cromwell v. Ferrier*, 19 N.Y.2d 263 (1967), quoted in Holme (51), p. 255 n. 22. One may question how "fruitless" that process is, however, It *is* descriptively accurate and determinate results *are* reached. (One may not derive an *ought* from an *is* alone, yet *ought* conclusions are derived from *is* premises associated with implicit *ought* premises. So may concepts be associated with decisional results, however arbitrary or conclusionary the procedure.)

On the conclusionary nature of the decisional language. see Kratovil and Harrison (58), pp. 601, 630; Elias (31), p. 31; Costonis (22), p. 1058; Dunham (28), p. 82; Harris (50), p. 667; Holme (51), pp. 255–256 n. 22; Sax (88), p. 60; Michelman (65), pp. 1203, 1203 n. 79; and Note (114), p. 1082.

On the tautological nature of the decisional language, see Costonis (22) pp. 1022,

1029 n. 37; Levi (64), p. 405; Olson (72), pp. 445, 446, 450, 457, 458; and Note (114), pp. 1034, 1039 n. 25.

On the failure to identify or classify conflicting interests, see Kratovil and Harrison (58), p. 610 n. 109; Stoebuck (100), p. 604; and Van Alstyne (106), pp. 39 and *passim*.

6. The problem is not unique, of course. In the late nineteenth century, for example, comparing two cases involving the same question, one commentator remarked that "It will not escape observation that the Court of Appeals of New York and the Supreme Court of Pennsylvania reached opposite conclusions on a question relating so vitally to the natural, inalienable, and primordial rights of the citizen. ... We have at all events that which is regarded as a fundamental right in New York considered not to be such in Pennsylvania"; Foster (33), p. 55. One does not have to be a complete rule skeptic; Friedman (40), pp. 789; Costonis (22), p. 1025, to appreciate that rules of law are neither precise nor mechanically applied and therefore ambiguous and uncertain. "Many rules of law are so framed as to be totally unpredictable in effect"; Friedman (39), p. 155. Nonetheless, it is striking to read of "the thorniest problem in modern property law, ... where to draw the line distinguishing compensable from noncompensable takings ..." Note (114), p. 1089, that "coherent principles defining the respective contours of the police power and the takings clause of the fifth amendment have proven ... elusive" Note (113), p. 1019 n. 28, and that "the fact is that the law in this area is a hopeless mess and one can find just about any statement for which he is looking if he reads enough cases" [Cal. Law Revision Comm'n, Memorandum 70–29, at 5; quoted in Fadem (32), p. 298, as are several of the above quoted statements and many others]. Thus, speaking of the case decisions, Michelman (65) offers "the hypothesis that decisional rules simply cannot be formulated which will yield other than a partial, imperfect, unsatisfactory solution and still be consonant with judicial action" (*ibid.*), p. 1171; and, of the "tests" of compensability, "that none of the standard criteria yields a sound and self-sufficient rule of decision—that each of them, when attempts are made to erect it into a general principle, is either seriously misguided, ruinously incomplete, or uselessly over-broad" (*ibid.*), p. 1184. Perhaps predictably, Carmichael (17), p. 754, concludes that "the 'taking' question is some metaphysical blend of factors ... "

7. "You can find law for both sides of any proposition on any issue that is going to arise in a condemnation case"; Fadem (32), p. 296. For examples of conflicts see: Sackman (80); Note (11) (overflights), Van Alstyne (106), pp. 14, 18, 21 (aesthetic aims); Kratovil and Harrison (58), p. 639 (platting of future streets); Carmichael (17), p. 763 (regarding "any and all" use); and Stubbs (102), pp. 211–212 (goodwill and profitability).

8. The right to pollute may be seen as the right (say, a private eminent domain right) to take others' rights; J. Smith (94), p. 394. Standardized or adhesion contracts may be seen as a mode of private taking; Goldberg (89). Regulation would be prevention of a private taking; Sax (89), p. 181, n. 64.

9. In re taking a right to impair others' access rights, explicitly stated, see Cormack (21), p. 248 n. 143.

10. Michelman (65), pp. 1178, 1179, 1180; Cormack (21), pp. 224 n. 21, 225 and n. 25, 228, 257, 259; Downs (27), pp. 70, 90, 98; Kottke (56), p. 407; Waite (108), pp. 287 and n. 7; Costonis (22), p. 1070; Note (111), pp. 1444, 1445; and Note (114), pp. 1064 n. 148, 1067, 1068, 1086, 1089.

11. Ackerman (1a) identifies two markedly different but coexisting legal analytics: Scientific Policymaking (and within it the also markedly different Utilitarian and Kantian modes of perception and adjudication) and Ordinary Observation (and Ordinary Adjudication). In addition, he identifies two corresponding different views of property, several different conceptions of judicial role, a multiplicity of conflicting lines of reasoning, and a heterogeneous Conventional View (or paradigmatic concep-

tion of social reality). Ackerman's two analytics have much in common with but are not strictly equivalent to analytical vis-à-vis realist jurisprudence. Ackerman applies the two legal analytics to the taking problem and finds the compensation principle approached and applied differently by various types of judicial roles within each.

12. Note (114), p. 1096.

13. Consider the following examples perception of which is likely to be selective: interests, rights, freedom, coercion, government, progress, growth, development, private, and public; benefits vis-à-vis costs; definition of problems: "Problems, as well as their solutions, are largely subjective. Perception of problem areas determines which property rights questions are relevant as well as which solution among the possible alternative solutions is appropriate. There are few objectively right or wrong property right laws"; Ditwiler (26), p. 663; cf. Arnold and Bromley (4), Miller (66), pp. 148, 162–163; when maximum individual freedom is consistent with the integrity of society [Levi (64), p. 405]; negative regulation vis-à-vis affirmative protection; legitimate expectations; government as intervener vis-à-vis (property) right producer; government largess as a right or a grant; public assistance as compensation for systematic disadvantage; abuse of power; whether sonic booms cause significant injury to persons and/or property; the reach of navigable servitude; "arbitrary" and "unreasonable"; "grievous social injustice," and "serious indignity" (Sax and Hiestand (90), pp. 875, 877, 881–882, 884); the definition of absolute rights and of fee simple absolute; whether a tariff establishes a "legitimate vested interest" (say, with a ten-year phase-out)—Simons (93), p. 70; what government acquires vis-à-vis what an owner loses [Olson (72), pp. 442–443; Ruegsegger (77), p. 336]; change within law vis-à-vis change of existing law; "exigencies" [Large (61), p. 1082]; "destruction by necessity" [Nichols (71), sec. 1.43]; reach of the public trust doctrine or of the life tenant concept, with respect to intergenerational relations [Large (61), pp. 1067ff]; Bosselman, Callies and Banta (13), pp. 24 and passim; Carmichael (17), pp. 759–760; reach of public rights, with respect to diffuse private interests [Sax (89)]; when Alpha's procedures are not reasonably related to Alpha's legitimate intended purposes and therefore violate Beta's rights (that is, when Beta's right is dependent upon the reasonableness of Alpha's procedures) [Dawes v. Philadelphia Gas Co., No. 73–2592 (E.D. Pa., Oct. 5, 1976)]; when regulation is "unduly restrictive"; what is "natural" [Holme (51), p. 268]; new priorities and needs [Carmichael (17), pp. 749, 750]; when progress in an area erodes and renders antiquated certain traditional legal doctrines and rights [United States v. Causby, 328 U.S. 256 (1946)]; Note (111), p. 1431; Note (115), p. 1020; when plausibility for compensation is lent by giving an economic claim a property-sounding name [Kratovil and Harrison (58), pp. 612, 613]; when losses are accidental and unavoidable; when a risk is voluntarily assumed; when "novel" property rights are federally protected by the Fifth Amendment taking provision (ibid.) pp. 632, 645; when zoning is no longer suitable for an area (ibid.) pp. 635–636; when an action represents "bad faith, manifest oppression or gross abuse" [Harris (50), p. 678]; what is the legitimate cost of doing business (in a world of reciprocal externalities) [Holme (51) p. 257]; when rights are "extreme," as in "'extreme rights' cannot be enforced" [Spur Industries, Inc. v. Del E. Webb Development Co., 494 Pac. Rep.2d 700, 707 (1972)]; what "the times dictate" [Haik (49), p. 25]; newly recognized externalities; when the legislature reflects rather than is out of touch with contemporary values; "bad faith or palpably unreasonable exercises of the police power" [Costonis (22), p. 1076]; mala in se vis-à-vis mala prohibita; the reach of "harshness of regulation is no objection" (compare the cases cited in Laitos (59), pp. 436, 436 n. 32); the definition of progress and the relation of pollution thereto; when regulation is "overly stringent," the police power "unfairly used" and "unfairly impinges on property owners," government "overreaches," and regulatory excursions "go too far" [Costonis

(22), pp. 1043, 1046, 1058, 1049, 1054, 1059]; rational relationship of a statute to its regulatory objective; the psychic value of "green open spaces"; market failure; and, *inter alia*, the parties at interest, or whose interest should be considered if not counted.

14. The role of injury is also variously given: "no one can obtain a vested right to injure the public" [Sax (88), p. 39]; "not every injury is legally remediable" [Cormack (21), p. 246]; "damage alone is not enough to require compensation" [Note (114), p. 1087]; "without a taking, damage alone is insufficient to require compensation" [*United States v. Willow River Co.*, 324 U.S. 499, 510 (1945)]; some losses must be considered the inescapable risks of ownership [Downs (27), p. 91]; some losses are accidental and unavoidable [Cormack (21), p. 228]; some risks are voluntarily assumed (*ibid.*), 231 and n. 54; some losses are collateral to assuming the rights of a citizen (*ibid.*), p. 258; and so on.

The nature of property is also variously given: emphasis may be on the physical integrity of the property, its use, or its value [Ackerman (1a) pp. 26 ff, 116 ff and *passim*; Olson (72), pp. 442, 457, 458; Sackman (80), p. 342]; even substantial damage may not be considered a taking so long as the property is not rendered uninhabitable, *or* the owner may be asserted to have freedom from substantial interference and the right to unrestricted use and enjoyment [Note (111), pp. 1440, 1441; Ackerman (1a), pp. 123ff]; the more or less traditional physical invasion test may be seen as outmoded for failing to encompass other types of losses [Roby (76), p. 513]; injury may count only if it is special or concentrated [Kratovil and Harrison (58), pp. 632, 648; Cormack (21), p. 245]; injury may have to be unforeseeable [Kratovil and Harrison (58), p. 648]; injury may have to involve the inability to earn a reasonable return [Waite (108), p. 289]; prevention of the highest and best, or most profitable, use [Lesser (62), p. 150; Harris (50), pp. 677, 679, 681–682]; "reasonable beneficial use" Costonis (22); compare C. J. Berger (7), Harris (50), p. 644); or no (or no reasonable) use (*ibid.*), pp. 636, 645, 677. Either an externality or the control thereof can be perceived as the legally relevant injury.

15. Concerning *de minimis*, see Kratovil and Harrison (58), pp. 626, 640, 648; Rayburn (75a), p. 259; *Dawes v. Philadelphia Gas Co.*, No. 73–2592 (E.D. Pa., Oct. 5, 1976). Concerning *damnum absque injuria*, see Stubbs (102), pp. 209–210; Rumble (78), pp. 300, 305, 310, 311, 314; Kratovil and Harrison (58), p. 611; Sackman (79) pp. 176, 189–191; Cormack (21), p. 237; Large (61), p. 1044 n. 23; Roby (76), p. 509; and Nichols (71), sec. 1.42 (17).

16. *Hadacheck v. Sebastian*, 239 U.S. 394 (1915); Harris (50), p. 640 n. 30; Large (71), pp. 1051–1053, 1064, 1066.

17. Cormack (21), pp. 235, 237; Dunham (28), pp. 81ff; Note (111), p. 1443.

18. For example, see *United States v. Willow River Co.*, 324 U.S. 499 (1945).

19. "The fact speaks for itself." The maxim also refers to the rebuttable presumption that the defendant was negligent because (1) the injury (say, due to a falling flowerpot) required negligence and (2) the instrument causing the injury was in the defendant's exclusive control. That is, the fact speaks for itself until challenged and rebutted.

20. The phrase "at common law," often found in the literature, is misleading. The common law evolved, and what were "rights" at one point may not have been at another; Parsons (73), p. 174; Large (61), p. 1069; Cohan (19), pp. 491, 492–493, 500; Holme (51), pp. 261–262.

21. Transformation from a seigneurial to a market system property and labor market regime required government decisions against traditional property rights, with loss felt by many, especially those who lost what they perceived or regarded as "perfectly legitimate forms of property"; Fox-Genovese (34), p. 228, cf. pp. 220, 245.

22. "…economic institutions are innovated or property rights are revised because

it appears desirable for individuals or groups to undertake the costs of such changes; they hope to capture some profit which is unattainable under the old arrangement" [Davis and North (24), p. 10]. "A set of principles is required for choosing among the various social arrangements which determine this division of advantages and for underwriting an agreement on the proper distributive shares" [Rawls (75), p. 4]. The conflict in legal history is precisely over which interests will secure rights, and thereby distributive advantages. History written or evaluated from the point of view of the conflict winners will be tautologically optimal.

23. The executive is less directly involved in taking cases. Administrative commissions, however, are often involved.

24. Kratovil and Harrison (58), pp. 609–610; Van Alstyne (106), pp. 5–7; Foster (33), pp. 57, 58, 66, 67; Sackman (79), p. 179; Funston (43), pp. 271, 279; Roby (76), p. 508; Dunham (28), pp. 91–92; and Holme (51), pp. 262–263.

25. For examples of a system of compensation perceived as existing outside of the formal system of property rights, see Highway Beautification Act of 1965, 23 U.S.C. sec. 131 (1965) and Uniform Relocation Assistance and Real Property Acquisition Policies Act of 1970, 42 U.S.C. sec. 4601 et seq. (1970). See Netherton (70), p. 52; Holme (51), p. 248 n. 4, p. 278 n. 87; and Bosselman (12), pp. 690ff.

26. Elias (31), pp. 30–32; Harris (50), p. 676; Dunham (28), p. 91; Stubbs (102), pp. 209–211; and Waite (108), p. 286 n. 5. With regard to (a) what the constitution compels compared to what it permits, see Sax and Hiestand (90), p. 922, (b) legislative assertions of rights which should be recognized at common law (ibid.), p. 914 n. 181; and (c) constitutional necessity versus legislative dole or charity; Sackman (79), pp. 186, 189.

27. With regard to different attitudes concerning the grounding of rights, and their consequences for which claims and expectations are legitimized, see Ackerman (1a), Michelman (65a).

28. United States v. Willow River Co., 324 U.S. 499, 503 (1945). The question is always "whether the asserted interest is one which the law will protect"; Batten v. United States, 306 F.2d 580, 587 (10th Cir.) (1962). Yet conclusionary and tautological statements are typical: "Such legislation does not disturb the owner in the control or use of his property for lawful purposes, nor restrict his right to dispose of it, but is only a declaration by the state that its use by any one, for certain forbidden purposes, is prejudicial to the public interest"; Mugler v. Kansas, 123 U.S. 623, 668–669 (1887). In each relevant case, what is lawful and what is forbidden is precisely at issue. The opinion just quoted was by the elder Harlan; for Holmes and the same problem, see Emery v. Boston Terminal Co., 178 Mass. 172, 185, 59 N.E. 763, 765 (1901) and McAuliffe v. Mayor, 155 Mass. 216, 220, 29 N.E. 517, 517–518 (1892). See also Cormack (21), p. 252, and Large (61), p. 1039. On the tautology of lawful vis-à-vis forbidden purposes, also see Cohan (19), p. 509.

29. Laitos (59), p. 433; Sax (88), p. 39; Harris (50), p. 641 n. 35; Kramon (57), p. 152.

30. Compare, for example, the Pennsylvania Constitution, Article I, Sec. 9: "the people have a right to clean air, pure water, and to the preservation of the natural, scenic, historic and esthetic values of the environment." See Lantz (60).

31. Radical indeterminacy and other considerations suggest that the formation of rights is a general interdependence process: Rights are a partial function of government (legal) policy which is a partial function of the competition over the use of government by interested parties which is a partial function of the extant total matrix and distribution of rights. Litigation based on certain rights and assertive of other rights is often rights-changing. Innovative claims accepted by courts produce new rights. In other cases, persons acquiesce in assertions of rights by other parties.

32. Sax (88), p. 61. Sax adopts a view close to what Ackerman (1a) calls the Scientific Policymaker's view of property in contrast with that of the Ordinary Observer. Sax also writes:

> ... a view founded on a recognition of the interconnectedness between various uses of seemingly unrelated pieces of property. Once property is seen as an interdependent network of competing uses, rather than as a number of independent and isolated entities, property rights and the law of takings are open for modification. ... Property does not exist in isolation. Particular parcels are tied to one another in complex ways, and property is more accurately described as being inextricably part of a network of relationships that is neither limited to, nor usefully defined by, the property boundaries with which the legal system is accustomed to dealing. Frequently, use of any given parcel of property is at the same time effectively a use of, or a demand upon, property beyond the border of the user (89), pp. 150, 152.

A similar view is held by Michelman (65), p. 1167:

> In a given period, a person enjoys a certain liberty to do as he wills with certain things which he "owns," and a certain flow of income (utility, welfare, good). The practical boundaries of his liberty, and the practical relationships between it and the sum of goods currently flowing to him, are in significant part determined by existing conditions of economic resource employment within his social universe—call it society, community, state.

33. See Samuels (85). In regard to the normative compensation rule requiring an unambiguous definition of status quo rights, see Goldberg (47), p. 568.

34. Even the law of nuisance is not exempt: "Mr. Justice Pitney said that while the legislature might legalize what otherwise would be a public nuisance, it could not 'confer immunity from action for a private nuisance of such a character as to amount in effect to a taking of private property for public use'" [Cormack (21), p. 241, quoting *Richards v. Washington Terminal Co.*, 233 U.S. 546, 553 (1914)]; cf. Laitos (59), pp. 431, 432. The issue, of course, is whether control of a nuisance or the granting of immunity from action for a private nuisance (also a control) is held to be a taking; both, in fact, are.

35. A subsidiary issue capable of misinterpretation is whether the definition of property rights is or can be so understood as to include perhaps all future exercises of the police power. See Large (61), p. 1080; Van Alstyne (106), p. 17; Haik (49, pp. 24–25; Michelman (65), pp. 1203 n. 79, 1240; Kratovil and Harrison (58), p. 603; Goldberg (47), pp. 566–567; Foster (53), pp. 52, 71, 74, 80; Stoebuck (100), pp. 558, 585, 592; and Note (111), p. 1442. Argument for or against this proposition is of no analytically effective use in disposing of the takings issue, although it often arises in discussions of the issue as if it could be dispositive. In re William Penn's reservation of the power to retake land, with grants larger than they would otherwise have been by 6 percent, as an historical exception to general practice, see Stoebuck (100), pp. 558–559. Absolute inclusion of police power limitations in property right definitions would prevent any holding of a taking: the putative owner cannot have had taken what he/she does not have. Absolute exclusion of police power limitations from property right definitions (the view that all rights claims not hitherto specifically limited are viable and subject to protection) seemingly would mean universal takings and require universal compensation, which is (perhaps a correct conclusion for the wrong reason) theoretically and

practically impossible, as above. The problem applies not only to the police power but also to nuisance, navigable servitude, taxation, and, *inter alia*, monetary controls [Van Alstyne (106), p. 17; Large (61), p. 1071 n. 127; Dunham (28), p. 77; Samuels and Schmid (87), p. 107]; property rights always can be defined so as to include or exclude the governmental action at issue. The question is part of the still larger and more complex problem of distinguishing "change of law" from "change within existing law"; Van Alstyne (106), p. 68; Michelman (65), p. 1240 n. 126; Carmichael (17), pp. 751, 752; Goldberg (47), pp. 566–567; Stubblebine (101), p. 43. All of the above discussion indicates the impossibility of any conclusive and nonpresumptive differentiation, which is characteristic of the normative legal-political process.

A further issue concerns the identification of the taking party, a problem in some airport zoning and noise cases; Dunham (28), p. 84; Harris (50), pp. 686–691. A more intriguing problem involves cases holding that economic change has produced a taking within an extant zoning ordinance (that is, there has been no change in the law, only a change in the circumstances in which the law applies); Harris (50), pp. 650, 651, 662–663.

36. The tests are adumbrated and critiqued in Sax (88, 89), Michelman (65), pp. 1183ff, 1203ff, 1224ff; Kratovil and Harrison (58); Stoebuck (100); Olson (72), pp. 442ff; and Downs (27), pp. 94ff.

37. Compare the positions taken by such otherwise like-minded justices as Holmes and Brandeis in *Pennsylvania Coal Co. v. Mahon*, 260 U.S. 393 (1922).

38. Kratovil and Harrison (58), p. 610; Cormack (21), p. 233; Van Alstyne (106), p. 68; Dunham (28), pp. 80–81.

39. Rules function to intellectualize conflict resolution; Parsons (73), p. 178.

40. Even without the Fifth Amendment taking provision, we can be confident that it would have been judicially read into another provision, say, the Fifth and Fourteenth Amendments' due process of law clause, or, for that matter, the Ninth Amendment. The existence of the Fifth Amendment taking provision does not suffice to explain the relevant belief system of legislators.

41. *Tyson v. Banton*, 273 U.S. 418, 446 (1927).

42. Attributed to Paul Weaver, in Moynihan (68), p. 59. See Samuels (81), p. 297 n. 80; and (86), p. 207.

43. Friedman (41), p. 52. See *Home Building and Loan Association v. Blaisdell*, 290 U.S. 398 (1934).

44. Birmingham (11), p. 273; Funston (43), p. 281 n. 10; and Note (114), p. 1074.

45. Among the ironies of the taking principle in relation to social control is the fair return on fair value fallacy of *Smyth v. Ames*, 169 U.S. 466 (1898). If fair value is the capitalized monopoly returns of the unregulated utility and no taking is allowed, then the fair return on fair value formula would function to protect and perpetuate the monopoly return. The courts in fact [insofar as they review rate cases as to "confiscation," which review is now less than prior to *Federal Power Commission v. Hope Natural Gas Co.*, 320 U.S. 591 (1944)] preside over the determination of how much expropriation of monopoly profits will be allowed. Indeed, the process may mask the continuation of monopoly returns and amount to ineffectual regulation; Stigler and Friedland (99).

REFERENCES

1. Abraham, Henry J. (Summer 1975) "'Human' Rights vs. 'Property' Rights: A Comment on the 'Double Standard,'" *Political Science Quarterly*, Vol. 90: 288–292.

1a. Ackerman, Bruce A. (1977) *Private Property and the Constitution*, New York, Yale University Press.

2. Aloi, F. A., and Goldberg, A. A. (April 1968) "A Reexamination of Value, Goodwill and Business Losses in Eminent Domain," *Cornell Law Review*, Vol. 53: 604.

3. Arnebergh, Roger. (1974) "Recent Developments in the Law of Inverse Condemnation," in *Proceedings*, Southwest Legal Foundation, Institute on Planning, Zoning and Eminent Domain, New York.

4. Arnold, Victor L., and Bromley, Daniel W. (1970) "Social Goals, Problem Perception, and Public Intervention: The Fishery," *San Diego Law Review*, Vol. 7: 469–487.

5. Auerbach, Carl A. (1959) "Law and Social Change in the United States," *University of California at Los Angeles Law Review*, Vol. 6: 516–532.

6. Barrows, Richard L., and Prenguber, Bruce A. (November 1975) "Transfer of Development Rights: An Analysis of a New Land Use Policy Tool," *American Journal of Agricultural Economics*, Vol. 57: 549–557.

7. Berger, Curits J. (1976) "The Accommodation Power in Land Use Controversies: A Reply to Professor Costonis," *Columbia Law Review*, Vol. 76: 799–823.

8. Berger, Lawrence. (May-June 1974) "A Policy Analysis of the Taking Problem," *New York University Law Review*, Vol. 49: 165–226.

9. Berger, Peter L. (1976) *Pyramids of Sacrifice*, Garden City, N.Y., Anchor Books.

10. ———, and Luckmann, Thomas. (1966) *The Social Construction of Reality*, Garden City, N.Y., Anchor Books.

11. Birmingham, Robert L. (1970) "Breach of Contract, Damage Measures, and Economic Efficiency," *Rutgers Law Review*, Vol. 24: 273–292.

12. Bosselman, Fred P. (October 1975) "Property Rights in Land: New Statutory Approaches," *Natural Resources Journal*, Vol. 15: 681–693.

13. ———, Callies, David, and Banta, John (1973) *The Taking Issue*, Washington, D.C., Council on Environmental Quality.

14. Broeder, D. W. (December 1965) "Torts and Just Compensation: Some Personal Reflections," *Hastings Law Journal*, Vol. 17: 217.

15. Buchanan, James M. (1975) *The Limits of Liberty*, Chicago, University of Chicago Press.

16. ———, and Tullock, Gordon. (March 1975) "Polluters' Profits and Political Response: Direct Controls versus Taxes," *American Economic Review*, Vol. 65: 139–147.

17. Carmichael, Donald M. (October 1975) "Fee Simple Absolute as a Variable Research Concept," *Natural Resources Journal*, Vol. 15: 749–764.

18. Coase, R. H. (1960) "The Problem of Social Cost," *Journal of Law and Economics*, Vol. 3: 1–44.

19. Cohan, Edward M. (1970) "Unemployment as a Taking without Just Compensation," *Southern California Law Review*, Vol. 43: 488–515.

20. Commons, John R. (1924) *The Legal Foundations of Capitalism*, New York, Macmillan.

21. Cormack, Joseph M. (1931) "Legal Concepts in Cases of Eminent Domain," *Yale Law Journal*, Vol. 41:221–261.

22. Costonis, John J. (October 1975) "'Fair' Compensation and the Accommodation Power: Antidotes for the Taking Impasse in Land Use Controversies," *Columbia Law Review*, Vol. 75: 1021–1082.

23. Dales, J. H. (November 1975) "Beyond the Marketplace," *Canadian Journal of Economics*, Vol. 8: 483–503.

24. Davis, Lance E., and North, Douglass C. (1971) *Institutional Change and American Economic Growth*, New York, Cambridge University Press.

25. Dewey, John. (1924) "Logical Method and Law," *Cornell Law Quarterly*, Vol. 10: 17–27.

26. Ditwiler, C. Dirck. (October 1975) "Water Problems and Property Rights—An Economic Perspective," *Natural Resources Journal*, Vol. 15:663–680.
27. Downs, Anthony. (1970) "Uncompensated Nonconstruction Costs Which Urban Highways and Urban Renewal Impose upon Residential Households," in Julius Margolis, ed., *The Analysis of Public Output*, New York, National Bureau of Economic Research.
28. Dunham, Allison. (1962) "Griggs v. Allegheny County in Perspective: Thirty Years of Supreme Court Expropriation Law," in Philip B. Kurland, ed., *The Supreme Court Review: 1962*, Chicago, University of Chicago Press.
29. Ehrlich, J. W. (1959) *Ehrlich's Blackstone*, Vol. 1, New York, Capricorn.
30. Eisenhower, David D. (1949) "The Middle of the Road: A Statement of Faith in America," *American Bar Association Journal*, Vol. 35: 810.
31. Elias, E. A. (1973) "Significant Developments and Trends in Zoning Litigation," in *Proceedings*: 1–46, New York, Southwest Legal Foundation, Institute on Planning, Zoning, and Eminent Domain.
32. Fadem, Jerrold A. (1973) "Trial Tactics to Make the Compensation Just to the Owner," in *Proceedings*: 261–302, New York, Southwest Legal Foundation, Institute on Planning, Zoning, and Eminent Domain.
33. Foster, W. Frederic (December 1895) "The Doctrine of the United States Supreme Court of Property Affected by a Public Interest, and Its Tendencies," *Yale Law Journal*, Vol. 5: 49–82.
34. Fox-Genovese, Elizabeth. (1976) *The Origins of Physiocracy*, Ithaca, N.Y., Cornell University Press.
35. Frank, Jerome. (1963) *Law and the Modern Mind*, New York, Anchor Books.
36. Frank, John P. (1966) "American Legal History; The Hurst Approach," *Journal of Legal Education*, Vol. 18: 395–410.
37. Frank, Lawrence K. (1960) "What Is Social Order?" in J. G. Manis and S. I. Clark, eds., *Man and Society*, New York, Macmillan.
38. Freud, Sigmund. (1962) *Civilization and Its Discontents*, New York, Norton.
39. Friedman, Lawrence M. (Winter 1966) "On Legalistic Reasoning—A Footnote to Weber," *Wisconsin Law Review*: 148–171.
40. ———. (April 1967) "Legal Rules and the Process of Social Change," *Stanford Law Review*, Vol. 19: 786–840.
41. ———. (1969) "On Legal Development," *Rutgers Law Review*, Vol. 24: 11–64.
42. ———. (1973) *A History of American Law*, New York, Simon and Schuster.
43. Funston, Richard. (Summer 1975) "The Double Standard of Constitutional Protection in the Era of the Welfare State," *Political Science Quarterly*, Vol. 90: 261–287.
44. Furubotn, Eirik G., and Pejovich, Svetozar. (December 1972) "Property Rights and Economic Theory: A Survey of Recent Literature," *Journal of Economic Literature*, Vol. 10: 1137–1162.
45. Fusfeld, Daniel R. (December 1974) Book review in *Journal of Economic Issues*, Vol. 8: 903–905.
46. Goedecke, Robert (October 1961) "Feelings, Facts, and Politics," *Ethics*, Vol. 72: 1–11.
47. Goldberg, Victor P. (September 1974) "Public Choice-Property Rights," *Journal of Economic Issues*, Vol. 8: 555–579.
48. ———. (October 1974) "Institutional Change and the Quasi-Invisible Hand," *Journal of Law and Economics*, Vol. 17: 461–492.
49. Haik, Raymond A. (Winter 1974) "Police Power versus Condemnation," *Natural Resources Lawyer*, Vol. 7: 21–26.

50. Harris, Charles E. (Summer 1973) "Environmental Regulations, Zoning, and Withheld Municipal Services: Takings of Property by Multi-Government Action," *Florida Law Review*, Vol. 25: 635–692.
51. Holme, Richard P. (1974) "Billboards and On-Premise Signs: Regulation and Elimination under the Fifth Amendment," in *Proceedings*: 247–292, New York, Southwest Legal Foundation, Institute on Planning, Zoning, and Eminent Domain.
52. Holsti, Ole R. (September-October 1976) "Cognitive Process Approaches to Decision-Making: Foreign Policy Actors Viewed Psychologically," *American Behavioral Scientist*, Vol. 20: 11–32.
53. Horwitz, Morton J. (1977) *The Transformation of American Law, 1780–1860*, Cambridge, Mass., Harvard University Press.
54. Kanner, G. (Fall 1969) "When is 'Property' not 'Property Itself': A Critical Examination of the Bases of Denial of Compensation for Loss of Goodwill in Eminent Domain," *California Western Law Review*, Vol. 6: 57.
55. Keeton, Page. (May 1966) "Products Liability—Some Observations about Allocation of Risks," *Michigan Law Review*, Vol. 64: 1329–1348.
56. Kottke, Frank. (June 1975) "Social Control of Corporate Power: Comment," *Journal of Economic Issues*, Vol. 9: 405–408.
57. Kramon, James M. (January 1971) "Inverse Condemnation and Air Pollution," *Natural Resources Journal*, Vol. 11: 148–161.
58. Kratovil, Robert, and Harrison, Frank J. Jr. (1954) "Eminent Domain—Policy and Concept," *California Law Review*, Vol. 42: 596–652.
59. Laitos, Jan G. (July 1975) "Legal Institutions and Pollution: Some Intersections Between Law and History," *Natural Resources Journal*, Vol. 15: 423–451.
60. Lantz, Delano M. (Winter 1973) "An Analysis of Pennsylvania's New Environmental Rights Amendment and the Gettysburg Tower Case," *Dickinson Law Review*, Vol. 78: 331–364.
61. Large, Donald W. (1973) "This Land Is Whose Land? Changing Concepts of Land as Property," *Wisconsin Law Review*: 1039–1083.
62. Lesser, Joseph. (1973) "The Dilemma of Airport Zoning—The Constitutionality of Police Power Regulation v. the Necessity of Eminent Domain Acquisition," in *Proceedings*: 117–156, New York Southwest Legal Foundation, Institute on Planning, Zoning, and Eminent Domain.
63. Levi, Edward H. (1961) *An Introduction to Legal Reasoning*, Chicago, University of Chicago Press.
64. ———. (Fall 1973) "The Collective Morality of a Maturing Society," *Washington and Lee University Law Review*, Vol. 30: 399–430.
65. Michelman, Frank I. (April 1967) "Property, Utility, and Fairness: Comments on the Ethical Foundations of 'Just Compensation' Law," *Harvard Law Review*, Vol. 80: 1165–1258.
65a. ———. (1973) "In Pursuit of Constitutional Welfare Rights: One View of Rawls' Theory of Justice," *University of Pennsylvania Law Review*, Vol. 121: 962–1019.
66. Miller, Arthur Selwyn. (1976) *The Modern Corporate State*, Westport, Conn., Greenwood Press.
67. Mises, Ludwig von. (1951) *Socialism*, New Haven, Yale University Press.
68. Moynihan, Daniel P. (January 22, 1977) "The Liberals' Dilemma," *The New Republic*, Vol. 176: 57–60.
69. Murphy, Cornelius. (1971) "Ideological Interpretations of Human Rights," *DePaul Law Review*, Vol. 21: 286–306.
70. Netherton, Ross D. (1968) "Implementation of Land Use Policy: Police Power vs.

Eminent Domain," *Land and Water Law Review*, Vol. 3: 33–57.
71. Nichols, P. (1975) *The Law of Eminent Domain*, 3d ed. rev., New York, Matthew Bender.
72. Olson, James M. (Summer 1971) "The Role of 'Fairness' in Establishing a Constitutional Theory of Taking," *Urban Lawyer*, Vol. 3: 440–465.
73. Parsons, Kenneth H. (1962) "The Contribution of Institutional Economics Analysis to Land Problems Research," in Joseph Ackerman *et al.*, eds., *Land Economics Research*, pp. 168–178, Washington, D.C., Resources for the Future.
74. Pound, Roscoe. (1908) "Common Law and Legislation," *Harvard Law Review*, Vol. 21: 383.
75. Rawls, John. (1971) *A Theory of Justice*, Cambridge, Mass., Harvard University Press.
75a. Rayburn, Madison S. (1973) "Legal Rights and Legal Fictions in Condemnation," *Houston Law Review*, Vol. 10: 251–265.
76. Roby, Ronald H. (October 1967) "Police Power in Aid of Condemnation?" *Appraisal Journal*, Vol. 35: 507–517.
77. Ruegsegger, Martin C. (1974) "Fifth Amendment Taking—Inverse Condemnation," *Journal of Air Law and Commerce*, Vol. 40: 332–341.
78. Rumble, H. H. (February 1918) "Limitations on the Use of Property by its Owner," *Virginia Law Review*, Vol. 5: 297–315.
79. Sackman, Julius J. (1973) "Condemnation Blight—A Problem in Compensability and Value," in *Proceedings*: 157–193, New York Southwest Legal Foundation, Institute on Planning, Zoning, and Eminent Domain.
80. ———. (1974) "Access—A Reevaluation," in *Proceedings*: 335–363, New York, Southwest Legal Foundation, Institute on Planning, Zoning, and Eminent Domain.
81. Samuels, Warren J. (1966) *The Classical Theory of Economic Policy*, Cleveland, World.
82. ———. (October 1971) "Interrelations Between Legal and Economic Processes," *Journal of Law and Economics*, Vol. 14: 435–450.
83. ———. (1972) "Welfare Economics, Power and Property," in G. Wunderlich and W. L. Gibson, Jr., eds., *Perspectives of Property*, pp. 61–148, University Park, Institute for Research on Land and Water Resources, Pennsylvania State University, 1972.
84. ———. (February 1974) "The Coase Theorem and the Study of Law and Economics," *Natural Resources Journal*, Vol. 14: 1–33.
85. ———. (November 1974) "An Economic Perspective on the Compensation Problem," *Wayne Law Review*, Vol. 21: 113–134.
86. ———. (1974) *Pareto on Policy*, New York, Elsevier.
87. ———. and Schmid, A. Allan. (Winter 1976) "Polluters' Profit and Political Response: The Dynamics of Rights Creation," *Public Choice*, Vol. 28: 99–105.
88. Sax, Joseph L. (November 1964) "Takings and the Police Power," *Yale Law Journal*, Vol. 74: 36–76.
89. ———. (December 1971) "Takings, Private Property and Public Rights," *Yale Law Journal*, Vol. 81: 149–186.
90. ———. and Hiestand, Fred J. (March 1967) "Slumlordism as a Tort," *Michigan Law Review*, Vol. 65: 869–922.
91. Schumpeter, Joseph A. (1950) *Capitalism, Socialism, and Democracy*, 3d ed., New York, Harper.

92. Shackle, G. L. S. (1967) *The Years of High Theory*, New York, Cambridge University Press.
93. Simons, Henry C. (1948) *Economic Policy for a Free Society*, Chicago, University of Chicago Press.
94. Smith, Jeremiah. (1917) "Reasonable Use of One's Own Property as a Justification for Damage to a Neighbor," *Columbia Law Review*, Vol. 17: 383–403.
95. Smith, Raymond. (April 1974) "The Economic Loss Cases—The Light at the End of the Tunnel?" *Journal of Business Law*: 119–127.
96. Solo, Robert A. (1974) *The Political Authority and the Market System*, Cincinnati, South-Western Publishing Co.
97. Spengler, Joseph J. (July 1948) "The Problem of Order in Economic Affairs," *Southern Economic Journal*, Vol. 15: 1–29.
98. ———. (September 1974) "Was 1922–1972 a Golden Age in the History of Economics?" *Journal of Economic Issues*, Vol. 8: 525–553.
99. Stigler, George J., and Friedland, Claire. (October 1962) "What Can Regulators Regulate? The Case of Electricity," *Journal of Law and Economics*, Vol. 5: 1–16.
100. Stoebuck, William B. (August 1972) "A General Theory of Eminent Domain," *Washington Law Review*, Vol. 47: 553–608.
101. Stubblebine, William Craig. (1972) "On Property Rights and Institutions," in Gordon Tullock, ed., *Explorations in the Theory of Anarchy*, pp. 39–50, Blacksburg, Center for Study of Public Choice, Virginia Polytechnic Institute and State University.
102. Stubbs, Robert C. (1973) "Compensable and Noncompensable Items and How to Handle the Evidence," in *Proceedings*: 209–259, New York, Southwest Legal Foundation, Institute on Planning, Zoning, and Eminent Domain.
103. Tapp, June L., and Kohlberg, Lawrence. (1971) "Developing Senses of Law and Legal Justice," *Journal of Social Issues*, Vol. 27: 65–91.
104. Tribe, Laurence H. (1975) "From Environmental Foundations to Constitutional Structures: Learning from Nature's Future," *Yale Law Journal*, Vol. 84: 545–546.
105. ——— et al., eds. (1976) *When Values Conflict*, Cambridge, Mass., Ballinger.
106. Van Alstyne, Arvo. (1971) "Taking or Damaging by Police Power: The Search for Inverse Condemnation Criteria," *Southern California Law Review*, Vol. 44: 1–73.
107. Viner, Jacob. (October 1960) "The Intellectual History of Laissez Faire," *Journal of Law and Economics*, Vol. 3: 45–69.
108. Waite, G. Graham. (September 1966) "Governmental Power and Private Property," *Catholic University Law Review*, Vol. 16: 283–296.
109. Waterman, Sterry R. (October 1972) "Whither the Concept 'Affected with a Public Interest'?" *Vanderbilt Law Review*, Vol. 25: 927–937.
110. Williamson, Oliver E. (1970) "Administrative Decision Making and Pricing: Externality and Compensation Analysis Applied," in Julius Margolis, ed., *The Analysis of Public Output*, pp. 115–138, New York, National Bureau of Economic Research.

Law Review Notes:

110a. Note. (1966) "Just Compensation for the Small Businessman," *Columbia Journal of Law and Social Problems*, Vol. 2: 144.
111. Note. (December 1965) "Airplane Noise, Property Rights, and the Constitution," *Columbia Law Review*, Vol. 65: 1428–1447.
112. Note. (January 1967) "The Unsoundness of California's Noncompensability Rule

as Applied to Business Losses in Condemnation Cases," *Hastings Law Journal*, Vol. 20: 675.

113. Note (1974) "Just Compensation and the Assassin's Bequest: A Utilitarian Approach," *University of Pennsylvania Law Review*, Vol. 122: 1012–1032.

114. Note (1973) "Utility, Fairness and the Takings Clause: Three Perspectives on *Laird v. Nelms*," *Virginia Law Review*, Vol. 59: 1034–1096.

115. Note. (1973) "Takings and the Public Interest in Railroad Reorganization," *Yale Law Journal*, Vol. 82: 1004–1022.

11
REGULATION AND REGULATORY REFORM:
SOME FUNDAMENTAL CONCEPTIONS
Warren J. Samuels, A. Allan Schmid, and James D. Shaffer

The general perspective taken here can be briefly
stated: Regulation is a fundamental, not epiphenomenal,
matter. It is part of larger social processes with respect to
which it is both a determined and determining (dependent
and independent) variable. Regulation has a dual nature: It
both controls and protects, it both restricts and enhances
opportunity sets, typically for different persons in each
instance. Accordingly, regulation is a relative, not absolute,
phenomenon capable of being selectively perceived. It is
deeply related to power structure: It governs and is
governed by power. Power is at the center of politics (law)
and economics, and regulation is not sui generis in the legal-
economic arena. The central problem is not whether or not
there should be regulation or greater or lesser government.
The juxtaposition of the market or competition to government or regulation typically if not inevitably involves one
set of legal rights (regulation) being given a privileged
position. The central problem is whose interests are to be
promoted by regulation, and how (insofar as interests conflict, some regulation receiving perhaps universal approval).
Regulation functions to promote interests, in part by channeling radical indeterminacy, uncertainty, and risk. The
question is, who shall use government, including regulation,
to advance their own interests. Finally, as will be seen
below, regulation must be comprehended in the context of a
general analysis of power and rights: Private regulation is
the alter ego of public regulation, the two are quite
interdependent, and regulation is a mode of, not antagonis-
tic to, rights.

Our approach may be compared with the practice of
economics in the regulatory area and the power play of
248

those in the legal-economic arena (with some of which the practice of economics comports more closely than others). The conduct of economic analysis, especially in its vulgar but also (more subtly) in its chaste uses, typically either rules regulation and power out of disciplinary bounds or makes selective implicit assumptions as to regulation and rights and therefore power.[1]

Although the economy comprises more than the market mechanism, the policy analytic perspective of economists ultimately derives from their abstract modeling of a narrowly defined economic mechanism as a closed system. This both permits and is congruent with the ideal of the market existing independent of government, especially regulation; in fact, the unregulated market is a fiction, and the market actually works within the structure of governmental and private regulatory power and indeed serves as an instrument of that power. Emphasis on the market, or on competition, is compatible with a variety of rights structures and regulatory patterns. Each market equilibrium is specific to a rights (and regulation) system. Accordingly, there is no unique Pareto optimum, and it is not logically permissible to argue that one set or one structure of rights is inconsistent with the market or welfare maximization. Welfare maximization, in part through output definition, is governed by rights and regulations; and rights govern efficiency, not the other way around. But the application of the abstract market model to the real world conveys the inherent limits of the model as if those limits were congruent with the real world. The emphasis here is on voluntary exchange within extant opportunity sets, largely abstracting from the political and legal forces governing entitlements, exposures to the choices of others, and the opportunity set structure brought to exchange.

Although the economy is more than the market, and regulation is more than an economic phenomenon, the application of the abstract market model also typically contemplates government action as permissible only insofar as it would reproduce what otherwise would have occurred through the market (except for perceived "imperfections" or "failures"). Such a view largely ignores the vast bodies of common, constitutional, statutory, and administrative laws which govern market performance independent of the "corrective" action in question. Most especially, however, the abstract economic model permits the juxtaposition of market to regulation as mutually exclusive categories, whereas market structure, operation, and performance are regulation-specific. Regulation is an economic alternative in constrained-maximization behavior as economic actors seek to use government to channel or preempt the market (ceteris paribus other government action). The demand for rights is a demand for regulation and, as is the demand for deregulation or regulatory reform, for government. Accordingly, the conduct of economic analysis less ignores regulation, rights, and power and more permits (if not requires) the introduction of selective antecedent normative premises as to whose interests are ultimately to count through rights and regulation and the definitions of problems and reality based thereon. Thus the economic analysis of markets ostensibly independent of rights structure and regulation can only lead to analytical conclusions that are congruent and tautological with selective perceived rights and regulations functional as rights (see below).[2]

The approach taken here must also be distinguished from the ideas expressed by two different types of legal-economic movements. These ideas may appear disparate but are analytically equivalent. There are those who want to use regulation, and government generally, to promote certain concepts of the "public interest;" to alter the power structure and/or performance results of market activity, for example, to protect the public from abuses and negligence; to limit the place of market relationships and the market mechanism as a decisional mode; and to reshape the U.S. economy and transform the social and economic order. There also are those who find regulation costly, excessive, unreasonable, useless, and so on, and/or desire to update, modernize, and streamline regulation. Thus, for some years, efforts to "extend" regulation and to "deregulate" or "reform" regulation have proliferated. In the context of this paper, these movements, although seemingly disparate, are "only" attempting to revise the rights-regulation-power structure and the performance of the system. None of these groups is homogeneous, but each is functioning to channel and control government in its interest-promoting role, eliminating neither government, regulation, nor power. Each group is aware that "The way government goes depends not so much upon the realities as upon the public perception of the realities at the time,"[3] and each attempts to manipulate perception as part of the power struggle over relative rights and the control of the regulatory uses of government.

Indeed, perhaps the most distinctive characteristic of the regulatory process and all discussions concerning regulation is <u>selective perception.</u>[4] This selectivity is possible because of the dual and relativist character of regulation and the diversity of perspectives from which regulation is perceived. There are selective perception and specification of regulation, government, rights, autonomy, competition, costs, benefits, interests, red tape, subsidies, performance, and so on. It is largely through the selective perception of implicit rights that (pejorative) regulation can be juxtaposed to (honorific) rights. Policy analysis is thoroughly imbued with the ramifications of selective perception, for example, through implicit rights' specifications governing definitions of output and productivity.[5]

It is not surprising, therefore, that much writing in this area is power and not knowledge oriented. Its aim is to persuade, not to describe objectively. There is much manipulation of images of an ostensibly unregulated economy in order to denigrate the regulation in question or to cast luster on some form of deregulation or reform. Part of the regulatory process, then, involves a contest of myths and symbols: "competition," "market," "rights," "bureaucracy," "free enterprise," "government," "the public interest," and so on. Myths are invoked and symbols manipulated to channel perception, opinion, and policy. For example, certain regulations are characterized as "artificial" or "excessive," whereas in fact these and other code words are euphemisms for claims that different interests should be protected by new uses of governmental regulatory authority or private regulatory control.

Part I will explore the nature of regulation in terms of the larger context in which it has meaning. Part II will examine the constituent elements which comprise the nature of regulation. In both parts implications will be drawn regarding the nature of deregulation and regulatory reform.

I. The Nature of Regulation: The Larger Context

It is characteristic of selective perception that individuals tend to perceive as regulation those governmental actions which are disliked and take as given (indeed, as natural) governmental actions which are liked or of which they are unaware. The perceived artificiality and distorting quality of the disliked regulation is rarely if ever seen clearly against the detailed background of all other regulation which, while of the same character, is taken as given. For example, a regulation often is said to distort private choice, whereas private choice actually is a partial product of vast regulatory systems in society. Regulation seen as an intrusion on consumer sovereignty assumes propriety of other rights and regulations. More broadly, regulation is said to negate individual freedom, but individual freedom (vis-a-vis the particular type of system of freedom) always and inevitably is intrinsically limited.

Regulation as an analytical concept or category must be comprehended within the broadest reach of the problem of order, namely, the necessity to reconcile the fundamental conflicts between freedom (or autonomy) and control, hierarchy and equality, and continuity and change. Regulation (again, as an analytical concept or category, not specific regulations) ultimately derives from the problem of order and its component conflicts as a characteristic of social and economic reality. The economy as we know it is in no small part what it is directly because of certain distinctive resolutions of the problem of order. There is a similar problem with freedom, for example. The freedom of Alpha is limited by that of Beta; one's freedom from is limited by another's freedom to; and freedom is restricted in order to enhance or make it more meaningful (as subjectively perceived by participants). What is here called regulation is a means through which the details of all this are worked out and revised. The structure and operation of every single industry are partly governed by regulatory statutes and other law typically the result of solutions to problems--as well as of power play--emanating from within the industry itself. The nature and structure of the economic system are partial functions of law (the state, government), one mode of which is typically (however, imperfectly) called regulation.

The problem of order emphasizes one condition which most discussions of regulation obscure: the inevitability of control in the society and the economy. It is fallacious to think that the economy can exist without an extraordinarily elaborate system of societal, including governmental, controls. That many of these are nondeliberative should not prevent recognition of the fact that many are conspicuous and deliberative regulations. Moreover, the behavior which permits a market economy to exist and persevere is culturally, socially, and governmentally socialized. The problem, then, is not one of control or no control, but of which, or whose, control. Regulation is relative to and must be understood within the larger system of control in which it exists.

Society is comprised of a number of regulatory systems which determine, interdependently, who can affect others and in what way. The market itself is one of these regulatory systems, despite the fact that it is often perceived and lauded as perfectly free. It, as do other institutions, governs individual behavior (the substance and constraints upon personal choice) and the structure of opportunity sets within which choices are made.

Another context in which regulation has meaning involves the problem of organization and control. Each economic system has an institutional structure which, among other things, functions to organize activity and distribute control. The market, as a regulatory system, is an institution which is comprised of and is shaped and channeled by other institutions typically legal in character. It organizes and controls economic activity or, more accurately, is a means through which other institutions and power centers operate. The market is at once both a check on and a vehicle of power.

The problem of organization and control may be expressed as the matter of the distribution of power in society. Power will exist; at issue is its structure. In that statement, either the word control or regulation may be substituted for power.

The market is not the equivalent of nonregulation, although it is often presented as such. This misconception arises because competition affecting the availabililty of alternatives does control one source of power and affect price. But competition does little to address sources of power which have their origins in the distribution of rights, exclusion costs, and transaction and information costs, and in situations of declining or zero marginal costs. The market is a regulatory system. It requires regulation in order to exist. It will give effect to the structure of nominally private power able to operate through a market as constituted.

One extremely important characteristic of regulation is that public (governmental) regulation is both an alternative to and a means of private regulation. Public regulation is the functional equivalent of private market control and is often its instrument. Private power will be operative through the market and through government. Another important characteristic of regulation is that it is not exogenous: It is part of the system of power in which the ostensibly regulated often dominate and write legislation in their own interests. The overriding point, however, is that regulation may be public or private; regulatory authority will exist, and the important question concerns its locus or loci. The economy comprises a system of organization and control, and it will be an object of control and use. The economy is an object of legal control, and the law is a means to private economic ends. Regulation, inevitably, exists in this process.

The problem of organization and control can be approached in terms either of social control or power play. Of significance is the fact that the institutions of social control are the chief power players in society. Social control is not exogenously imposed; it arises from and within the context of power play in society. It is only or chiefly through the selective identification of a regulation against the background of (presumably) exogenously given social control that one regulatory activity can be segregated from others. Arguments over regulation, then, concern the pattern of freedom versus exposure to the freedom of others, and not freedom alone; they are arguments about the substance of social control, not its existence; and they are made by the power-playing actors participating in the drama of working out social control.

Government regulation must be seen and understood within the problems of order and of the organization and control of the economic system, within the ambit of the struggle for power in society, and the resultant system of social control. Any regulatory action by government is relative to these processes and, moreover, to the private exercise of regulatory control which is the functional equivalent of public control, and often its master.

It seems to follow that government regulation (and its functional equivalent, private control) also must be comprehended in a particular context: The contest for control of government. Government is an instrument available for the use of those who can manage to control it. It is an instrument for controlling the social structure, the opportunity set structure, and the distributions of power, income, wealth, and realized interests in society. Determinations of rights, regulation, taxation, and spending are among the means by which such control is undertaken. Government is both an object of capture and use and an arena in which the contest for its use is fought. Regulation is sought as a means--within the opportunity sets of economic actors--of restricting or channeling the opportunity sets of other economic actors. The allocation of resources and the distributions of income and wealth are functions of market forces which themselves give effect to the structure of power (opportunity sets) in society. The structure of power in the market is a partial function of the distribution of rights and regulation, which are a function of the uses to which government is put. Markets tend to capitalize the differential benefits of law (secured by rights and regulation) into asset values. Regulation is used to create property values. Regulation is a weapon in the contest over the use of the state to manipulate income and wealth distribution. It is an inevitable means because of the necessity to define and redefine rights. That process will have inevitable distributive effects, as will the conflict resolution process in general. The legal system, including regulation, will necessarily be a major determinant of the distribution of income, wealth, and welfare. The contest over the use of government to those ends will take the form of a struggle over who is regulated and for what (whose) purposes.

Deregulation and regulatory reform involve something quite different than is typically adduced for them, such as less control and greater freedom, especially from government. Deregulation and regulatory reform, no less than regulation per se (vis-a-vis a hitherto "unregulated" situation), constitute a facet of the continuing struggle surrounding, indeed comprising, the problem of order: change in the patterns of freedom and control, hierarchy and equality, and continuity and change--as well as change in the organization and control of the economic system, its power structure, and its distributions of opportunity, income, wealth, and welfare. Above all, regulatory reform and deregulation involve not less government control, but a change in the uses to which government is put, a change in the interests which government is used to support, and by inference a change in the control of government itself. That certain uses of government appear to constitute regulation and their reciprocals or reverses and others do not, only suggests the

enormity and selectivity of perception. Government regulation, deregulation, and regulatory reform exist within and as
facets of the structure of private power and as part of, an
alternative to, and a mode of, the system of private control.
Government is fundamentally an ubiquitous process in which
rights are created and destroyed, as different interests are
given the protection of government, as new users and uses
characterize government.   Some of this legal change is
called regulation and some is called deregulation (or regulatory reform), but it is all of one piece. At issue is the use of
government to protect interests in a context of the problem
of order, the organization and control of the economic
system, social control, power play, and/or the contest for
the control of government for nominally private purposes.
That being the case, regulation, deregulation, and regulatory
reform involve a great deal, but typically something quite
different from their usual rationalization, whether that be
phrased as protecting against abuse of power, promoting the
public interest, or letting the market work.

II. The Nature of Regulation: Constitutive Elements

If it is paradoxical and ironic that regulation and
deregulation, as those terms (and regulatory reform as well)
are conventionally used, are functional equivalents (although
serving different interests in particular cases) with regard
to resolving the problem of order, power, organization and
control, and the use of government, much more ironic and
paradoxical will be the following argument. We maintain
that regulation and deregulation are the functional equivalent of rights, and that regulation, as do rights, has a dual
and therefore relativist nature seldom recognized and, indeed, typically obscured in conventional discussions.

Rights--sanctioned claims, as contrasted with claims
per se and recognized claims--function to protect interests.
To have a right is to have one's interest protected; not to
have a right means to have one's interest exposed to the
rights-based choosing capacity of others. What then of
regulation-deregulation?

First, regulation protects interests and is the functional equivalent of a right(s). The imposition of what is perceived to be regulation constitutes a legal change of the interest(s) protected by government.

Second, regulation is a mode through which rights are determined and redetermined. Many of what are implicitly or explicitly considered rights are the result of an earlier regulatory action of government, perhaps one explicitly changing the interests to which government was giving its protection, perhaps one which was seen as regulation in the pejorative sense.

Third, regulation is the functional equivalent of rights not only in protecting interests but also in governing the distribution of income and wealth, that is, the entitlements with which market exchange begins and is conducted and which are produced also in part (say, for the next period) by market exchange as well as by new regulations produced through investment in legal change. Regulation is the functional equivalent of rights as a means of establishing opportunity sets within which individual choice takes place.

Fourth, deregulation (and regulatory reform) is the functional equivalent of regulation and therefore of rights in protecting interests (through changing the interests to be protected by law) and in governing the distribution of opportunity, power, income, and wealth. For precisely the same reason that regulation can be considered so-called government intervention, deregulation and regulatory reform also can be so characterized. That one is perceived to be pejorative intervention and the other is a function of selective identification with certain interests and not others. (When one agrees with the interest to be regulated, deregulation would appear reactionary; when one agrees with the interest being deregulated, continued regulation would appear to be unreasonable interference.) But both regulation and deregulation function to protect interests, albeit different interests in any specific case. There is further irony in the fact that whichever interest is protected is the status quo, and deregulation simply means a

reversal of the interest given government protection.   If
Alpha's interest is protected initially, deregulation would
protect Beta's; if Beta's interest is protected initially,
deregulation would protect Alpha's.   Quite aside from the
rationalizations given in particular cases, the specific content of deregulation (or regulatory reform) is a function of
the status quo point defined by the initially protected right.
Regulation and deregulation restructure, redefine, and reas-
sign private rights.   Deregulation, no less than regulation,
revises rights governing economic structure, behavior, and
performance.

One characteristic of rights is that they too protect
(more or less adequately) interests.   Another is their dual
nature.   When Alpha and Beta are in the same field of
action, for one party to have a right means that the other
has no right and perforce is exposed to the exercise of the
right of the other.   The right guaranteed to Alpha protects
Alpha but leaves Beta exposed or limited.   Every right has
this dual aspect: Every right implies a nonright, or exposure.   The same is true of regulation: Every regulation or
regulatory activity both protects or enhances and exposes or
inhibits.   The same is true of deregulation: For every
deregulated Alpha, there now is an exposed, unprotected
Beta.   Whereas the regulation of Alpha implied rights
(protection) for Beta, the deregulation of Alpha implies
rights for Alpha and exposure and no right for Beta. (It may
have been true, of course, that regulation of Alpha protected Alpha, not Beta, and that deregulation will protect Beta,
not Alpha.)

Another characteristic shared by rights, regulation,
and deregulation (and regulatory reform) is their functioning
to govern whose interests are a cost to others (and in what
way). Consider a regulation changing the relative rights to
upstream polluter and downstream pollutee, or a regulatory
safety requirement that a worker (possibly otherwise unoc-
cupied) be placed at the manhole entrance to a cable tunnel
in which other employees are working on the lines.   These
regulations may be perceived as unreasonable, cost-

increasing, and featherbedding. But each regulation changes the determination of whose interest will count as a cost to others and in what way. The pollution case is also a good example of the reciprocal nature of externalities: If the upstream producer has the right, then the externality is downstream pollution; if the downstream party has the right, then the externality is the upstream producer's inability to produce with pollution effects; the two are inextricably connected, given the state of technology. Regulation, or deregulation, does not create the costs but helps determine their imposition or incidence. We are not saying that regulation never increases costs; we are saying that in the typical case in which the argument is raised, it is false and misleading. In the situation illustrated by the pollution and safety examples, regulation, deregulation, or rights adopted to protect certain interests tend to increase the costs for others by their very nature. Others now must view the right of the protected party as, in effect, a factor of production to be considered. Notwithstanding such reasoning, there is a common asymmetry of perception between rights and regulations regarding costs. We rarely perceive that costs are consequent to rights. The acceptance of the rights as given leads us to accept the costs in the form of prices as natural or given but we commonly recognize the costs of regulation, as no such status of background acceptability is accorded it. The costs stemming from the fact that Alpha has a property or other right are not perceived in the same manner as the costs specific to a health or safety regulation. Similarly, the dual nature of red tape is usually ignored. The costs of delay are obvious; the protection to conserved interests is not. But while the operation of selective perception is a significant factor and its recognition should be an important corrective, the principal argument here is this: Neither regulation, deregulation, rights, nor red tape actually create costs. Costs are a consequence in each case of the parties' interdependence (given the technology). The reciprocal character of externalities and the dual nature of rights dominate in such a way that the law (in whatever form and however perceived) governs cost registration and assignment, not its existence.

A good example of this point arises in the context of the special-pleading argument that regulation is inflationary (which may be but is not typically true in the cases in which the argument is raised). It is true that regulation (say, of the upstream polluter) will increase the polluter's costs or that safety regulations will increase the firm's production costs. But notice that costs to others likely will be lowered: the costs being borne by the downstream pollutee, by the worker, and by society in the form of medical costs. These costs were not hitherto registered by the newly regulated party. Regulation has not created the costs, only reassigned them. Costs hitherto borne by one party are now imposed on another and are passed on as a cost of production to the consumer of the final product. Notice also that the imposition, for example, of safety regulations means that the output of the industry for social purposes is not solely the physical product but also worker safety. The former price associated with the industry was for its physical product alone. The price now is for both the physical product and worker safety. It is a higher price, covering two products (and therefore not strictly comparable with the former price), and it substitutes for the price, now lower, hitherto borne by others when the costs of unsafe working conditions were visited upon them. The apparently obvious evidence that regulation causes costs to increase and thereby contributes to inflation is misleading. Regulation, deregulation, and rights are modes of cost registration and assignment, not the causes of costs, and are so because regulation, deregulation, and rights are the means by which interests in conflict are differentially protected.

Deregulation, as is the case with regulation and rights, is always selective in effect, however selectively perceived (as we have seen, the actual selective effect may be quite different from the selective perception). Regulations requiring that mortgage contracts be written in understandable language, for example, signify that mortgages hitherto were standardized contracts written largely by lenders to minimize their risks, but now there may be a change in the distribution of risk and cost of information. Similarly, change from a caveat emptor to a caveat venditor rule does not create costs but reassigns them selectively. Selectivity enters in a somewhat different way but to the same effect in the case of so-called sunset legislation providing for regular review of certain governmental programs. Insofar as not all interest-protecting modes of governmental action are covered, there will be quite distinct selective and differential treatment of interests. As we perceive the matter, certain social reform programs and competition restricting agencies may be inhibited, along with the interests they protect, whereas a wide range of government actions protecting interests in property and organizations will not be reviewed. Notice, finally, that the argument is once again the same regardless of the status quo point: A change from caveat venditor to caveat emptor is analytically identical to a change from caveat emptor to caveat venditor, as is a change newly protecting the pollutee vis-a-vis a change newly protecting the pollutor, or the imposition of regulation vis-a-vis the imposition of deregulation.

Deregulation and regulatory reform are modes of protecting interests akin to rights and regulation itself. Deregulation has a quite relativist significance vis-a-vis regulation derived from the more or less arbitrary content of the status quo point. Moreover, it is true that regulatory reform is the functional equivalent to property right reform, inasmuch as they both change the interests for which governmental protection is provided, and that regulation and deregulation are functional equivalents insofar as they each constitute government intervention (meaning a change of the interests to which government is providing support). Regulation, in short, is dual, relativist, and the functional equivalent of rights, and so are deregulation and regulatory reform. Regulation, deregulation, and rights all function to achieve some set of interests and pari passu are dysfunctional for the related conflicting interests. The debate over regulation, deregulation, and regulatory reform is part of the contest over the control and use of government as an instrument for protecting interests. Deregulation only changes the interests protected; it constitutes a different regulatory system, analytically considered. The ultimate problem is: Whose interests are to be protected, whether through regulation, deregulation, or regulatory reform?

Regulation, deregulation, and regulatory reform are modes of securing protection of interests. Some parties believe that they are able to secure their interests better through one mode than another, and some parties will use any mode depending on their private calculations of advantage (as is the case with the choice of litigation, lobbying, or private contract in other connections). In some circumstances, the best choice will appear to be regulation, in others deregulation. But these denominations are quite subjective and, as we have seen, the functional equivalent of each other.

III. In Conclusion

The question that has analytical meaning is not whether or not there should be regulation, but which system of regulation, rights, power, and social control and whose interests are to be protected and in what way. Vilfredo Pareto once wrote that if the trade unions conquer, government will be comprised of a system of trade union law. The implication is that if trade unions do not conquer, bourgeois society will be ruled by a system of bourgeois law. If development interests dominate government, there will be prodevelopment law; if environmentalists dominate government, there will be proenvironment law. Each would favor, indeed constitute, its own system of regulation and mixture of private and public organization and control. From whichever system of law or particular regulation one starts, deregulation will mean a change to a different system of law or regulatory scheme. Regulation and deregulation are a mixture of episodic and continuing facets of power play over the system of law, the control of government, and the use of government to protect interests and channel economic performance. Movements for regulation and deregulation, so-called, are part of the total regulatory process, each operating through selective perception to determine whose interests to protect. Given that scarcity implies inevitable opportunity cost, frustration, and conflict; given the reciprocal character of externalities and the dual nature of rights; given that "problems" from one perspective or another are inevitable; and given that some state of the law (interest protection) must prevail, there is ineluctable pressure for regulation and/or deregulation. Whatever the word used, the functional and analytical results are the same. And it is the same whether the regulations promote competition, monopoly or market control, or health and safety. What differs are the interests protected.

Finally, we wish to reiterate the qualification that we have not intended to present a complete theory of regulation. The analysis does not mean a policy analyst could not conclude that the cost of a regulation is greater than its benefit (depending upon perspective) and that net benefits can accrue from regulatory reform independent of the problem of weighting different groups (although we continue to stress this is an important problem). We certainly also are aware that one of the interest groups at stake in regulation, deregulation, and regulatory reform is bureaucratic personnel in addition to the private Alphas and Betas. The realms of politics and bureaucracy have lives of their own. While attempts to expand (or contract) the bureaucratic empire are seldom neutral in their effects on Alpha and Beta, and there are instances when both Alpha and Beta could be better off with a different regulatory system, the bureaucracy is a distinct interest in the parallelogram of power in which regulation and deregulation must be located. This is true of both the local police and the administrative commissions on both state and federal levels. At the level of fundamental conceptions, regulation, deregulation, and regulatory reform are infinitely more complicated than the usual discussion--especially those directed at partisan change--permits to be seen. Central is the normative process through which is determined whose interests regulation, deregulation, and regulatory reform will be used to promote.

Footnotes

[1]This paper is written with the conviction that much, if not most, of the work on the subject is normative (although often masquerading as positive) and neglects, among other things, fundamentals of social order bearing on the nature of regulation and deregulation and the dynamics of the distribution of welfare in society. These are considerations which dwarf (but do not substitute for) the usual arguments surrounding specific regulatory arrangements and which place those arguments in an important perspective. The purpose here is to conduct a discussion that will, first, enable analytically meaningful and intelligent decisions to be reached and, second, enable comprehension as to what is actually involved in policy changes.

We would not be misunderstood. We offer neither an apologia for nor a normative evaluation of existing regulation, regulatory reform, or deregulation. We intend that our analysis be wholly independent thereof. We do not attempt a total theory of the origins, practices, and consequences of regulation. Rather, we analyze certain facets of regulation and the nature of regulation at an abstract level. We are not concerned with wishful thinking on the political left or right, although we will indicate the fundamental role of symbol manipulation in regulatory policy. We are not concerned with particular solutions to perceived problems or with alternative ways of achieving regulatory movements, although we will indicate their fundamental role in regulatory systems operating, in part, on and through selective perception. Moreover, we abstract from the varying sources of regulation within government and from identifying whose interests regulation may in fact advance, including the uncertain performance results of regulation in all its aspects. The analysis is intended to be completely positive and independent of the fact that there is regulation which we individually like and other regulation which we individually dislike, and on which we, just as does everyone else, disagree.

[2]Warren J. Samuels, "Normative Premises in Regulatory Theory," Journal of Post Keynesian Economics, Vol. 1 (Fall 1978), pp. 100-114; and A. Allan Schmid, "Regulatory Policy: Literature Review," Policy Studies Journal, Vol. 6 (Summer 1978), pp. 555-557.

[3]Antonin Scalia, in Paul W. MacAvoy, ed., Unsettled Questions on Regulatory Reform (Washington, D.C.: American Enterprise Institute for Public Policy Research, 1978), p. 1.   Thus, for example, Richard E. Wiley, 1974-1977 Chairman of the Federal Communications Commission, reports that the commission "considered the term 'deregulation' too controversial, and so we coined the phrase 'reregulation.'" (P. 5) After leaving the FCC, Wiley became trustee of a group which distributed broadcasting industry campaign contributions to political candidates. New York Times, February 12, 1978, p. 29.

[4]Warren J. Samuels and Nicholas Mercuro, "The Role and Resolution of the Compensation Principle in Society: Part One--The Role," Research in Law and Economics, Vol. 1 (1979), especially pp. 163-166.

[5]Samuels, "Normative Premises in Regulatory Theory," op. cit.

INDEX